True Murder Stories

From Marie —
For Christmas, 2005

Frank Jones

True Murder Stories

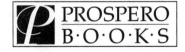
PROSPERO
B·O·O·K·S

Library and Archives Canada Cataloguing in Publication

Jones, Frank, 1937–
   True murder stories / Frank Jones.

Includes stories previously published in Murderous women, Beyond
   suspicion and Murderous innocents.
ISBN 1-55267-866-0

1. Murderers—Biography. 2. Murder. I. Jones, Frank,
1937– . Murderous women. II. Jones, Frank, 1937– . Beyond suspicion. III.
Jones, Frank, 1937– . Murderous innocents. IV. Title.

HV6515.J656 2004   364.152'3'0922   C2004-905968-8

This collection produced for Prospero Books.

Key Porter Books Limited
70 The Esplanade
Toronto, Ontario
Canada M5E 1R2

www.keyporter.com

Text design: Peter Maher
Electronic formatting: Jean Lightfoot Peters

Printed and bound in Canada

04 05 06 07 08 5 4 3 2 1

To my daughter, Fazia,
For all the help she gives me

Contents

Introduction
A Taste for Murder

See the guy halfway down the subway car? The one reading a book? That would be me. Can you make out the title? It's hard to miss—it's in bold yellow capitals on the cover: *How to Commit a Murder*.

The book was written in 1930 by a small-time New York hood named Danny Ahearn. In addition to useful tips on how to dispose of awkward customers "and get away with it," it also has chapters on "How to Stick Up a Fur Joint," "How to Steal a Car" and "Taking a Crap Game."

But don't worry—I have no homicidal intentions, and larceny is the furthest thought from my mind.

The book is simply a collector's item, a curiosity, and I am conducting an experiment. I want to see if the things they say about Toronto people being cold fish are really true. I want to see if it's true that they turn the other way, cross over to the other side, do anything in their power to avoid becoming involved or making a scene.

My idea is to flaunt this sensational book in their faces, act like I'm sitting here on the train plotting to assassinate some unsuspecting sap, and see what happens. So I let everyone get a good look at the title. I apply myself to the book as if I'm committing the whole thing to memory. Then I wait for a hint of anxiety, a suspicious glance, even a subtle shuffling away. But nothing! The other passengers can't help seeing the title, but they simple stare up at the ads overhead or return to reading their newspapers.

Which leads me to conclude that Toronto, which we like to think of as a go-go, multinational city, still puts up an icy wall of English reserve that makes it simply the best place in the world to plot a murder. Sit in Nathan Phillips Square in front of City Hall, go for a ride on one of the famous Red Rocket streetcars, ride to the top of the CN Tower, if you like. Then get out your plan marked "Murder" and don't be afraid to discuss details like disposing of the body in a loud, overbearing voice—no one will take a bit of notice. In Toronto, murder is none of our business.

Which is odd, because we live in a culture of murder. The Bible, from Cain and Abel to the Crucifixion, is all about murder, Shakespeare's plays are saturated with blood, and today, from Hollywood movies to the latest blockbuster mystery book, we turn to murder for entertainment.

It's just that we don't expect real-life murder to intrude in our lives.

I am as guilty as anyone. When I was twelve years old, I lived with my parents in a former monastery called Strawberry Hole in an English village, Northiam. The ghost of a monk, victim of some long-ago outrage, was reputed to walk in the chapel at night. But that was centuries ago. No one was more surprised than me when, in the course of researching a book on hired killers in more recent years, I found that a woman just up the lane from Strawberry Hole had conspired with her grown son to hire a man to come to their door at night and shoot her husband dead when he answered the door. Like everyone else, I never expected murder to come so close to home.

But like nearly everyone else, I am fascinated with murder. As the writer of some half-dozen true-crime books, though, I have been privileged to indulge that fascination, meeting social historians, police officers and people who have been involved one way or another in murder—even a murderer or two.

It is not that I am morbid. On the contrary, I love stories that illuminate the human condition, joys as well as tears. And that is what attracts me to real-life murders. They tell us what people are really like, what they say, what they do, and what their neighbors think of it or do about it. They are the best sort of unvarnished history, conveying what happens in the homes of the great and of the humble, revealing strong emotions and, sometimes, love.

If they happened long enough ago, they can even be funny. I have a soft spot for Dr. William Palmer (see "Saintly Billy"), the British punter and mass murderer who, anticipating the death sentence, declared, "I knew it was the gooser for me!" It's hard not to giggle when reading about Dr. Arthur Warren Waite's repeated failed attempts (in "Dr. Waite's Curious Germs") to hurry his wealthy father-in-law into the next life.

The thread connecting these stories is that, in each case, I feel a strong sense of personal involvement. When researching "He Was My Master, and He Kissed Me," about a housemaid who shot her employer, I never imagined that I would end up telling her daughter about it seventy years after the event. In the account of the Karla Homolka and Paul Bernardo case ("Karla: An Old-fashioned Kind of Girl"), I tell a horrifying tale of police ineptitude. But that was the exception. I have met countless police officers whose dedication and real sense of outrage on behalf of victims has been exemplary. In the course of researching another notorious woman murderer, Myra Hindley ("Wherever He Has Gone, I Have Gone"), I met Joe Mounsey, a cop whose decency and a concern kept him in touch with the mother of an abducted twelve-year-old boy long after others had forgotten the crime. Mounsey is my hero.

Sometimes I found myself taken unawares by powerful sympathy, even for a woman such as Alma Rattenbury ("Silk Pajamas for the Chauffeur"), whose foolishness cost her husband his life. And I could only hug—carefully because of their burns—Pauline Leyshon and Ivor Stokle, a brave couple whose lives were all but snuffed out by three brutal assailants ("Horse Crazy").

The cases often read like fiction. When writing about the duel of wits between Abbé Adélard Delorme, the murderous Montreal priest, and Detective Georges Farah-Lajoie ("The House on Rue Saint-Hubert"), I kept picturing Lieutenant Columbo, the bumbling TV sleuth, holding up a finger, scratching his head and saying, "But just a minute, Father..."

Time and time again, I find that the story is in the details. When murders happen, everything is recorded—giving us an instant snapshot of another time, another place. It is hard to imagine a fuller and more fascinating picture of nineteenth-century rural life in Upper Canada than that derived from the pursuit, capture and trial of Dr. William King ("The Devil Said, Try Chloroform")—from King's flowery love letter to his sweetheart, Melinda, to the bottle containing the unfortunate victim's stomach that the coroner insisted on keeping on the desk in front of him, where he could keep an eye on it.

Murder, as if I needed to tell you, is fascinating.

Karla: An Old-fashioned Kind of Girl

She was leaving her job to move to another newspaper, and Christie Blatchford knew she would have to do something with the notebooks she had filled while covering the Karla Homolka and Paul Bernardo trials several years earlier. "They formed piles of four or five notebooks all around the perimeter of my little office," Blatchford, one of Canada's best-known journalists and now a columnist for *The Globe and Mail*, told me. "I went through them all, and I was astonished to see there were pages in each notebook that were illegible because I had wept so hard. The ink had run. Some of the pages were stuck together from snot from my nose. Because these were not the sort of trials where you just have a few tears."

No other case in Canadian legal history has inspired as many tears. Tears of sorrow; tears of outrage. More than a decade has passed since Homolka's and Bernardo's crimes became known, yet for many the details are still vivid. Karla Homolka is the most reviled woman in Canada. There is still a festering anger over the way the case was bungled and over the travesty of her light sentence. Although Canadians are famously mild and capital punishment has long been abolished in Canada, many would make an exception for Karla. At one point, a website called "The Karla Homolka Death Poll (When the Game Is Over, We All Win!)" invited people to bet on the date of Homolka's death.

Why is Homolka hated even more than her husband, Bernardo? Because Homolka is not just a monster; she also succeeded in hoodwinking the psychiatric and legal professionals, convincing them that she just was a poor coerced battered wife, a victim forced to stand by while her handsome, curly-headed husband raped and murdered teenage girls. Now—too late—everyone knows she was as much an instigator and participant as he was. In fact, Blatchford believes that, without Homolka to urge him on and act as his facilitator, the beast we call Paul Bernardo might never have progressed from serial rape to murder. There were, at one time, plans for a movie about the case, but they came to nothing after many people protested that such a film would be exploitive. That's a shame, because the Homolka-Bernardo story is a modern-day *Heart of Darkness*, reminding us of the depravity of which humans are capable.

The movie-that-never-was could easily have opened with a little girl, blonde and startlingly pretty, running home in her Pioneer Girls uniform to a house on Dundonald Street, in the pleasant city of St. Catharines, not far from Niagara Falls. One day *Newsweek* would call Karla and Paul "the Ken and Barbie of murder and mayhem." At this stage in Karla's life, though, it is Little Bo Peep that comes to mind.

Her father, Karel Homolka, a Czechoslovakian-born traveling salesman, and her mother, Dorothy, had had a difficult start, living in trailer parks and small apartments. But after moving to the Dundonald Street house in 1978, the family, which included Karla's two younger sisters, Lori and Tammy, enjoyed a modest version of the Canadian dream. Summertime social life centered on the small backyard swimming pool, and the house was noisy with the infectious laughter of the three girls and their friends.

Apart from early bouts of asthma, Karla seems to have led a perfectly normal childhood. Her IQ registered at a bright 131, her marks, apart from a blind spot for math and science, were usually in the 80s and, given more encouragement, it's quite possible that Karla Leanne Homolka might have gone to university and ended up as a professional—likely a veterinarian. Always fond of animals (her job as a veterinarian's assistant would play a significant role in the crimes) little Karla trained the family cat to perform tricks. She was outgoing, an excellent figure skater and a participant in school shows, and she enjoyed writing poetry and stories.

As she progressed through Sir Winston Churchill High School, however, a darker side of Karla emerged. She gave her friends personally inscribed horror books, wore black nail polish and developed a taste for the occult. She took to carrying a pair of handcuffs, supposedly because she wanted to be a police officer, and her friends found her increasingly bossy and domineering. Suddenly, death fascinated her. She talked to a boyfriend about suicide, and inscribed a friend's yearbook: "Death rules...I love death. Kill the fucking world."

She lost interest in school, but still the little girl who tried her best, she got a full-time job at the Number One Pet Centre while keeping up a couple of grade twelve courses. And it's quite possible that Karla might soon have forgotten her silly teenage fascination with death and got on with her life, if she had not, in October 1987, chosen to attend a pet supply convention at a hotel in Toronto.

There, she and a friend ran into a couple of guys in a Howard Johnson restaurant and invited them back to their room. Karla

3

had enjoyed a previous fling, defying her parents and flying to Kansas to join a boyfriend for two weeks, but even her friend was startled when she jumped into bed with the tall, handsome guy she had just met, making love with him for four hours. His name was Paul Bernardo. He was twenty-three; Karla was seventeen.

Invited home to St. Catharines the following weekend, Paul made a good impression on the Homolkas. A university graduate, he was a charmer who had honed his powers of persuasion flogging soap powder to the gullible on behalf of Amway. Now turned respectable, he had a bright future ahead of him as a trainee at the prestigious accounting firm of Price Waterhouse. A motto taped to his bedroom wall summed Paul up: "If you can dream it, you can do it." Soon, Karla's parents were inviting the new favorite to sleep on the couch on weekends instead of driving home to his parents' house ninety minutes away in Toronto.

As for Karla, she would say, "He treated me like a princess. He totally swept me off my feet." Other guys she had been able to push around. Not Paul. She liked that. And when she shut and locked her basement bedroom door and produced her handcuffs—just like a pair he had—Paul realized he had met a girl who shared his sexual tastes. "I love fucking you with my parents in the house," she wrote in one of the first of what would be many letters and cards, which she often signed "your princess." The hint of danger only added to his allure.

When she met him, for all his fresh-faced boyishness and fair curls, Paul was damaged goods. As a child he had been cute, always smiling and, just like Karla, everyone's darling. He was a keen Boy Scout, popular with smaller boys, and he soon found he could work his charms on girls too. Then, when he was sixteen, his mother did the unforgivable. In the course of an argument, she threw a photograph onto Paul's bed and told him the man in the picture was his real father—he was illegitimate. The man had been her first love, but bowing to pressure from her parents, she had married Ken Bernardo, who abused her and would ultimately go to prison for sexually assaulting Paul's half-sister.

The hatred he now felt for his mother found an outlet in his increasingly abusive relationships with girls. He demanded anal sex and often beat them up. One girlfriend reported to the police that he had beaten and raped her, but nothing was done about it. In the months before he met Karla, he began haunting bus stops at night in the Guildwood Village area of Scarborough, where his parents lived. He would approach women getting off buses, show them a knife and fondle them.

"What would you think," he asked Karla one day, "if I was a rapist?"

It was fine with her. And that was the permission he had been waiting for. In the following two years, the "Scarborough Rapist" inspired a wave of fear among women in the Toronto suburb. His method was always the same: the bus stop, a grab from behind, the knife and a demand for anal sex and fellatio. One of the thirteen victims reported that her assailant was accompanied at the scene of the crime by a woman carrying a video camera. From descriptions given by victims, police soon had a composite drawing of the rapist—a drawing that would prove to be an uncanny likeness of Paul Bernardo. However, for unknown reasons, they never released it to the media. It was the first of many police bungles.

As far as Karla was concerned, Paul could act out his rape fantasies as much as he liked, as long as she retained her power over the violent, unpredictable man she called "my prince." Then he got a bit too close to home. One night in July 1990, on one of his weekend visits to St. Catharines, he took Karla's fifteen-year-old sister, Tammy, out to buy liquor. They did not return for six hours, and he freely admitted they had been kissing near the Niagara Gorge.

Karla, already planning her picture-perfect wedding to Paul for the following May, was desperate. Paul had been resentful that Karla was not a virgin when they met, and Tammy was in a position to give him what Karla could not. Then she had a brilliant idea: she would make him a gift of her sister's virginity.

That summer, Paul and Karla experimented with putting crushed Valium in Tammy's and a friend's drinks to knock them out, but it did not work. Ditto when they sprinkled Valium on Tammy's spaghetti. By late November, Karla was studying the pharmaceutical compendium to find a drug that would work better. She settled on halothane, an anesthetic used at the veterinary clinic that she could easily obtain.

On December 23, Paul received his special Christmas present— Tammy. It was all recorded on Paul's brand-new video camcorder for enjoyment later. The videotape, which would one day be viewed by jurors, shows the girls in high spirits that evening, and Paul giving Tammy drinks laced with the sedative Halcion.

The girls' parents had gone to bed. Karla and Paul waited like vultures as Tammy, watching television on the couch in the basement, became drowsy and then dropped off. Karla poured halothane on a rag and held it over Tammy's mouth and nose. While Paul pulled down Tammy's green track pants, Karla pulled up her top. "Hurry up," she urged.

"Yeah, okay...keep her down...here we go," he grunted.

Karla, surprisingly, insisted that Paul wear a condom. It wasn't out of concern for her sister: she just didn't want her wedding ruined by the arrival of a surprise baby. It was one aspect, though, that they had not discussed, and he didn't have one. "Don't get all worked up," he told her. "Shut up."

"Put it on," she said again. "Fucking put it on!"

Meanwhile, she was dripping more halothane on the rag and checking Tammy's breathing.

"Suck on her breasts," Paul ordered. A few minutes later, Karla's head was between Tammy's legs. "Put your tongue out, probe," he urged her.

While Karla held the cloth over her sister's face, administering many times the correct dose, Paul entered Tammy anally, only to stop suddenly when Tammy vomited. Realizing that administering an anesthetic after Tammy had eaten was not the wisest move, Karla grabbed her sister with surprising strength and held her upside down to clear her air passages.

Paul and Karla knew by now that they were in trouble. They dragged Tammy across the floor to her bedroom, and while Karla went upstairs to get a mirror to see if Tammy was breathing, Paul tried mouth-to-mouth. In a panic now, Karla called 911, disposed of the halothane down the drain and hid the sleeping pills.

The girls' parents woke to the sounds of sirens and tramping footsteps.

"Tammy just stopped breathing," Paul told them.

"Her color's coming back," Karla reassured them as the paramedics worked on Tammy.

But as they put her into the ambulance to take her away, Tammy was already dead. A cop coming down the basement stairs after a doctor had officially declared her dead at the hospital found Karla washing the blanket on which her sister had thrown up.

It had been a shock to the pair. Things had gone horribly wrong. Yet it did not take them long to adjust to and even revel in the events of that night. Three weeks later, Karla and Paul were lounging naked on a bed in the basement, the camcorder running.

"I loved it when you fucked my little sister," she said. "Do you think we can do that [rape another young girl]? Do you want to do it fifty times more? Do it every week?"

Paul was surprised. "Why would you want to?"

"'Cause I love you. 'Cause you're the king. You can take their virginity. They'll be our children." Pandering to his fantasies, she dressed up in a shirt and sweater that had belonged to her sister. "I am your little virgin," she simpered, imitating Tammy's voice as she fellated him. "I'm glad Kar doesn't know about us."

By February, though, problems had arisen. The wedding plans were great, Karla wrote a friend, "except my parents are being assholes. They pulled money out saying they can't afford it. Bullshit! Only thinking of themselves. Screw that."

Her parents also objected to Paul living in the basement full-time and wanted him out during the week. So Paul and Karla rented 57 Bayview Drive, in St. Catharines, an attractive Cape Cod–style property that would be their playhouse.

They lavished gifts on each other. He bought her a Rottweiler puppy that they named Buddy. One night, as he was driving home, she called him on his car phone to tell him she had a surprise for him. When he got home, he couldn't believe it: a girl was lying asleep on their bedroom floor. The girl, who would be called "Jane" in the trials, was the same age as Tammy and bore a striking resemblance to the dead teenager. Jane had met and admired Karla, and was flattered when the older girl called her and invited her over for pizza and a video.

Karla had secured new supplies of sleeping pills and halothane, and this time she got the dosages right. Jane woke up the next morning feeling ill and sore and, after Paul and Karla drove her home, went to bed with the "flu." If it were not for the videos, which show first Karla assaulting her and then Paul taking her virginity while Karla administers the halothane, nothing further might ever have been known of this incident.

Karla and Paul were urban jackals now, prowling the streets, sometimes snapping at each other, always alert for an opportunity, gorging themselves on their prey. In the early hours of June 14, 1991, Paul moved quietly through a neighborhood in Burlington, Ontario, thirty minutes from home, looking for license plates to steal. He needed them for his new sideline: smuggling cheap American cigarettes across the nearby border into Canada and reselling them.

A girl came around the corner of a house and tried the door.

"Hi," Paul said. "What are you doing?"

"I live here."

"Locked out, huh?"

It was one of those moments from every parent's nightmares. One of those moments when we wish we could turn back the clock. If only...

Fourteen-year-old Leslie Mahaffy was in that rebellious teenage stage, no worse than thousands of other young girls, but a continuing source of frustration and anger for her parents. She skipped school and came home any old time, if at all. Her parents, asleep upstairs when she tried the door, made a mistake for which they will always blame themselves: they locked her out. It was 2:00 A.M. when she walked to a nearby pay phone, called a friend and asked if she could come over for the night. That might not be such a good idea, her friend replied: when she stayed over before, Leslie's parents were annoyed. After half an hour of girl talk, Leslie hung up. She was back at the house to try ringing the bell one last time when she met Paul.

Karla and Paul's wedding two weeks later was a dream. The videos and photographs taken of the beautiful young couple would play big across the world when the truth emerged. They show the Hollywood-handsome groom and his radiant bride in her $3,000 wedding dress riding in a carriage to the dollhouse church at Queenston Heights, a famous 1815 battleground above the Niagara River.

For Paul, always on the make, the wedding was also a chance to make a buck. The idea was to put on a big show and invite the maximum number of people, asking them to give money rather than gifts.

The next day, as the couple rested up and packed for their honeymoon in Hawaii, a man canoeing on Lake Gibson, near St. Catharines, noticed what looked like an unfamiliar sort of fish beneath a slab of concrete in the water. He poked it with his paddle. Not believing what he had seen, he returned later and, with the help of a man fishing nearby, pulled out the slab. Underneath was the calf and foot of a young woman. Police would recover seven concrete blocks containing body parts, plus a torso. The body, crudely dismembered with a power saw, was identified from dental braces as that of Leslie Mahaffy.

The first thing Paul and Karla did when they returned from their honeymoon was call the police to report that wedding gifts worth $30,286 had been stolen in a break-in. The officer who came to get the details was suspicious of their claim, but had to leave to resume more important work: tracking down the killer of Leslie Mahaffy.

A few weeks later, there was another call for official assistance. This time, Karla called 911 in the early hours of an August morning. "Please hurry!" she pleaded. "My friend has stopped breathing." A few minutes later, she called back to say the friend was breathing again. After inviting Jane around to the house again, Karla had been a little too heavy-handed with the halothane. Jane recovered.

Meanwhile, the police finally released the composite drawing of the Scarborough rapist, and several people called in to say it was Paul Bernardo. Eventually, an officer went to Bayview Drive, interviewed Paul about the rapes and even took blood, saliva and hair samples. But the tidy house, the wedding pictures on the shelf and the neatly dressed, well-spoken trainee accountant who answered questions in a straightforward manner did not fit the cop's idea of a serial rapist. The officer went away satisfied, and the samples were not examined at that time.

And so it went. A St. Catharines woman, after being followed several times by a man in a gold Nissan 240SX, gave police the license number. It belonged to Paul Bernardo. That information was also filed away.

Nearly a year had passed since the disappearance of Leslie Mahaffy. Karla and Paul felt invulnerable: no one could touch them. On April 16, 1992, Kristen French, a pretty, popular fifteen-year-old honors student was leaving her St. Catharines school in the mid-afternoon when a woman with long blonde hair standing beside a gold Nissan sports car in a church parking lot called her over for help with directions. Paul bundled her into the back of the car at knifepoint. As with Myra Hindley and Ian Brady, the Moors murderers (see "Wherever He Has Gone, I Have Gone"), the combination of male and female predators working together was lethal, disarming their victims' natural caution.

Two weeks later, Kristen's naked body was found in a ditch. That week, on her twenty-second birthday, Karla sent Paul a card: "You're the greatest husband in the world. All my love, and sweet dreams of you and me together forever. Karly Curls."

It was just the sort of card you'd expect from a woman who would describe herself to a psychiatrist as "an old-fashioned kind of girl, a stay-at-home, Girl Guides, have a bunch of kids, have doors opened for me kind of girl."

Initially, police did not connect Kristen's murder with that of Leslie—the methods used to dispose of the bodies were entirely different.

On May 23, 1992, the body of Terry Anderson, a personable fourteen-year-old who had disappeared the previous November, turned up in the water at nearby Port Dalhousie. The coroner found no evidence of foul play, and her death was put down to beer combined with a small amount of LSD, which had caused her to fall into the water. It was an explanation her father could never accept.

By now, Inspector Vince Bevan, the officer in charge of the Mahaffy and French murder investigations, and half the police in Ontario were preoccupied with the Great Camaro Wild Goose Chase. A woman who had been driving by the church when Kristen was abducted remembered seeing what looked like a struggle beside a car that, after being shown car identity books, she would label a cream Camaro. It was the strongest clue yet. Thousands of police hours were spent checking 1982 and more recent cream-colored Camaros. Three months after Kristen disappeared, Inspector Bevan starred in one of the most-watched Canadian crime shows ever—a re-enactment of the abduction, culminating with an appeal to the public to report sightings of cream-colored Camaros. Police telephone lines were jammed with people phoning in sightings. Karla and Paul hugged themselves with glee. They would never be caught.

It was not until February 1993—six months later—that the forensics lab got around to testing the samples made available long before by Paul Bernardo, and found that they linked him conclusively to three of the Scarborough rapes. By then, Paul had very unwisely turned his aggressive tendencies against his "princess."

In January, Karla's mother had received two anonymous phone calls urging her to look at her daughter's face. Stopping by the veterinary clinic where Karla worked, she found Karla sporting two hideous blue-black eyes. She must leave him, Dorothy Homolka urged her daughter. Karla finally agreed. After checking her bruises, a doctor at St. Catharines General said it was the worst case of wife abuse he'd seen. She had been beaten on the back of the head with a heavy flashlight, forcing the brain to collide violently with the front of her skull, which caused the "raccoon eyes." Karla's parents moved her to an aunt and uncle's apartment in Brampton, an hour away. No one noticed at the time, but photographs taken at the hospital showing Karla's injuries also show her wearing a Mickey Mouse watch just like the one Kristen was wearing when she disappeared.

Police, following up on the positive rape tests, were interested to discover that Paul's wife had laid a charge of assault against him. That suggested she might be willing to testify against him. A detective would thank her for her courage in speaking to them: "You're innocent. You're a victim," he reassured her. "We're not here to get you. We need you to get him." The vote of confidence must have cheered Karla no end. It also gave her the line that would carry her through the coming ordeal: "I'm innocent. I'm a victim."

Just to be on the safe side, she went to see George Walker, a Niagara Falls lawyer whose Dalmatian she had taken special care of when he brought it to the veterinary clinic. It was Walker who, after hearing as much of the truth as Karla was willing to tell him, got the Crown prosecutors to agree to the deal that to this day outrages Canadians. In return for testifying against Paul, Karla would plead guilty to manslaughter in the deaths of Leslie and Kristen and get the deal of a lifetime:

- She would receive in each case a twelve-year sentence, to be served concurrently.
- She would be eligible for parole in a little over three years.
- The Crown would try to have her assigned to a psychiatric hospital instead of prison.
- The Crown would write to the parole board, asking it to go easy on poor Karla.

Bernardo's lawyer, Ken Murray, would describe it as "a deal with the devil."

Why were the Crown officers willing to kiss away Karla's role in the murders? By this time, forensics specialists were tearing apart the house on Bayview Drive. They found a meticulous list of details of each of the Scarborough rapes, and hundreds of books and videos about sex and crime, from Dostoevsky's *Crime and Punishment* to *Lesbian Vibrator Bitches*. Missing, though, considering Bernardo's well-known love affair with his camcorder, were any videos of their crimes.

It would be no great task to convict Bernardo of rape, but that would leave the Mahaffy and French murders still on the books, officially unsolved. It must be remembered that the Crown and the police were under tremendous public pressure to get murder convictions, especially after snafus such as the Camaro fiasco. Karla's testimony, it was felt, was the Crown's only hope of pinning the big ones on her husband.

Karla's trial, which began in St. Catharines on June 28, 1993, was supposed to be little more than a one-day formality, with the judge imposing a gag order on publication of the proceedings. The Crown argued that if the public knew some of the gruesome details, it would be almost impossible to find an unbiased jury to try Paul Bernardo later. Newspapers and television stations had lawyers in court to oppose the ban, but their lawyers lost, and the gag was imposed. *The Washington Post* and the American TV tabloid show *A Current Affair* ignored the ban with impunity; Canadian media, meanwhile, could report none of the details.

There was, as it turned out, no need for the Crown to have signed its "deal with the devil." In May 1993, soon after his arrest, Bernardo directed his lawyer, Ken Murray, to visit the now thoroughly ransacked Bayview Drive home. Following directions given to him by Bernardo over a portable phone from his cell, Murray recovered a package of videotapes hidden inside a light fixture in the bathroom ceiling. Murray should have handed over the evidence to the Crown; instead, he kept it for more than sixteen months, believing he could use the tapes to defend his client, although his conscience would be increasingly troubled. Finally, frustrated by the ethical and tactical difficulties of his position, he turned to a widely respected defense lawyer, John Rosen. After Rosen viewed the tapes, he went into his bathroom and cried. Finally, too late to have any impact on Karla's sentence, the Crown got the evidence.

The farce continued. The court believed that the sensibilities of the Canadian public, and the victims' families in particular, had to be protected at all costs. So when Bernardo appeared in court in May 1995, charged with two counts each of first-degree murder, aggravated sexual assault, forcible confinement and kidnapping and one count of performing an indignity on a human body, only the jury was allowed to see the crucial videotapes. It is thanks to the courage of writer Stephen Williams, who revealed the contents of the tapes in his masterly account of the case, *Invisible Darkness*, that the public was finally allowed to know what happened in the Bayview Drive house of horrors (which has since been torn down).

Lead prosecutor Ray Houlahan was left with a problem. There was a real danger that the defense would try to switch the spotlight to Karla, making her, not her husband, seem like the devil incarnate. Houlahan was relentless in hammering home the horror of Bernardo's five-and-a-half-year rampage of rape and murder. But he tried to portray Homolka, his chief witness, as just another of Paul's victims. Even when Karla, on the tapes, showed every sign of enjoying the degradation of their victims and urged her husband on in his depravities, Houlahan argued that these scenes were scripted by Paul and demonstrated his control over her.

The first shot of the Mahaffy sequence shows the fourteen-year-old kneeling half-undressed by the fireplace, with Paul's red turtleneck wrapped around her head as a blindfold. "Tell me your name," he says.

"Leslie Mahaffy," she says in a frightened, little-girl voice.

"Oh my god," she says a little later, realizing from the sound of the camcorder that he is videotaping her on the toilet.

Karla has slept through all this. Coming downstairs, she is furious—that Paul has used her best champagne flutes to entertain his latest catch. Knowing he will be busy for a while, she takes the dog for a walk and then goes up to her room to read. The book? The extremely violent *American Psycho*.

Later, in the bedroom, Leslie cries when Paul asks her, "Would you like to have sex with two people?"

"Tell her the other person is a woman," says Karla, out of camera range.

"Make me feel good," he tells Leslie at one point, as Karla alternately sucks and licks her man and the submissive girl. "I'm judging you right now, okay? The next two hours are going to determine what I am going to do with you."

And later: "Is she making you feel okay?" he asks Karla, who smiles. "Put your tongue right in her asshole," he tells Leslie brutally. "Push it right in."

Then it is Karla's turn to hold the camera. Her hand is steady as a rock as Paul enters the girl from behind and she screams.

"I gave Leslie some sleeping pills and Bunky [Karla's teddy bear] to hold," she would tell a psychiatrist later. "I didn't want her to have any pain. Holding on to Bunky, Leslie just went to sleep. But I knew she'd get killed. I was there when he strangled her... I saw discoloration, and I had to help him carry her down to the root cellar. Because it was Father's Day, and my parents were coming to dinner."

Her only bad moment, she would say, was when her mother offered to go down to the root cellar to get the potatoes to prepare for dinner. "Don't worry. I'll get 'em," Karla said quickly, but she claimed it grossed her out to get the potatoes from beside the body in the cellar.

If Kristen French ever had a chance of escaping from the Bayview Drive house, it was lost when, soon after she was dragged in, she vomited and her blindfold fell off. After that, Karla and Paul did not bother with the blindfold. "I love you, Karla," she said at one point, trying to ingratiate herself as she was forced to masturbate the older woman. "Is that your name?" It didn't matter any more: her fate was sealed.

Now Karla took to her role as movie director. "Smile!" she ordered Kristen, as Paul pounded the girl in her lower back and told her to arch her back to make entry from the rear easier. "Suck his dick, Kristen," she said at one point during the girl's three days of torture. "Good girl!" Then she told Paul, "I got some good mouth shots."

In the midst of the torture sessions, she found time to write an Easter card to "the most wonderful man in the entire world, who means everything to me. All my love, Karly Curls."

At one point on Saturday afternoon, Paul left Kristen and Karla alone for an hour while he went out for pizza and to rent a movie. Was he worried Karla would try to save Kristen? Paul knew his wife better than that. All she did wrong while he was out was to let Kristen watch the TV news. When the girl saw her father making an appeal for his lost daughter, Kristen cried and threw up on the carpet. Paul was furious.

By Easter Sunday, Karla was becoming impatient. "They had been attacking [Kristen] for two-and-a-half days," says Christie Blatchford, who attended the trials. "Karla got up that morning, and you can just see her tapping her watch and saying, 'Well, you know, Paul, we gotta get this done. We're going to my parents' for Easter dinner.'" And when it was done, Karla, by her own admission, went downstairs to blow-dry her hair.

It could have been a zombie in the witness box for all the emotion Karla showed as she was taken through the devastating tapes. One of the psychiatric reports had mentioned her "moral vacuity." But she had learned well from the books she had been reading about battered wife syndrome. All the bad stuff, she kept saying, left her "numb." Except that in the tapes she seems to be having a good time.

Did Karla ever express one moment's regret or revulsion? The one instance seems to occur on the Tammy tape when Karla wrinkles her nose and says, "Fucking disgusting!"

But John Rosen, replaying the tape in slow motion for the jury, was able to point to Tammy's sanitary napkin and belt on the floor near the sofa. Bernardo had told her to put her fingers into her sister's vagina. "You take the hand out," Rosen said to Karla, indicating the screen images, "and you wipe it on the bed because it has blood on it, and he's telling you to lick it, and you don't want to lick your sister's menstrual blood, right? And that's why you say, 'Fucking disgusting!'"

"That's a lie," she said coolly.

The one crucial issue that the tapes did not settle was who had killed Leslie and Kristen. The murders were not videotaped. No one doubted that Paul Bernardo would be found guilty of all the lesser charges, but there was no hard evidence—except Karla's word—that it was he who had killed the girls. Now, in defending Bernardo, Rosen found himself raising the question that should have been confronted by the prosecution long ago: was Karla, in fact, the murderer?

She claimed that Paul had beaten Leslie and then strangled her with an electrical cord. Because her neck had been severed with a power saw, it was impossible for the pathologist to determine whether Leslie had been strangled. But other classic symptoms of strangulation were not present, and there were no signs she had been beaten. However, there were two deep-muscle bruises on either side of her back.

"What we do know," Rosen said to Homolka, "is that these two little red marks are consistent with a pair of knees about the size of your knees pushing the muscle against the ribs while you held her head down on a pillow and suffocated her, isn't that right?"

Similarly, and ignoring her denials, Rosen put it to Karla that deep hemorrhages inside Kristen's head above each ear were not from being punched by Bernardo, as Karla claimed, but were from blows Karla had administered with a rubber mallet. (Karla

19

had admitted to having the mallet handy when she was guarding Kristen while Bernardo was out.)

"I have never hit anyone in my life, Mr. Rosen," she responded.

Rosen was changing the equation. Where the prosecution saw Paul as a murderous sexual deviant who abused his wife, Rosen saw him as a violent sexual deviant teamed with a woman capable of and well equipped to murder. She had a knowledge of drugs. Moreover, although she claimed Paul had done all the work of dismembering Leslie Mahaffy, cutting up the body with a power saw and encasing the parts in concrete, it was she, said Rosen, who from her work with animals had a knowledge of anatomy and dismemberment.

Bernardo's version would be that they had dismembered the body together, working under a tarpaulin to prevent flesh and blood from splattering, and that he had handed the parts to her to wash. Not surprisingly, he denied killing the two girls, claiming that, in both cases, Karla killed them in his absence.

To no one's surprise, Bernardo, after a four-month trial, was found guilty on all counts and sentenced to life imprisonment with no possibility of parole for twenty-five years. The sentence brought little satisfaction. To this day, it is "the deal with the devil" that rankles with the Canadian public.

"I never saw her as a victim," says Blatchford. "I never bought this thing that she was afraid of him. She was part of it, she understood him, and she got her power through sex. It's like people say she was scared when she handed over her sister to him. Well, that's crap. She was living at home in the bosom of her family in St. Catharines, and this clown was a weekend boyfriend living in Toronto. And one day, he said, 'You know, I'd really like to fuck your little sister.' Every woman I know would say, 'What are you talking about?' and never see the guy again. That was probably her single worst act, and she did that before she had any reason to be afraid of him."

Karla's applications for parole have been rigorously opposed, and in March 2001 the National Parole Board denied her early release and told her, "If released, you are likely to commit an offense causing death or serious harm to another person." But in 2005, her sentence will be up and she will released.

In the meantime, imprisonment seems to have been no great burden: in 2000, a leaked photograph showed her partying in a slinky evening dress at a birthday party with other inmates at a medium-security institution in Quebec that guards refer to as "the love shack."

She has spoken about leaving Canada when she is released. "She doesn't need to," suggests Blatchford. "She's remarkably bland. She dyes her hair, she puts on a pair of glasses, you would never know who she was—until too late."

He Was My Master, and
He Kissed Me

It was raining as I walked up the front path to the 1950s suburban house. I didn't know what to expect. It had taken me weeks to track down this woman, who, I believed, might be Carrie Davies' daughter. I knew that several years after the trial, Carrie had married a man named Brown, and someone had told me they had moved to the small town of Huttonville, northwest of Toronto.

After a number of phone calls to people called Brown in the area, a man said he knew Carrie. "That would be my mother."

"Your mother?"

"Yes. She died in 1961."

Had she ever talked to him about a court case she was involved in back in 1915?

"No, I can't say as she did," he said. "Maybe you better speak to my sister, Margaret, in the city. She knows more about Mother's background than I do. Hold on, I'll get the number."

I called his sister, Margaret Grainger, and told her I was doing some historical research and wished to speak to her about her mother. I wasn't going to use the word "murder" on the phone.

She sounded a little puzzled, but said she would be happy to see me on Monday morning. As I drove out to Margaret's home in the Toronto suburb of Etobicoke, I wondered whether Carrie Davies was indeed her mother. Carrie was a common enough name around the early part of the twentieth century.

But all doubt disappeared the moment she opened the door. "Come in, won't you?" she said. "What a dreadful day!" Perhaps the surprise showed on my face. It was Carrie Davies standing before me—sort of. Her daughter, at sixty-two, had the same high, almost oriental cheekbones, the same straight, no-nonsense mouth I was familiar with from newspaper photographs published at the time of the trial.

"Let me take your coat," she said, leading me into the kitchen and offering me coffee and cookies. I set the cardboard tube containing old newspaper clippings on the floor beside me. Had she been wondering why I wanted to speak to her about her mother?

"To tell you the truth, I've been puzzling about it ever since you called. She was never well known or anything like that."

She didn't know. She had no clue that her mother's name was once on every Canadian's lips. That she was at the center of a scandal involving Toronto's leading family, the super-rich and powerful Masseys, of whom the humorist B.K. Sandwell had written:

Toronto has no social classes,
Only the Masseys and the masses.

She didn't know. I had thought she might be reluctant to talk about the shooting, but it had seemed so unlikely that she wouldn't know about it that I had prepared no strategy to meet that situation.

The cuckoo clock went off in the hall. I took a deep breath.

Toronto in the first year of the Great War was a city wearing its heart on its sleeve. Recruits dug trenches in Exhibition Park, practicing for a reality they could not possibly imagine, and the carnage in the trenches in France only redoubled the fanatical support for "our boys at the front." In Ottawa, lights were turned off for fear of German plane attacks—and this long before any plane had flown across the Atlantic.

For the most part, though, life in Toronto appeared surprisingly normal. The population was mostly of British stock, and any event was an excuse to take to the streets and break out the Union Jacks. The hits of the day were "It's a Long Way to Tipperary," recorded by John McCormack, and "Sister Susie's Sewing Shirts for Soldiers," lisped by Al Jolson.

On February 8, 1915, the Toronto newspapers were full of news from battles at Ypres and the Argonne Forest. A small item reported that the ocean liner *Lusitania* had arrived safely at Liverpool from New York (three months later she would be sunk off the coast of Ireland by a German submarine).

On Walmer Road, in the well-to-do Annex area, men trudged home along sidewalks swept clear of snow, anticipating a hot evening meal that had, likely as not, been prepared by a cook.

Shortly after 6:00 P.M., Charles A. "Bertie" Massey, returning home from his job selling cars downtown, left the Dupont streetcar and walked south toward his home at 169 Walmer Road. He would be having dinner with his only son, Charlie, age fourteen, because his wife, Rhoda, was away in Hartford, Connecticut, on a family visit.

Outside the house, paperboy Ernie Pelletier stopped Massey to collect his weekly bill—twenty-five cents. Beatrice Dennis, walking by, saw Massey turn up the front path. Then she heard a shot. As she turned, she heard him exclaim, "Oh!" and saw him backing down the path. He was halfway to the sidewalk when there was a flash from the porch—another gunshot. Massey toppled onto his back in the snow.

Nothing had been said and there was no light on the porch, but other witnesses said they could see a maid's white apron and cap standing out luminously in the darkness of the porch. Then the door was shut quietly, like the curtain falling on a melodrama.

Dr. John Mitchell, on his way home to 140 Walmer Road, was at Massey's side in seconds. He found him gasping. He could feel no pulse, and by the time the victim was carried into the house next door and laid on the carpet, he was dead.

Ten minutes later, Police Sergeant Larry Brown arrived. Stationing constables at the back and front of 169, he opened the front door. In the rich, oak-trimmed hallway, he was met by a confused Charlie, a scientifically inclined teen who had been conducting glass-blowing experiments in the basement, and who knew nothing of the shooting.

Brown searched the ground and second floors without finding anyone. Then, as he went to climb the stairs to the third floor, a girl's voice called, "Who's there?"

"Police," he replied gruffly.

"Come up."

"No, you come down," he called.

He climbed to the first landing, where he saw Carrie, a slim, almost childish figure, dressed in her coat, as if to go out. She was holding the gun, an Ivor Johnson revolver, by the muzzle. "Here it is," she said, handing it to him. He noted that it contained three live bullets. Two empty shells were found on her bedroom floor.

"You'll have to come with me, Miss," he said, not unkindly.

"Can I get my hat?" He nodded, and she fixed her slightly shabby black hat with a hatpin in front of the hall mirror.

Carrie put her hand on the sergeant's arm. She had to make him understand. "You see," she said, "He ruined my life. I've been good to them, and they've been good to me. He disgraced my life." For several minutes, her shoulders shook with sobs. "Take me away," she gulped.

"He ruined my life." Her words have a melodramatic ring to them, like the subtitle from some scratchy old silent movie. But at that time, servant girls trod a perilous line between respectability and disgrace. A Social Service Commission appointed by the Toronto city council that year to investigate deplorable social conditions had interviewed seventy-five prostitutes and had found that thirty-six of them had previously been in domestic service. The path to ruin was all too simple: seduced by an employer or some member of the family, the young woman would be discharged immediately upon discovery. Without references, she would find it impossible to secure another position and would end up on the street. Seduction of a female employee under the age of twenty-one was an offense punishable under the Criminal Code. But this provision applied only to owners of stores and factories. When the government attempted to extend the provisions to employers of domestic servants, the all-male Senate, mindful perhaps of their own failings, threw out the bill.

There was no doubt that Carrie had been strictly brought up. She was just past her sixteenth birthday when she arrived in Toronto from the village of Sandy Beds, in rural Bedfordshire, England, in May 1913. Her father, a retired British Army sergeant major, had been a disciplinarian at home, and his daughters went out little, except to Sunday school. On their two nights out a week, they had to be home by 9:00 P.M.

But now Carrie's father was chronically ill in the hospital, and her mother, with five smaller children to care for, had given up her sewing job because her eyes were failing. Carrie's married older sister, Maude, who lived in Toronto, paid Carrie's fare to Canada so that she could work as a domestic to help out her siblings back home. Carrie had immediately secured employment with Mr. and Mrs. Massey and, out of her salary of $14 a month, had begun repaying Maude her passage money. Eventually, her pay was increased to $16 a month; she sent most of it home to her mother.

Carrie's employer, Bertie Massey, had also experienced difficulties early in life. He had seen the best and worst of times, thanks to the capriciousness of his vindictive grandfather, Hart Massey.

Bertie could boast, and sometimes did, that it was his father, also named Charles, who was responsible for the dramatic growth of the giant Massey farm machinery company. The Masseys were of Yankee stock and founded Watertown, New York. Hart was a boy of seventeen when his father, Daniel, moved the family across Lake Ontario to Newcastle in Upper Canada. Typical of the Yankee inventors and tinkerers of the age, they set up a modestly successful farm machinery business. But in 1870, when he was forty-seven, Hart, citing ill health, moved to Cleveland, Ohio, leaving his oldest son, Charles Albert, then twenty-three, in charge of the business.

It was a wise choice. Over the next dozen years, Charles Albert traveled the length and breadth of the continent, seeking out new ideas and convincing farmers that it was Massey machinery they needed to open up the prairies to agriculture. In 1880, with his father's approval, he bought a large tract of land in west-end Toronto and built the largest factory in the British Empire. Soon, goods trains were rolling west, carrying machines with such names as the King of the Meadows and the Mighty Monarch of the Harvest Field.

Meanwhile, Charles Albert had bought a handsome row house on Clarence Square, not far from the new factory, where he installed his pretty wife, originally from Kalamazoo, Michigan, and their growing family.

It may have been that Hart, in distant Cleveland, was jealous of his son's success. At any rate, he moved his family back to Toronto, setting up in a twenty-five-room mansion, which he named Euclid Hall, on fashionable Jarvis Street. Charles Albert soon moved his family to a nearby mansion. It was as if father and son were in a contest to see who could work the hardest— and it was Charles who faltered. In early 1884, he fell ill with typhoid fever and died.

Hart commemorated his son with a stained-glass window in the company's new office building that showed Charles Albert flanked by a wheat field and the company's newest creation, the Perfect Binder. But he treated his daughter-in-law, Jessie, miserably. Forced to vacate the Jarvis Street mansion, Jessie found a modest, semi-detached home on Ontario Street. The children lived in two worlds—enjoying the opulence of their grandparents' surroundings at Euclid Hall, where they were treated like little potentates, and a very ordinary life at Ontario Street.

When Jessie decided to marry a bank clerk named John Haydn Horsey, Hart virtually kidnapped the two youngest children, Bertie and Bessie, setting them up at Euclid Hall. Bitterly resentful, Jessie reclaimed them one day as they left school. Hart would not forward their clothes or toys, and Charles Albert and Jessie's children grew up as virtual outcasts from the Massey clan. They carried the name, but Hart's attention and hopes had now switched to their cousins, including Vincent, who would one day be Canada's Governor General, and Raymond, who would make a name for himself as a Hollywood star.

In death as in life, Hart was vindictive. His fortune of $2 million went largely to charity, and the five children of Charles Albert, the son who had done more even than Hart to create the family fortune, were left $75,000 between them. Which explains why Bertie, not a great businessman in his own right, was at the time of his death working as a car salesman.

But he still bore the family name, which was enough for the Toronto *Globe*. The next day, the newspaper referred to his death as "a murder of sensational, dramatic and personal interest."

There is nothing on the public record to indicate how the Masseys in their mansions on Jarvis Street were reacting, but it is not hard to imagine. A discreet call to Daniel Thompson, KC, the Massey family lawyer, perhaps from the chief of police, likely alerted him to the incident on Walmer Road, leaving him in no doubt about the probable motive for the shooting. Thompson, in turn, would have contacted Chester Massey, the nominal and ineffectual head of the family, and Chester's first call would have been to Vincent, his clever son, who was making a name for himself as an academic at the University of Toronto.

We can see Vincent—a snob and a bigot remembered now for his wartime warning to the Canadian government about admitting Jewish refugees fleeing Hitler: "None is too many"—arriving at his father's home for what would have been a council of war.

Vincent would have been outraged that his cousin, in death, might besmirch the family name. More than likely, though, it would have been Thompson who put forward a possible solution: as the law stood, if Carrie Davies was judged by an alienist (as psychiatrists were then known) to be insane, there need be no trial, and she could be committed immediately to an insane asylum.

Hadn't there been an incident the previous summer when the poor girl had gone off her head when Bertie and Rhoda were staying at their cottage on Toronto Island? Carrie had become hysterical while out for a walk with a friend, and her employers had called in two doctors to examine her. True, her sweetheart, to whom she would say she was engaged, was just going overseas with his unit, and her father was at the point of death in hospital. But her attack, from which she had soon recovered, certainly indicated a fragile state of mind.

The Masseys, meanwhile, attended to one other small piece of business. Bertie, after a quiet service held in his brother's home rather than in church, and with the Masons, to which he had belonged, refusing to take part, was buried in a remote corner of Mount Pleasant Cemetery. The grave, unmarked to this day, is a good distance from the Massey family mausoleum, built in the form of a Scottish castle.

The morning after her arrest, Carrie, with her plain features and straight, no-nonsense mouth, and still wearing her long brown coat and the black velvet hat trimmed with pink feathers, looked sadly out of place sitting beside prostitutes and small-time offenders in the women's court. She seemed oblivious to her surroundings until her name was called. "The charge is murder," the magistrate told her. "That you, Carrie Davies, did contrary to the law murder Charles Albert Massey on the 8th instant." She seemed about to collapse, until a court official hastily gave her a chair while the magistrate remanded the case.

And then something quite odd occurred. Mrs. Arthur Massey, Bertie's sister-in-law, gave a lengthy interview to the press. Normally, the Masseys did not talk to newspaper people. On this occasion, though, Mary Massey held nothing back. "Motive?" she said in reply to a question. "Why, there wasn't any motive. We are all perfectly satisfied the girl was not mentally responsible when she shot Bert."

"I know," she added, "that it has been hinted that Mr. Massey may have been indiscreet and acted improperly toward the girl, but the whole story is ridiculous. No person who knew Bert will believe that for a minute."

And she cited Carrie's illness at the island the summer before as irrefutable proof that the girl was mentally unstable.

Suddenly, the police were talking to reporters about the likelihood that there would be no trial and that Carrie Davies would be committed to an asylum. "Girl Had Periodic Fits of Depression," read one headline.

The Masseys and their supporters, however, had counted without John Ross Robertson. The fiery publisher of the *Telegram* was strongly pro-British and no friend of the Masseys—and he smelled a rat. "Has the Government Taken a Hand in Carrie Davies' Case?" the *Telegram* asked, after coroner A.J. Johnson, conducting the inquest into Bertie's death, speculated about Carrie's sanity. Another headline, aimed at the *Telegram*'s newspaper rivals, read, "Slide to Asylum via Trial by Newspaper."

For the *Telegram*'s colorful, moody editor, John "Black Jack" Robinson, it was a dream issue. While British and Canadian soldiers were giving their lives at the front, here was a daughter of the Old Country, abused and probably assaulted by her employer, being railroaded into the asylum! One headline read, "British Fair Play for British Soldier's Daughter." In no time, the newspaper was able to announce that the local Bedfordshire Society was launching a defense fund on Carrie's behalf. No one stopped to ask if a "Bedfordshire Society" had even existed before Black Jack saw the need for one. And with the *Telegram* beating the drum, more than $1,000 was donated—a remarkable sum for the time.

There was pandemonium at City Hall when Carrie faced trial on February 26, less than three weeks after the shooting. A coroner's jury had stated unequivocally that "Carrie Davies did feloniously and with malice aforethought kill and slay Charles A. Massey." There was no dodging the central fact, so what possible verdict could there be but guilty?

But in the intervening weeks, public opinion, offended at the apparent attempt by the Masseys to sweep the scandal under the rug, and egged on by the *Telegram*, had swung solidly in Carrie's favor. So when the Crown prosecutor, E.E.A. Du Vernet, got to his feet, he struck a chord of sympathy. "It is the most unpleasant duty I have had to perform during my career to prosecute a poor, unfortunate girl like this," he declared.

So what were the facts? Carrie, a tiny figure with crimped hair, told her story in a low, clear voice. Before leaving for a two-week stay in Hartford, her mistress, Mrs. Rhoda Massey, had told Carrie to look after her husband and not to leave the house unattended. Everything went well until three days before Mrs. Massey was due home, when Bertie gave a Friday night dinner for twelve.

We can wonder at working conditions that called for an eighteen-year-old, in addition to keeping the house clean, doing the laundry and so forth, to prepare, serve and clear up after a dinner for twelve—and all for $16 a month! The heavy drinking and merrymaking went on until 1:00 A.M., when the guests gave three cheers for Bertie and made their unsteady way home.

On Sunday, Carrie was surprised to see her employer come down for his midday meal in his bathrobe. After dinner, when young Charlie had gone out, Bertie approached Carrie as she was clearing up the dining room. "Carrie, I must thank you for what you did on Friday," he said. "I have a present here for you." He produced a shamrock ring, made of pearls, and tried to put it on her finger. But it was too small, so he told her to take it to Eaton's department store and have it made larger.

Shortly thereafter, he approached her again, looking restless and excited. "Did you notice anything Friday night?" he asked. She shook her head. "Did you see a lady drop her table napkin several times, and did you see me run my hand up and down the lady's stocking?"

Carrie felt herself blushing. She looked at him reprovingly. Mrs. Massey, he told her, had gone to the States to have a good time. "But," he said, laughing, "you must know I have a lady friend of my own. Did you not see any kissing going on Friday night?"

With that, he slid his hands around her waist and kissed her. She struggled, but he kissed her again, trembling and excited. Carrie broke away and went into the kitchen. A few minutes later, she heard him running his bath upstairs. "Carrie, would you be so good as to make my bed while I have a bath?" he called down.

When she went into the bedroom, he was still there, rummaging through the drawers where his wife kept her underwear. "Here, Carrie," he said. "Why don't you try some of these on? You'd look marvelous." The next instant, he had hold of her wrist and was pulling her toward the bed. She cried and struggled, then broke away, ran up to her room and locked the door.

She took off her uniform, put on her outdoor clothes and, though it was not her day off, crept down the stairs and fled to her sister Maude's house. She was, apparently, too embarrassed to tell her sister and brother-in-law, Edmund, the whole story. Mr. Massey, she said, had tried to kiss her. That was not so unusual for an employer. If he tried it again, said Edmund, she should leave the house for good.

That night, Carrie returned to Walmer Road. The next morning, at 8:45, she knocked on her master's bedroom door to wake him, then scampered downstairs to put his breakfast on the table. Then she hid herself in the cellar until she heard the front door close behind him.

She couldn't keep her mind on her work. Mrs. Massey was due home that day, and once she arrived, Carrie would be safe. Periodically, Carrie peered out the front windows to see if there was any sign of her mistress. She feared that if she spent the night in the house, Bertie would make another attempt. She knew she should leave. But what would she say to Mrs. Massey if she came home and found Carrie not there?

"He was my master, and he kissed me. I kept thinking that," she testified. "I could only think of him doing me harm. He would disgrace me."

Just after 6:00 P.M., her anxiety growing, she heard the doorbell ring. It was the paperboy, Ernie, to collect his money. "Mr. Massey is not home," she told him.

"Oh, is that him coming down the street?" the boy asked.

Carrie looked up the street and saw the familiar figure in his dress coat. Not stopping to think, she ran upstairs to Charlie's room, where she knew he kept an old revolver that he used for target practice in the basement. Charlie had even shown her how to fire it. She opened the drawer where he kept his bullets, grabbed a handful and loaded five into the gun as she came downstairs.

Her employer was coming toward the front door as she opened it. She fired blindly. He said, "Oh!" and then it seemed to her he was walking backwards down the path. Thinking she had missed him, she ran out on the verandah and fired again. "I still kept pulling the trigger when someone called out 'Stop it!' I saw him lying there, and I thought he was just lying there to avoid the bullets."

She then ran up to her room, and dimly remembered writing two letters—one to her sister, one to a friend.

"What kind of harm did you think Mr. Massey meant to do you?" her counsel, Hartley Dewart, asked. The jury craned forward.

"That he was going to disgrace me."

"What do you mean by that? That he would forcibly have connection with you? That he would ravish you and accomplish his purpose?"

"Yes," she said in a small voice.

"Do you think Mrs. Massey would have discharged you rather than have this trouble?"

"Yes, I do."

In his speech to the jury the following morning, Dewart wrapped himself and his client in the flag. "Carrie was loyal, devoted and true. Never before," he proclaimed in shocked disbelief, "has an honorable, high-minded girl like this been tried for murder. Her only motive was the defense of her honor against a treacherous assailant. While this girl's lover is at the front, fighting for the honor of Britain"—he paused as if listening to the distant sound of bugles—"this girl was battling for her honor." (Doctors, incidentally, had established that Carrie was a virgin.)

Dewart had been careful in jury selection to pick stolid middle-aged men, most of them farmers, and now he capitalized on that advantage. "Look the facts in the face," he cried. "You have a wife, a daughter or perhaps a sister at home. Can you look them squarely in the face with a clear conscience and say you did your duty upon the facts of this case if you leave a stain upon this girl with your verdict? Put any one of your own in this girl's position and think what you would say if a jury found them guilty in the same set of circumstances."

Prosecutor Du Vernet reminded the jurors that Canada was not a society where arguments were settled with guns. "If you can honestly say that she lost control," he said, giving them an out, "the law allows you to say so. But let us brush away all this nonsense about justification." His voice gathered strength. "We must do our duty, even if it is hard. We must not let down the barriers of law and order."

The bearded chief justice, Sir William Mulock, instructed the jury that there were only three possible verdicts: guilty of murder, guilty of manslaughter or not guilty. The jurors were hardly listening. In less than half an hour, they were back with their verdict: "We find Carrie Davies not guilty."

There was an explosion of emotion and cheering in the courtroom. Even Sir William had tears in his eyes. "Miss Davies," he said, when he had secured silence. "You have heard the verdict?"

"Yes, sir."

"A verdict," continued the judge, "in which I concur, if that is any comfort to you... You were between two fires, one of them the promise to Mrs. Massey, and the other your terror of being there. So, trying to do your duty under all these circumstances, you found yourself in this tragedy. You are free to go now."

When I had finished telling the story, I handed Margaret Grainger photocopies of 1915 newspapers detailing the case. She spent some time studying them, and then she cried.

Finally, wiping away her tears, she got up and poured more coffee. "She had such a hard life, such a hard life," she said.

She looked out the window, where the last few leaves of autumn clung to the trees. Her mother, she said, had never told them about the war years, except to say that she had tried nursing in England but had been so upset by the sight of blood that she had given it up. By 1917, she was back in Canada, where she married Charles Brown, an Englishman some ten years older than herself. They were always moving from one farm to another, living on the edge of poverty.

At one point, while her husband ran a roofing business, Carrie cared for a thirteen-acre market garden, as well as working as caretaker of the local school. She gave birth to two children, Richard in 1918, and Margaret in 1919; a third child was stillborn after Carrie was thrown from a buggy while fetching water.

What set Carrie Brown's life apart from those of thousands of other wives of subsistence farmers was her constant effort to help others. "She was always willing hands," said Margaret. "When a neighbor's wife became ill with cancer, it was Mother who nursed her to the end. She was always the one who closed the eyes of the dying." On Sundays she was the first to arrive at Norval Presbyterian Church to fire up the furnace, and she pumped the organ during services. Later she started the Mission Band for children at Huttonville United Church and began a branch of the Temperance Union.

At the time, Margaret wondered why, when her girlfriend's sister got into trouble, Carrie went out of her way to help her. It was as if she couldn't do enough. Then, in the 1950s, she achieved what must have been a long-standing ambition: she became housemother at the Cedarvale Home for Wayward Girls, where her husband also worked as a maintenance man.

It is not hard to make the connection. Having once been in trouble herself, Carrie wanted to be there for other girls in difficulty.

Margaret left me for a few minutes, and when she returned from the basement, she handed me a hardcover notebook in which her mother had recorded her thoughts while at Cedarvale. "My possessions of this world's goods," she had written in June 1952, "are still very few, but my spiritual blessings are many."

Now and then, telling her story, Margaret would weep. She wondered how she had been so incurious, not to ask about the missing years in her mother's life. "I guess I was the kind of kid who accepted things as they were," she said.

Her mother had bouts of illness throughout her life, but not even a broken bone in her foot kept her from her chores. It was a bout of rheumatic fever that finally weakened her, and she died on October 5, 1961. Her husband lived another seventeen years, dying at the age of ninety.

The odd thing was, Margaret said, that when they'd checked her mother's documents, although her passport showed her as having been born in 1900—the year she had always led them to believe she was born—her birth certificate showed that she was born on April 28, 1897. "Perhaps she was trying to wipe those early years in Toronto out of her life," Margaret said. Knowing what had happened in 1915 suddenly made sense of her mother's life.

I gathered up my photocopies and put them away. Margaret accompanied me to the front door. "Wait a minute," she said as I was going out. She went down to the basement again. When she returned, she was carrying a large brown paper bag. "Here's some apples," she said. "They come from mother's old orchard in Huttonville. She always used to pick them."

Another Case for the No. 1 Lady Detective

What would Mma Ramotswe have done? That's what I keep asking myself as I review the tragedy of Mariette Bosch.

Mariette was a middle-aged white woman caught up in a tangled love triangle that ended in two deaths; Precious Ramotswe, as millions of readers know, is the proprietor of the No. 1 Ladies' Detective Agency. She is a woman of classical African proportions, the fictional creation of Alexander McCall Smith, and her feats are described in a series of bestselling books that began with *The No. 1 Ladies' Detective Agency*.

What the two women have in common is that they are both from Botswana, a desert-like, diamond-rich country on South Africa's northern border. Mma Ramotswe is a woman of enormous wisdom, humor and intuition who, after selling her late father's cattle to raise money, starts her detective agency and goes about solving life's little mysteries—like the tricks of two-timing husbands, the paternity of an illegitimate child, or the mischievous influence of witch doctors. Mariette, on the other hand, was foolish and impetuous. If she could only have consulted Mma Ramotswe, all might have been well.

Even Mma Ramotswe's fans, who have learned a good deal about Botswana from her stories, might have been able to help. They know that Botswana sets itself apart from its more violent neighbor, South Africa, in that it has an almost pathological abhorrence of guns. Possession of an illegal firearm is an offense that Botswana courts treat with the greatest severity. Mariette knew that, and it was in trying to get around the gun laws that she made her biggest mistakes.

Mariette was probably the last person in Gaberone, the capital of Botswana, who would have been suspected of murder—which helps to explain why it took a long time to catch her. Home videos taken in happier days show the plump, attractive blonde sitting beside the family swimming pool with her husband, Justin, in the well-to-do suburb of Phakalane.

It would seem ironic that the main reason Mariette and Justin and many other white families moved from South Africa to Botswana in the early 1990s was to escape crime. With the end of apartheid in South Africa, and the coming of the first truly democratic elections in 1994, many white South Africans feared for the future. They saw moving to Botswana as a chance to step back in time and preserve the kind of coddled life they were used to. There were black servants to serve breakfast beneath the jacaranda trees and to take care of chores like looking after the children. Best of all, there was an absence of fear. They could look back pityingly on a flawed South Africa, where the prosperous cowered behind barbed wire–topped fences and went in fear of being yanked from their Audis and BMWs at stoplights by carjackers. Gaberone—though it was close enough to the South African border that in a few hours you could be back in Jo'burg, visiting the folks—felt as safe and peaceful as...well, apartheid-era South Africa.

The Botswanan government, run by President Festus Mogae and his ministers (Botswana gained its independence from Britain in 1966), kept crime under firm control, a situation almost unique in Africa. Guns were forbidden and, while the death penalty had been abolished in South Africa, the hangman still found employment in Botswana. That was a comfort.

But on June 26, 1996, Mariette's best friend, Ria Wolmarans, a forty-six-year-old company executive, was murdered in her home two blocks from where the Bosch family lived. A ripple of fear went through the white community.

Ria's nineteen-year-old daughter, Maryna, had gone out to dinner that evening. "When I left," she said later, "I didn't know what time I was going to be back, so my mother gave me the keys so she wouldn't have to get up to let me in. She was going to bed early."

Maryna arrived home at about 11:00 P.M. "I went to my mom's room to let her know I was back. As I went through the passage that connects the garage to the house, I stepped on something. I thought it was the dog, but when I turned on the light, my mom was there. I didn't know what was going on. It never crossed my mind she might be dead."

Ria Wolmarans had been shot in the back and in the side at close quarters, and two spent 9 mm cartridges were found. "She didn't stand a chance," the pathologist said. The killing, the police said, appeared to be the work of an amateur burglar who, not suspecting Ria was home, had panicked. Nothing was stolen.

No arrest followed. Ria's husband, Marthinus—called "Tienie"—who had been away working in the north of the country when she was murdered, resumed life as best he could with their two daughters and their son. And Phakalane neighbors, driving past on their way to golf or bridge, would experience a small shiver of disquiet.

The police, though, had kept to themselves two vital pieces of information. First, there had been no sign of a break-in. Second, a neighbor, Janet Squire, had told them she was making dinner at about 8:45 the evening of the murder when she thought she heard a gun go off and then a cry for help, followed by a second shot. She ran to an upstairs window that overlooked the Wolmarans' property and saw a faint red light, but heard nothing more.

"Did you hear something?" she asked her husband, who was watching television. He did not reply. Satisfied that she had done her duty, she returned to the kitchen and continued cooking.

One more thing: the Wolmarans' dog had not barked. Janet Squire was sure of that.

Then, unexpectedly, police arrested Mariette Bosch. She not only worked alongside Ria at the Kwena Rocla concrete products company, where Ria was chief financial officer, but was the dead woman's best friend.

Most people in Phakalane simply thought there had been a police cock-up. Certainly, people who knew her did not believe Mariette was capable of murder. She was a type familiar at any suburban golf club or horse meet: tall, blonde, attractive, a bit of a flirt. And what was particularly puzzling was that this was a story of two families—and two women, in particular—drawn together by adversity.

Ria was unhappy when Tienie (pronounced "Tinny"), seeking new work opportunities, had moved them to Gaberone in 1991. They separated in 1993, but got together again the following year. "My mom was not a housewife-style person," her older daughter, Marianne, told a British Broadcasting Corporation (BBC) interviewer. "At the beginning, it was hard for her to adapt. She was basically the backbone of the family. My father was more soft than my mom." Ria found an outlet for her energies when Tienie used his contacts to get her a job at Kwena Rocla, and it was there that she met Mariette, who had also recently moved to Botswana with her husband, Justin.

There was tension in the Bosch household too: Justin was an overbearing man, quick to lose his temper and unfaithful. But with so much in common—the Bosch couple also had two daughters and a son—the Wolmarans and the Bosches were drawn together. They enjoyed *braais* (barbecues) at each others' homes, and on Sundays the two families sat across from each other in the front pews at the local Dutch reformed church. "They were close friends," said the minister, Reverend Arthur Cloete. "When Tienie had to go and work up north, Mariette was always around, making sure that Ria and her children were all right." (Congregation members would eventually put up bail to get Mariette released from prison.) The two women took classes together, learning how to decorate porcelain dolls, and experimented in the kitchen, making "the most decadent cakes." They even went on holiday together, leaving the husbands to look after the children.

As a matter of convenience and economy, the two families took it in turns to drive their kids to private school in Zeerust, across the border in South Africa. "Sometimes it was our mother who took us to school," said Charmaine, the oldest Bosch girl, "and Ria would pick us up." It was on one of these school runs that Justin Bosch, returning from dropping off the children, crashed his brand-new car and was killed. "It was hard, but we coped quite well," said Charmaine. Mariette became even more reliant on Ria at this time. "My mother was the strong-willed one," said Marianne. "Mariette was the dependent one. She needed a strong person to help her."

Then Ria was murdered. Within a month of her death, to the surprise of those closest to them, Tienie and Mariette rented a two-storey house just around the corner from their family homes. With a straight face, Tienie insisted their relationship was platonic and mumbled an excuse about needing a second home where Maryna could stay while he was away working (presumably she was afraid to be alone in the house where her mother was murdered).

He and Mariette, he insists to this day, did not begin a relationship until she joined him in northern Botswana for a holiday two months after Ria's death. In Tienie's words, "I said to her, 'You know, as we get along so well and are alone, maybe we should face the future together.' At the time, she just laughed at me and said she was not ready for such a relationship again. She must have thought about it, because she asked me if I was serious about it, and from that it started just slowly developing. You know," he added, "when you are married to a person for twenty-six years and suddenly that person is not there any more, it's a large adaptation to your life. Your companion is gone. Suddenly you don't have anyone to talk to. You have to adapt to so many things."

The bigger adjustment was for the children when they heard the news. "When my dad told me he was going to remarry," Marianne said, "I was quite angry, quite upset. I asked him, 'How could you do it so soon after my mother's death? It's not proper.' He told me he was lonely. I asked him, 'Who is the lady?' He said, 'Mariette.' I was furious about it. I said, 'Why? What happened?'"

Charmaine said, "They could have waited two or three or maybe five years. It's hard on us children as well." They would marry some fifteen months after the murder.

"Maybe it was too soon," Tienie, a man with the beefy profile of a Hereford bull, said in retrospect. "I am not making excuses for myself. It happened. I am sad for all the consequences of it. I

45

am not sorry for the relationship that developed between Mariette and myself. I loved Mariette very, very much."

And, in the blithe belief that all the world loves a lover, in September 1996 Mariette ordered a wedding dress from a designer in Pretoria and announced the upcoming wedding to their friends.

Meanwhile, in Kempton Park, Johannesburg, Mariette's sister-in-law, Judith Bosch, was worrying about a phone call she had received before Ria's death. It was from Dennie Weber, an old family friend in Pietersburg in Northern Province, where, coincidentally, Mariette had been born forty-eight years earlier. Dennie told Judith that Mariette was with him. She had driven the 250 miles from Gaberone to ask for a gun that had belonged to her late husband and that Dennie had in safe keeping. She wanted the 9 mm pistol and ammunition to use for target practice. Troubled by the request, he phoned Judith.

"Put her on the line," said Judith. "You are not allowed to take a weapon into Botswana," she reminded her-sister-in-law. "If they catch you, they will lock you up."

"Don't worry," Mariette assured her. "I just want to take the weapon."

As Mariette drove off with the gun, Dennie was still puzzled. She had asked for only four bullets. "You will need at least twenty-five for target practice," he suggested. So she had taken twenty-five.

Judith and her husband, Mike, were going on holiday, and there were other things to think about. On their return, a friend called from Botswana to ask if she had heard the news: "Ria is dead."

"I didn't know she was ill," said Judith.

"No, she was murdered," her friend said.

"My tummy went upside down," Judith said later. Comparing dates, she realized the telephone call from Dennie had come the day before Ria was shot. It could have been a coincidence. Perhaps Mariette did want the gun for target practice. If Judith told the police, it might make huge trouble for her sister-in-law. And maybe all for nothing. She was torn. She put off doing anything. Finally, though, she spoke to her minister, who told her it was her moral duty to report the telephone call to the police.

Which is why, shortly thereafter, Mariette got a call from Judith, reminding her about the gun episode. It really would be better, she suggested, if Mariette returned the gun to Dennie so that Justin's gun collection could be preserved intact as part of the children's inheritance. If she liked, said Judith helpfully, Mariette could drop the gun off to her, and she would see it was returned to Dennie.

One evening, after smuggling the gun back across the border, Mariette arrived at Judith's home with Tienie—and news of their engagement. To Judith, it almost didn't matter. Her mind was wholly on the gun. "[Mariette] stood in the door with her hand-bag under her arm, and she was shaking," she recalled.

Mike continued, "She said she'd got the weapon and I must take it. As I put it in the drawer, she moved off. She was very nervous. I knew Mariette for about twenty-one years and she was not herself at that moment."

As you may have guessed, it was all a police setup. Judith turned the gun in to local police, who returned it to Gaberone, where it was sent for ballistic tests. Mariette was arrested, and Tienie, too, was brought in for questioning. "I pray the gun and cartridges don't match," he told his interrogators. They did. Captain Victor van der Merwe, a South African Police Service ballistics expert, established that the cartridges found at the murder scene had been fired from the gun Mariette had given Mike. With no evidence that Tienie was anywhere but up north working when his wife was murdered, he was allowed to go home. In her cell, Mariette refused to see anyone except Tienie and their children and, acting on Tienie's advice, she refused to give the police a statement.

The general impression among whites in Gaberone was that the police had made a mistake. No one could imagine a woman like Mariette scaling a two-meter wall at night and shooting her friend. Ria's daughter Maryna would say, "I could not believe someone so kind would do something like that."

Charmaine described her mother as a soft person, very loving. "She was never screaming or giving us hidings when we were naughty."

With Marianne about to take exams at university in South Africa, Tienie kept the news of the arrest from her. When she finally heard, her reaction was one commonly heard at *braais* and bridge games in Phakalane: "How could they arrest Mariette! I mean, she's not the kind of person that could do it. I never once, honestly, doubted her innocence."

Angry that she had been kept in the dark, Marianne insisted that Tienie should take her to see Mariette in prison. "I asked her straight out, 'Did you kill my mother?' She broke, she just broke. There was no acting or anything. She said she would never harm my mother."

But what about her trip to pick up the gun from Dennie? If Mariette was not talking, Tienie was. And he had a bizarre story to tell police. The real culprit, he said, was another South African, Hennie Coetzee, the general manager at the firm where the two women were employed. There had been financial irregularities at the company, Tienie claimed, and Ria, as financial officer, had removed an incriminating file, intending to blow the whistle. With an audit due, Hennie had seen murder as the only answer and had offered Mariette $1,500 to get a gun for him. The story, though wildly implausible—why would Mariette cooperate in the murder of her best friend?—gained credibility with the news that, around the time of the murder, the firm had transferred Hennie to Ghana, in west Africa.

After three months of silence, Mariette was finally ready to make a statement to police. Working with a hypnotist, Evans Brown, hired by Tienie, she had recalled that "a powerful man" had forced her to get the gun from Pietersburg. The man? By coincidence, Hennie Coetzee. Her story was that Hennie had come to her home one evening with a bottle of wine. She believed that, while pouring two glasses in the kitchen, he had spiked her wine with a drug to make her suggestible. She experienced a powerful headache and then Hennie became aggressive, "looked deep into my eyes and told me I must go to Pietersburg [to col-lect] the pistol," she would say in court. A few days after she had given him the gun, she said, he returned it to her, saying he hadn't needed it after all.

Brown, the president of the South African Association of Hypnotherapists, would say in court that he was satisfied from his sessions with Mariette that she was at home with her daughter Charmaine and the maid at the time of the killing. "Either she's bloody good [at lying under hypnosis], or she's telling the truth. I have no doubt about it," he said.

After ten months in prison, Mariette was finally released on bail put up by church members. It was the first time in the coun-try's history that an accused murderer had gotten out on bail. If her earlier actions had shown a lack of judgment, her next step showed she had learned nothing at all: she and Tienie got married.

For fourteen subsequent months, living with their children in the northern safari town of Maun, six hundred miles from Gaberone and its gossip, she and Tienie could pretend that it was all a bad dream. The case against Mariette, as their barrister, Edward W. Fashole-Luke II, explained to them, was not a strong one. Certainly she had been in possession of the murder weapon, and that would tell against her—unless she could show she had given it to someone else. Now, after her sessions with the hypnotist, she could claim she had given it to Hennie Coetzee. No one could place her at the murder scene, there were no telltale fingerprints, and Charmaine would say that her mother was home all evening.

When Mariette arrived at the courtroom in Gaberone for her trial, she looked older. Her hair was drawn back unbecomingly in a ponytail, but she was animated and smiling and exuded confidence. That confidence evaporated in the face of the prosecution evidence. Hennie Coetzee had been brought back from Ghana to deny the whole bizarre drugged-wine story. There had been no financial irregularities at the company, and if he needed a gun, he already owned three—two in South Africa and one in Botswana. He denied, of course, having any ill will toward Ria Wolmarans.

Once again, Mariette discovered that her sister-in-law, Judith, was her worst enemy. Judith not only related the gun story, but also told of a conversation some time before Ria's murder in which Mariette said she was having an affair with Tienie and that they had driven together to Johannesburg, where they had stayed in a motel. They had enjoyed "good intercourse," she told her sister-in-law, and as soon as Tienie got his divorce from Ria, they planned to marry.

"You are playing with fire," Judith recalled telling her. "He's a married man—and I don't like him at all."

"No," protested Mariette, "he's not a bad guy. I love him very much."

Another time, said Judith, while on a trip to Gaberone, she had called at Mariette's place, accompanied by a friend. The gate was open, but there was no reply when they knocked. Walking around to the back, they found Mariette and Tienie drinking wine beside the swimming pool. It was not the situation that surprised Judith—surely two old friends could share a drink—but the couple's reaction: "They were so shocked to see us."

Even Mariette's barrister admitted after the trial that Judith's evidence "was crucial, and it was believed. It went a long way towards convicting her." A final piece of evidence completed the job: although Mariette's daughter Charmaine claimed that her mother was home the whole evening, the maid testified that Mariette had gone out at about 8:00 P.M. She did not know when Mariette had returned.

After being found guilty, Mariette covered her face with her hand as she was taken back to prison.

Interviewed by a Johannesburg *Sunday Times* reporter a few days later while sitting under a jacaranda tree in the prison yard, she told of dreaming that she was standing on the gallows surrounded by strangers whispering in a foreign tongue. "But when I am awake," she insisted, "I don't think about it. I believe that God will deliver me from this nightmare. I have been framed. People have turned against me. I loved Ria," she added.

Trying, perhaps, to preserve vestiges of the life she had known, she was wearing a bright, floral dress, blue eye shadow, rust-colored polish on her toenails and a turquoise hairclip. "I shouldn't be in this disgusting place," she complained. She could not abide the regular prison diet, saying it was mostly tripe, and she claimed she had not eaten for three days.

When she appeared in court two months later, in February 2000, for a pre-sentence hearing, her dress hung loosely following a dramatic twenty-kilogram weight loss. It was a day of farce. Dr. Louise Olivier, a psychologist called by the defense, testified that Mariette simply did not conform to the personality profile of a violent offender. "The most valued predictor of future violence is past violence," she said. Mariette, she suggested, might have been in a dream state, receptive to others' suggestions and not realizing the consequences. Dr. Olivier's loud pink suit and her admission that she was a magazine sex doctor did not add to her credibility. And waves of laughter swept the courtroom when Judge Isaac Aboagye asked her, "Let's suppose you are my wife—ha, ha, ha—and I knew you were going around with some guy...then suppose I go to Pretoria to get a gun and come back and shoot you—wouldn't you call that premeditation?"

Tienie winced as Dr. Olivier continued to dodge crucial questions and show off her knowledge, while Mariette frowned.

There was pathos, too, as her fourteen-year-old daughter, Suné, tearfully told the judge, "You have made a mistake. She is not guilty. I need my mom. I need her."

The judge was unmoved. "I have not been able to find one moral extenuating circumstance," he told Mariette. "You are not very young, you were not drunk, and you were not provoked by the deceased. The crime committed by the accused was carefully planned, carried out with evil motive, without mercy for an innocent victim who had done no harm."

Given her chance to speak, Mariette faced the judge. "I am not guilty," she said. "And you, my lord, are sentencing a woman for a thing I have not done."

"Is that so?" the judge replied mildly. Then, taking a sip of water, he placed the black cap on his head and pronounced, "Mrs.

Bosch, listen to your sentence. From here you will be taken to prison, where you will be hanged by the neck until dead. From there your body will be taken and buried where the president sees fit. May the Lord have mercy on your soul."

As his wife was taken to the Gaberone maximum-security prison, where she would remain for more than a year in solitary confinement, allowed only one fifteen-minute visit per month, Tienie declared, "We know she is innocent and the death penalty will not be carried out."

Suddenly, the world's media woke up to the fact that a white woman was about to be executed for the first time in Botswana's history. Journalists arrived from the United Kingdom and South Africa. And from London's hallowed Inns of Court, to handle the appeal, would come the Scarlet Pimpernel himself, barrister Desmond de Silva, QC, who had earned his sobriquet by saving from the gallows thirty-five of thirty-eight convicted murderers he had represented.

De Silva would tell me, "I have never had a case in which the trial judge had the burden of proof so completely wrong." Justice, he said, had been turned on its head, with Mariette having to prove her innocence rather than the prosecution having to prove her guilt. No evidence, he told me, placed her at the murder scene, and within a short time of arriving in Gaberone he called Tienie to inform him that he would be suggesting to the court that it was Tienie who had influenced Mariette to go to Pietersburg for the gun.

Shortly before the appeal was to be heard, de Silva also learned that in order to get Hennie Coetzee to return to Botswana to testify, the government had guaranteed him immunity from prosecution for murder or for gun offences. This development would have made a significant difference to the questions

Mariette's counsel could have put to Coetzee. Its concealment from the defense, de Silva told me, "would, in a British or American court, have automatically resulted in an acquittal."

But this was not the Old Bailey. Giving their decision in a courtroom packed with security officers, many armed, the judges acknowledged the force of de Silva's arguments—but then said none of them counted in the face of the woman's obvious guilt. Barely able to contain their indignation, the judges described her as "a wicked and despicable woman" who had been prepared to see her former boss, Coetzee, hang to save her skin.

De Silva had suggested that it must have been Tienie, as a domineering character, who had influenced the suggestible Mariette. The judges found no evidence of this and said it was mere speculation. In fact, the Gaberone police, still suspecting Mariette had not acted alone, had investigated Tienie's possible involvement following Mariette's conviction.

Most of the ex-pat community in Gaberone would still have given Mariette a better than fifty-fifty chance of cheating the noose. Although ninety percent of the population supported the death penalty in principle, voices were being raised in favor of commuting her sentence. South African human rights activists appealed to their president, Thabo Mbeki, to intervene.

But Botswana's president, Festus Mogae, was firm. "These events are not pleasant ones," he told a press conference. "One wishes they were not happening or had not happened, but here our view is that we are retaining the death penalty... We think we are doing the right thing for our country."

On Friday, March 30, 2001, Tienie drove to the prison with Suné to visit Mariette. De Silva had ordered a new psychological assessment, and this made up part of a new appeal to President Mogae for clemency. But Tienie and his daughter were turned away at the prison gates with the explanation that an inspection was going on. They were told to return on Monday. When they did, they were told that Mariette had been hanged on Saturday. A prison official opened the back door of the family Toyota and dumped in her belongings.

Desmond de Silva was outraged when he heard what had happened. "It was absolutely awful," he told me. "The children were in a state of very great distress. They were told when they came back on Monday they would have plenty of time with their mother." The defense had received an assurance that nothing would happen until May. When asked about clemency, the president, on business in England, said that he would consider the matter. He had, in fact, already issued a warrant for Mariette's execution.

Why did Botswana act in such an apparently brutal and inhumane fashion? It could only have been that it feared a growing tide of criticism around the world for its unwavering stand on capital punishment. A BBC team was in Botswana filming a documentary, while ETV, in Cape Town, had already broadcast a documentary questioning some of the evidence in the case. "If they had announced the execution a week ahead of time," Chris Bishop, head of Botswana TV, told me, "there would have been a CNN camera outside the prison interviewing the family."

Nothing had done more to arouse pity and feelings of disquiet than a photograph taken of Mariette on the way out of court after her failed appeal. It may be the most striking photograph ever taken of a woman murderer. Mariette is being led away by two female police officers; her hand is held up as if to attract attention to something that is happening. Her plump good looks are gone. Her receding hair is pulled back severely, revealing her skull; her face has lost every trace of softness and is harsh, lined and surprisingly masculine. Her eyes glare. Yet, in this portrait of contrasts, an elaborate and very feminine lace collar reminds us this was a woman after all.

"Perhaps what is really terrible about the picture," journalist Michael Morris wrote in South Africa's *Cape Argus*, "is that it seems to embody some demonic quality while also evoking wrenching pity."

The decision to execute Mariette was a harsh one but, in its way, a just one. Botswana retains the death penalty in order to keep a lid on crime that threatens to sweep across its border from South Africa. To spare a white woman clearly guilty of a heinous murder while executing black murderers with less appeal to the international media would have been rank injustice.

Tienie Wolmarans, hearing that he might be arrested, remained in South Africa for some time. When he returned to northern Botswana to resume his building work, his work permit was revoked—Botswana wanted no more of him.

It is quite likely that, had she been tried in the United States, Canada or the United Kingdom, Mariette Bosch would not have been found guilty of murder. The case against her was circumstantial and, with a good lawyer, she likely would have been convicted only as an accessory to murder.

What really happened? The whole story of the murder of Ria Wolmarans will probably never be told. I believe, though, that Mariette murdered her friend because she was afraid of finding herself alone. She had lost her first husband in a car accident. With three children to bring up and no one to comfort her, she turned to the man closest at hand, Tienie Wolmarans. And she planned to have him for herself.

Tienie, however, was a weak man. I suspect he did not even get to the point of asking Ria for a divorce. He may not have had the guts to tell his wife of his affair with Mariette. Like a million men before him, he may have thought the easiest thing was to keep both wife and lover. Ria likely had no suspicions, or she certainly would not have regarded Mariette as her friend. As Tienie prevaricated, hesitated and postponed taking any action, Mariette fumed. At the same time, she did not dare give him an ultimatum—in case Tienie chose to stay with his wife.

Working in the same office as Ria, seeing her after hours, doing things together with the children, Mariette must have been beside herself. It was so unfair! Tienie, perhaps an unhappy shambles of a man to many, was the apple of her eye. It was her he loved, not Ria. And day by day she grew to hate Ria.

Tienie was away in the north working most of the time, so Mariette had time to stew and plot. Killing Ria, she finally decided, was the only answer. Moreover, it would not be difficult. Random violence was a concept familiar to her from South Africa—the householder shot at night in his or her home by some drug-crazed criminal looking for jewelry.

The murder itself was executed with surprising competence. Mariette likely knew that Maryna, Ria's daughter, was going out that night. She would simply have knocked at the door and been welcomed by Ria. Letting herself out through the gate afterwards, she must have been horrified and yet thrilled at how easy it had been. And at first everything went as planned. The police bought the theory that it was a bungled burglary, and as the weeks and months went by, Ria Wolmarans' murder looked more and more like a cold case that might never be solved. It was only Mariette's carelessness in blabbing to her sister-in-law about her affair and then brazenly securing the pistol that finally gave the police a break.

Now, if Mma Ramotswe had been on the job, the whole thing

would have been cleared up in a few days. The key to the case? The maid, of course.

The proprietor of the No. 1 Ladies' Detective Agency has frequently solved stubborn cases by ignoring the front door and heading for the kitchen. Servants see and hear everything—and usually never tell. But under the power of that remarkable lady's charm, they soon reveal the house's secrets.

In this case, the dog that didn't bark—just as in the famous Sherlock Holmes story—gives the first clue. Mma Ramotswe would have quickly concluded that the murderer was someone Ria Wolmarans knew. Mariette, as Ria's best friend, would have immediately attracted the formidable lady's attention.

She would not, however, have wasted her breath asking questions of Mariette directly, but would have gone to the kitchen, perhaps in search of a recipe or to admire the maid's baking. In the course of a pleasant afternoon chat, the maid would have told her of Tienie and Mariette's affair. And, as she would testify in court, the maid would have told Mma Ramotswe that her employer was simply lying when she said she was home all evening the night of the murder.

Mma Ramotswe would have returned to her office next to Tlokweng Road Speedy Motors, the garage owned and operated by her fiancé, Mr. J.L.B. Matekone, with another case solved and another recipe in her ample handbag.

Lord Somerset's
Clever Scheme

It's not a great drawing. It hangs on my office wall, a little faded and yellow, and it shows a Victorian lady in her ball gown. Cecil "Nobby" Clark, former deputy commissioner of the British Columbia provincial police, gave it to me twenty-five years ago. We had spent a congenial morning at his home in Victoria, B.C., talking about one of his famous cases from the 1920s. Recognizing a fellow crime aficionado, Nobby, quite elderly at the time, went to his office and returned with the framed drawing. "Here," he said, "I've had a lot of fun with this. I hope you do too."

He was right: I was fascinated. The interest, of course, lies in the inscription: it was sketched in pen and ink by Reginald Birchall, otherwise known as Lord Somerset, while he was awaiting execution in the Oxford County Jail in southwestern Ontario in the 1890s. By coincidence, only a few weeks before I met Nobby, I had been sitting in Birchall's death cell at the by then unused jail, fingering the revolver he used to murder Fred Benwell and posing for a photograph with Birchall's high boots, borrowed for the occasion from the Woodstock Museum.

Morbid? Of course! But Birchall would have approved. Because he was one of the great showmen murderers of the nineteenth century. It was a feature of that self-confident era—killers who experienced not a moment of introspection or guilt, who went about their grisly trade as casually as if they were carriage makers or carpenters, and whose main concern often seemed to be their place in history. The stories of two other larger-than-life killers of that era, Dr. William Palmer, "Saintly Billy," and the casually homicidal Dr. Arthur Warren Waite, the New York dentist, appear later in this book.

Birchall, who seemed to feel no animosity toward his victim, spent his last days making drawings, which he sold to souvenir hunters, and writing his self-serving memoirs, which were published in installments in the Toronto *Globe*. Checkbook journalism has an old, if disreputable, history!

His crime may have been sordid, but there was nothing sordid at all about Reginald Birchall's beginnings. He was the son of the Reverend Joseph Birchall, the local rural dean of Whalley, in Lancashire in the north of England, and his father's plan was that he should enter the clergy. Getting into Oxford University on his second attempt, Birchall showed little aptitude for theology, but a gift for gambling, boozing and high living.

He left Oxford without a degree, worked briefly as manager of a touring theatrical company, then eloped with Florence Stevenson, whose father had been general traffic superintendent of the London and North Western Railway Company. Birchall was confident that his elderly father-in-law would soon die, leaving his daughter well fixed. Meanwhile, though, there were pressing debts, and in 1891 he was forced to sell a $20,000 inheritance due to him for $15,000 to stay ahead of his creditors.

To make a clean start—and to escape other creditors—Birchall sailed for Canada with Florence. He later claimed that he had been duped by a money-making scam under which the young sons of English gentry would, for a handsome consideration, be placed as agricultural students on Canadian farms, many of them in southwest Ontario. The English customers visualized farms where the young master would have little to do but ride around giving orders and getting in a good bit of hunting and fishing. Parents putting up funds were usually glad enough to see the backs of idle young troublemakers. The reality of the nineteenth-century Canadian farm was very different. Birchall claimed that, on arrival at the farm outside Woodstock to which he had been assigned, he found it "a pigsty" and he stayed only one night.

It is hard to believe Birchall was ever duped by anyone and, as we shall see, the crooked scheme seems to have originated in his own imagination.

Returning to Woodstock, he and Florence assumed new identities, Lord and Lady Somerset, and were welcomed by local gentry thrilled at the thought of rubbing shoulders with titled folk. Merchants were only too happy to extend credit to the couple, but were left whistling for their money when Birchall returned suddenly to England in 1899, claiming his father had died.

In London, Birchall would later state in his autobiography, he was given a sure-fire tip on the Derby. To raise the wager money, he devised what he called "a great scheme which, I thought, would land me safely upon the shore of comparative affluence and comfort." The first the world knew of the scheme was an advertisement placed in the *Daily Telegraph* in December 1889 that read:

CANADA. University man having farm, wishes to meet gentleman's son to live with him and learn the business with a view to partnership; must invest $500 to extend stock. Board, lodging and 5-per cent interest until partnership arranged. Address: J.R. Burchett, Primrose Club, 4 Park Place, St. James, London.

The advertisement, with the deliberate misspelling "Burchett" to put Birchall's creditors off the track, brought two promising replies. One was from Frederick C. Benwell, son of Colonel Benwell of fashionable Cheltenham, the other from Douglas Pelly, son of the Reverend R.P. Pelly, vicar of Saffron Walden and a cousin of Lady Pelly, a society beauty who had been lady-in-waiting at Rideau Hall, the Ottawa residence of the Queen's official representative in Canada.

Up to that point, Birchall would likely have been satisfied to dupe just one young Englishman and, as he explained in his memoirs, once he had made his big killing on the Derby, he intended to pay back the money to his victim. (A likely story!) But suddenly Birchall found himself with two fish on his hook and, always the opportunist, he decided he could play them both. He told the applicants glowing tales of his magnificent farm near Niagara Falls, the house lit by gas, the brick barns by electricity, and of his profitable business supplying the Canadian Pacific Railway with horses.

Pelly, who had traveled the world after getting a degree from Oxford, was bowled over by Birchall, gave the scoundrel a check for $850 and arranged passage for himself to New York. Benwell and his father were more cautious; they were willing to hand over the money only once young Benwell had had a chance to check out the farm in person. That would prove difficult.

On board the *Britannic*, bound for New York with his wife and his two protégés, Birchall skillfully kept the young men apart as much as possible, even creating ill will between them by telling stories behind about each of them behind their backs. The group arrived in Buffalo, just across the Niagara River from Canada, on February 16, 1890. Significantly, Birchall and Benwell, at the former's suggestion, amused themselves that evening by imitating each other's signatures.

At dawn the next morning, after asking Pelly to stay with Florence, Birchall accompanied Benwell on the train to visit the "farm." At 8:30 that evening, Birchall returned alone. Benwell, he said, had not liked the farm, which was run-down after being let to tenants, and had continued to London, Ontario, to view other farms.

Pelly smelled a rat. He questioned Birchall closely, but all he got was a yawn, as Birchall, claiming he was tired out, went off to bed. The next day, Pelly, Birchall and his wife crossed to Niagara Falls, Ontario, and took rooms at Baldwin's boarding house.

Someday, perhaps, someone will make a movie about Lord Somerset. The shame is that neither Alec Guinness nor Peter Sellers, those masters of muddled murder, will be around to play the role. Think *The Ladykillers* or maybe *Kind Hearts and Coronets*, those two comic murder classics.

Here comes Guinness, I mean Birchall, on their first morning at the Niagara Falls boarding house, wearing a conspiratorial leer. "Grand morning for a walk," he tells young Pelly. "We should see the Falls."

"We walked along the river road, which goes from the village up to the Falls," Pelly would relate. "I had told him about ten minutes before that he was failing to fulfill the representations he had made to me. He had replied with a shuffling explanation, and I mentally decided to give him another week, and if matters did not change, I would leave him."

Birchall had quite made up his mind not to give Pelly another week. They came to a stairway leading down the cliff, and Birchall said, "Oh, you have never been down here? You ought to go. It is the best way to see the Falls."

"I went down first," said Pelly, "and soon noticed it was a rotten, unsafe stairway. It led down close to the Falls. 'Birchall,' I said, 'this is a horrid place.'

"He was following and he said, 'Go on, [the view] will pay you.' I wondered afterwards that I did not slip or miss my footing. We landed at the bottom finally. To my surprise, there stood a man gazing into the swirling water. This man turned and looked at me."

The man's hostile look aroused fear even in unsuspicious Pelly. "I sprang past Birchall and started back up the stairs. The man turned and resumed his gazing into the water."

Whether or not the man had been hired by Birchall to toss Pelly into the Falls, the young man should have trusted his instinct. He did not. Or perhaps Birchall was just a convincing liar. At any rate, the next day, Birchall was at it again. A walk by the Falls? Why not! "He led the way down to the cliffs close to the cantilever bridge," Pelly reported. "Underneath the bridge, you cannot be seen. Birchall took me in there so as to get a better view of the rapids. He tried to persuade me to stand close by the edge, but his manner seemed so coldly quiet that instinctively I drew back. A little push and all would have been over."

Pelly was proving tiresome. Birchall had to think up some new ploy. That was it! Would Pelly be so kind as to accompany him back across the border to settle a baggage matter? He was still anxious, too, for his young companion to appreciate this great wonder of the world. "We started to walk back to Canada across the lower suspension bridge," Pelly said. "It was storming and blowing. When out near the center of the bridge, Birchall walked over by the edge and looked down at the roaring rapids. 'Come see the view. It is superb,' he called. I drew back. He grew white and walked on to Canada. I lagged behind, out of his reach." Before they reached the other side, Birchall stopped once again, turned around and looked back. "Then he advanced a step toward me," said Pelly. "I stepped back and was about to run over the bridge, when two men came walking across and Birchall turned and walked on to Canada."

Meanwhile, on February 21, two brothers, Joseph and George Eldridge, ventured into what was then called Blenheim Swamp, outside Woodstock, to cut saplings. George, pushing through the thick bush, put his foot on a solid, unyielding object. It was a frozen body.

Called to the scene, Ontario's first full-time detective, the legendary John Wilson Murray, established that, although all identifying documents and labels had been removed, the clothing worn by the corpse was of English cut.

Two days later, a photograph of the body appeared in local newspapers, and Birchall knew he had a problem. Improvising cleverly, he told Pelly he had just received a message from Benwell, who wrote that he was going to the Fifth Avenue Hotel in New York. Birchall directed Pelly to go to New York at once to make contact with him.

With remarkable cool-headedness, Birchall then decided to travel to Woodstock to assist the police. Yes, he said, he believed he knew the dead man. He had met him aboard the *Britannic* on a recent crossing of the Atlantic.

The body, which had been buried in Princeton Cemetery, not far from the swamp, was disinterred, and Birchall, holding on to a constable's arm for support, said, yes, that was the man he had met aboard ship.

Murray interviewed Birchall and Florence at a nearby hotel. The dead man's name? "I think it was Bentwell, or Benswell or Benwell," dead-panned Birchall. Murray noted that Florence was walking up and down nervously.

Bentwell, Birchall recalled, had been on his way to London, Ontario, the last time he'd seen him, in Niagara Falls.

"Did you hear from him?"

"Just a line."

"Have you got it?"

"Have I got Fred's note, my dear?" he asked his wife.

"His first name was Fred?" said the detective, picking up on the giveaway detail.

"I think so. It was so signed on the note," replied the nimble Birchall.

Murray recorded, "The man was lying. I was sure of it." He wired Niagara Falls police to keep an eye on Birchall but not to arrest him unless he tried to cross the border into the United States.

Murray did not have long to wait: the case resolved itself when the slow-witted Pelly finally learned of Benwell's fate and made a statement to a magistrate. The Birchalls were arrested immediately, although Florence was never charged.

The town of Woodstock would briefly draw international attention when Birchall was put on trial the following September. A special effort was made to spruce the place up, including new carpets and draperies for the town hall, where the trial would take place. The square outside was packed with hundreds of people hoping to get a glimpse of "his lordship."

What might have been the world's first closed-circuit coverage was offered by a local hotel, which had installed telephones in the town hall to relay the proceedings to guests, who paid for their receivers by the hour. And across the street at the Oxford Hotel, telegraph wires linked the little market town to the U.S. and Europe as readers waited for word on the trial.

Murray and the prosecution had done their job well, spinning a flawless web of circumstantial evidence around Birchall. Most tellingly, numerous witnesses described seeing Birchall, wearing a distinctive fur cap, and Benwell on their fateful journey from Buffalo to Eastwood railway station and then on their walk of close to five miles to Blenheim Swamp. Others saw Birchall, whom they recognized as "Lord Somerset," returning alone to the railway station.

The defense rather forlornly challenged the ability of some of the witnesses to identify Birchall at a distance.

But the most damning evidence of the scam Birchall had practiced was a letter he had mailed to Benwell's father three days after the murder, announcing that young Benwell had inspected the farm and found it entirely satisfactory. They had entered into a partnership, and it was now an appropriate time for Benwell Senior to forward the $500.

"Your son, I think, is writing you by this post," Birchall wrote. "Kindly excuse bad handwriting on my part. My letters are generally written by typewriter." Could he have been preparing the older Benwell to receive a typewritten letter from his son, signed, of course, with Birchall's well-practiced hand.

The jury took only ninety minutes to find Birchall guilty, and he was sentenced to be hanged on November 14. Ever-faithful Florence took a petition containing five thousand signatures to Ottawa, appealing for clemency, but to no avail.

Birchall was a fraud, an imposter and a murderer, but give the man this: he had style. For his final supper he had oysters and venison steak. The next morning he enjoyed a hearty breakfast of three poached eggs on toast, but passed up the bramble preserve.

The hangman, J.R.R. Radclive of Toronto, on visiting the prisoner to measure him for final adjustments to the rope, was so disconcerted at Birchall's friendly and forthright manner that he went out the night before and got roaring drunk.

"Goodbye, Flo," Birchall told his wife on her last visit. "Be brave." He told Murray in his last interview, "I have found you, sir, always a gentleman. You did your duty. I have no hard feelings against you."

As he prepared to leave the death cell, he told an old Oxford friend who had come to offer his support, "Take hold of my arm, old man, and walk with me as we used to do in the old days together."

On the scaffold in the prison yard, as a hung-over Radclive prepared to slip the black mask over his head, Birchall said, "Do you mind shaking hands with me?"

"Certainly not," replied a shattered Radclive. "Well, goodbye, old fellow," he said, moving to the lever.

Newspapers of the day, very thorough in these matters, reported that Birchall's body jerked upwards, his chest heaved, and his legs were drawn up. Then he went limp.

I don't want to leave you with the impression that Birchall was some kind of hero. Stylish he may have been, but his fraudulent scheme could have only one outcome: murder. He may have thought that, having secured Pelly's money, he could simply give him the slip. But there was no way to get Benwell's deposit without killing him.

The spot where the crime occurred is now called Benwell Swamp, and today it is just as wild as and even more remote than it was when Birchall led his victim down the country road. At that

time, this rural area was quite populated, the farms were occupied, and families were large. There were plenty of people
walking the roads who saw Birchall's comings and goings.
Today, you don't see a soul, and cars pass only infrequently.

In the swamp, tree stumps stick up like old molars, dense
undergrowth drags at your clothes, and black, water-filled sink-
holes threaten every footstep. It's a puzzle how Birchall
persuaded Benwell to come here. Perhaps he described it as a
shortcut to his farm. Birchall came up behind his victim as they
staggered through the bush, pulled out his small-caliber gun and
killed him with two shots to the head. Then he rolled him on his
back, cut off all identifying buttons and pulled open his topcoat
so that he could snip off every label in his clothing. Finally,
Birchall flung the revolver as far as he could into the brush—but
not so far that it was not found later.

Walking breezily back toward the railway station, he must have
felt confident that, in that remote spot, the body might not be discovered for weeks or months. It was his bad luck that it was
found only five days later.

At the Princeton Cemetery, not far away, Benwell's gravestone
bears a warning that Birchall might have taken to heart:

What I do thou knowest not now,
But thou shalt know hereafter.

Horse Crazy

At murder trials, there is always someone missing. The judge, bewigged or otherwise, sits in solitary dignity, the lawyers prepare to scrap like snapping terriers, the jury members squirm self-consciously in their seats, and in the prisoner's box sit the accused, turned out in their best clothes, often conveying an air of blithe innocence.

It seems to me, though, that in every courtroom where murder trials are heard there should be a box at the front and a chair that remains empty. That would be the victim's box. Because, by the time these cases ever reach trial, the victims, except for those close to them, are largely forgotten. They are not there to speak for themselves, to describe what may have been unspeakable suffering and pain that preceded the snuffing out of their lives. The prosecution, and even the judge, may do their best to compensate for that missing voice, but the odds are against them: the pendulum all too often swings in favor of the accused, who, even though they may be found guilty, are there in the flesh to put forward their own self-serving account of events.

That is why I found myself walking up a front path in Frampton on Severn, an idyllic English village that looks like a piece of the eighteenth century preserved. In one of the most painful interviews I can remember, I would hear a couple describe what it is like to be murdered. That Pauline Leyshon and Ivor Stokle are still alive is amazing. The three monsters who kidnapped them with the intention of killing them went home the night of the crime satisfied they had done a good job. This, though, was one of those rare instances in which the victims lived to tell their story.

Ivor should have known that Sheila Stroud, his former girlfriend, cared about only one thing: her horses. She cared enough to kill for them.

He met Sheila at the Walls' ice cream factory, where they both worked, near Gloucester, in the west of England. In no time, Sheila was talking to him about horses. She came from a gypsy background and had grown up with them.

Ivor had never given much thought to horses, but as Sheila introduced him to her passion, he couldn't help getting interested. She even persuaded him they should start a horse-feed business together, although that failed, and Ivor started taking horses to trotting meets for her stepfather.

Real estate initially proved a better bet than horse feed. The couple bought an old house, renovated it and sold it for twice the price. But when they tried to repeat their success, they found themselves stuck with an expensive property and were forced to sell it at a loss.

By this time, Sheila, a strong-willed woman with a nasty temper, was losing interest in their nine-year relationship. Mark

Evans, a traveler (or gypsy) whom she had known since child-hood, moved in as a boarder and became her romantic interest. Ivor was planning to move out.

Then she came to him one day, sweet as honey, with a plan. "You've got to see it," she told him. "It's a great property. We'll make a killing." What she showed him was a run-down bungalow near Staunton. Fixed up, it would fetch a tidy price, she promised. But hadn't she been listening? He was moving out. They were splitting up. Well, she argued, this deal would give him the money to start a new life. He was not keen, but she kept it up. She wouldn't let him alone. It was a great chance. It might never come again.

And, of course, the property came with a five-acre paddock and barn where she could keep her horses. It didn't register with Ivor that breeding thoroughbreds was the ambition Sheila had always spoken of.

Finally, he gave in. They put together their savings, took out a $240,000 mortgage and bought the property for $336,000.

Then Ivor lost his current job as a building surveyor. Short of money, he moved back into the bungalow with Sheila and Mark as a temporary expedient. But when he got another job working at the Lucas electronic plant, he soon found himself paying the living expenses for all three of them.

In the meantime, he had met Pauline Leyshon in the cafeteria at work. She was everything Sheila wasn't: quiet, affectionate and easy to get along with. It was a tricky situation. Pauline, who had four grown children, was leaving her marriage—and it wasn't an amicable separation. And Ivor didn't know what to expect from the hot-tempered Sheila.

Which is why, on summer evenings or during lunch hours, Ivor would drive Pauline to Barrow Wake, a scenic spot on the edge of the Cotswolds near Gloucester where you could see for miles around. There, they felt safe and far away from any prying eyes. "We always used to call it 'our spot,'" Pauline would tell me.

Ivor's caution proved justified when, one day, he told Sheila he was moving in with Pauline. Sheila simply exploded. Couples break up every day; there are spats, resentments. But this was different. Sheila cared nothing for Ivor. But without his money, who would pay for her beloved horses? Her financial adviser, John Slade, told her what she already knew: she would have to sell. "I hate everything about him," Sheila wrote in a letter to her family. "He was the worst thing I ever met in my life, but I will make sure he never has any rest." The words were prophetic.

In a black moment, she even wrote a suicide note: "I cannot go on any longer. Life was just torture. I was not going to have my home, land and horses taken away from me, so instead I went in peace and took my life."

But Sheila Stroud was not one to give up the ghost. That was no way to win. Ivor Stokle was the problem, not her. When they took out the mortgage, she and Ivor also bought life insurance. If one of them died, the other would receive $264,000. As well, Sheila remembered that Ivor had a $70,000 life insurance policy at work naming her as beneficiary (she didn't know he had now named Pauline in her stead). Ivor, under pressure from Sheila, had also paid up the premiums on the mortgage insurance payments until the end of the year. It made you think.

And Mark Evans had an answer. On his most recent stay in prison, he'd met a truly frightening man, a thug from Bristol who was now Mark's drug dealer. He would do anything for money.

So, that summer of 1991, Mark and Sheila drove around the rolling Gloucestershire countryside, talking always about possible solutions to the Ivor problem. And then it got worse. Ivor and

Pauline found a cute little bungalow in the storybook village of Frampton on Severn that they planned to buy. Their offer had been accepted, and the deal would close in September. Ivor figured Sheila owed him $70,000, but to avoid an argument, he was willing to settle for $50,000. She wouldn't have to sell the house, he explained. If she sold three of her six valuable horses, that would cover it.

Was he crazy? Sell her horses! She would do anything rather than that.

Sheila and Mark would later claim that they had hired the thug from Bristol to give Ivor a beating so that he would stop his demands for money. Doesn't seem likely. A beating might stall Ivor for a while, but the mortgage was already $5,000 in arrears. One way or another, Sheila would lose her precious horse farm— unless Ivor died and the insurance money saved the day. That was the only answer.

Ivor was driving through Gloucester one day that summer when he noticed someone following him in a white BMW with tinted windows. Suspecting it might be Pauline's ex-husband, he drove to a police station and made a complaint. An officer approached the BMW and asked the driver to roll down the window. Sheila was driving, and Mark was in the front passenger seat. In the back was a man who, when asked to show identification, produced a driver's license in the name of Harris. When police checked the license later, they found it belonged to a man who was still in prison.

The car belonged to a dealer, Sheila said. They were taking it for a test drive. Was she following Ivor? What nonsense! Ivor, thinking Sheila was just trying to find out where he lived, told the policeman to forget it. Big mistake.

Sheila was now obsessed with finding a way to kill Ivor. She could think of little else. In October, fate intervened. While out one evening with Mark, she dropped in on Reg Fear, a neighbor. "Want to watch a film on Sky[TV]?" he asked. Sheila, Mark, Reg and his wife settled down to watch *Fighting Mad*, an utterly forgettable gangster film starring Peter Fonda. But Sheila and Mark were transfixed. They sat on the edge of their seats, absorbing every detail. At one point in the movie, three armed men burst into a house, beat up the occupants, a young couple, tie them up and bundle them into a car. They drive them to a remote quarry and douse the car with gasoline. Then, to make it look like an accident, they set the car ablaze and push it over a cliff with the couple inside. Mark and Sheila seemed quite excited as they left for home.

Sheila had not paid Ivor his $50,000. Now he gave her until January 1, 1992, to come up with the money. The couple had a new deadline to work with.

One day, while Ivor was out at a rugby practice, Pauline received a call from Sheila. Not bad-tempered, ranting Sheila, but sweet-as-honey Sheila. "I don't want to argue any more," she told Pauline. "Let's get together and talk this over. Are you and Ivor free tonight? We could meet you at the Air Balloon at nine o'clock. Would that be all right?"

The Air Balloon is the favorite pub of thirsty hikers and other beauty seekers on the way up to take in the wonderful views from Barrow Wake, and Pauline and Ivor knew it well. They were there promptly at nine, and Sheila arrived soon after—alone. She explained that Mark had stayed home because there were prowlers about, and he had to keep an eye on the horses.

Would she like a drink? Sheila shook her head. She seemed agitated. She asked if they would mind coming back to the bungalow, where they would talk matters over.

Ivor was still drinking his shandy (a mild beer and ginger ale mix), and Pauline had not finished her juice. "We'll finish our drinks and follow you," Ivor said.

It all seemed rather odd. Staunton was fifteen miles away. Why had Sheila driven her white Toyota pickup so far just to invite them back to her home? Ivor would tell me later that, unbeknownst to them, Sheila was following the movie script. Her plan was to have them seen at the pub so that, after the "accident," witnesses would recall them drinking and then driving away. Their choice of drinks must have been a disappointment to her.

It was a chilly November night as Pauline and Ivor climbed into his small 1976 Vauxhall Viva. He was teaching her to drive, so it had learner's plates on the bumpers. The country lanes were quiet and empty. As they pulled into the driveway, Ivor told Pauline, "Something seems wrong." Months later, he realized that the yard had been in darkness. Why were the lights off if Sheila and Mark feared intruders?

As Sheila's dogs came rushing up to make a fuss of them, Mark led them into the house. He, too, seemed in a conciliatory mood. "Is there anything here belongs to you?" he asked Ivor. "If there's anything, I can get it for you."

"I left my battery charger in the garage," said Ivor. "If you could leave it by the car, I'll take it." While Mark went to fetch the charger, Sheila put the kettle on for tea so they could talk.

It all seemed to be going remarkably well. As they reached for their cups, Ivor waited for Sheila to say what she had in mind.

Before she could say anything, there was a sound of heavy footsteps, and a man wearing a mask burst into the room. Ivor's first thought was that it was Mark, playing a joke. But, unlike Mark, the man had a husky build and was black. This was no joke. The stranger grabbed Ivor and held a long carving knife to his throat. Even in his panic, Ivor recognized it as the very knife he'd used to carve the roast on many past occasions.

"Get down, get down!" the man ordered. When Ivor lay down on the floor, the man pulled Ivor's sweater over his head while holding the knife to his back.

Pauline, realizing it was a setup, made a dash for the door. But, unfamiliar with the house, she ran into a bedroom by mistake. No one followed her. She could hear nothing from the living room. She could only imagine what was happening. Then Sheila and the stranger found her sobbing behind the door. "It's all right, love," Ivor shouted to her. "Do what they say."

As they brought her back into the room, she saw Ivor trussed up on the floor with a set of reins. "Give me a glass of water, please," said Pauline. "I'm shaking." Surprisingly, Mark fetched her one. Their friend was more versed in the ways of terror. "You're not having it," he growled. He pulled her sweater over her head, kicked her in the ribs and punched her in the mouth. "Now shut up!" he said, turning his attention to Ivor. "Where's your fucking credit cards?" he yelled.

Ivor—stupidly, he told me later—decided he might get beaten up, but he wasn't going to let the man have his money. "I get my money through work," he said. "I don't use credit cards."

It was one of those odd moments that months later would have a surprising sequel when the three would-be murderers were tried. As Ivor testified to that frightening conversation and revealed that he did, in fact, have credit cards, the man, whose name was Norman White, and who had been sitting impassively in the dock, suddenly registered an expression of outrage. He had been conned! He had been lied to. His furious expression helped to convince the jurors that this was a truly frightening individual, capable of anything.

While White tied Pauline up, Sheila vented her anger: "This will teach you to shit on me!" she hissed at Ivor.

Using Ivor's head as a battering ram to open the door, they carried the trussed couple into the conservatory. What would happen now? Ivor was completely puzzled. If the trio beat them up, how could they expect to get away with it? He didn't want to think about the other possibility.

He heard someone start Sheila's truck. It was backed up to the conservatory doors. They were hoisted into the back, and the plastic tonneau cover was put in place so they could not be seen.

Anyone walking by that night would have seen the white truck emerge from the driveway, a woman at the wheel, a black man beside her. The little Viva followed behind, with Mark at the wheel. The procession proceeded unnoticed along the darkened roads. To Ivor and Pauline, it seemed the trio was driving aimlessly, perhaps to pass time until no one was around.

"Let's make a jump for it," Ivor urged Pauline a couple of times. "I can't, I'm scared," she said.

At one point the truck stopped, and the stranger came back and told them, "Shut the fuck up or you're going to get it."

They were climbing now. When they stopped, and the cover was removed, Ivor knew exactly where they were. The distant lights of Gloucester told him they were on top of Barrow Wake, where he and Pauline had spent many happy times. There was no time to think. Someone grabbed his feet and yanked him out of the back of the truck, causing him to fall heavily to the ground. He was dragged to his little sixteen-year-old car. Then, while the other two watched, White approached, carrying something heavy. Ivor felt a shock of pain in the back of his head. With casual viciousness, White had fractured Ivor's skull, apparently using a car jack. Lights blazed in his head, and his world whirled, but

Ivor was still conscious. He knew that if he showed any sign of life he would be hit again. He kept absolutely still as the stranger lifted him into the passenger seat of the car.

Mark's behavior was no better. He struck Pauline on the head with a piece of lumber. "Mark," she cried, as he pushed her behind the wheel of the car, "Why are you doing this? We don't deserve this!"

"Blade her," he snapped, meaning slash her face. That didn't make sense. The plan was to put Pauline in the driver's seat so that, when their bodies were found, it would be assumed that, as a learner, she had lost control of the car and driven it over the cliff.

The car doors were slammed. "Don't worry, love," Ivor yelled, "They're not going to kill us." He was being over-optimistic.

They heard the truck engine fire, a bang, and then the car lurched forward over the curb and onto the shaggy grass that fell away to the edge of a 250-foot sheer cliff.

Ivor told me, "I knew by then that they were going to push us over the cliff, but never in my wildest dreams did I think they would set fire to the car." He realized that was the plan when, as the car began to roll, they both smelled gasoline. "Flame-o!" shouted Mark, and flames engulfed the car interior.

This sounds like the climatic moment in an episode of an old-fashioned Saturday morning movie serial. With the hero facing certain death, how can he possibly escape? Watch for the next episode!

As far as Sheila Stroud, Mark Evans and Norman White were concerned, there would be no next episode—except for that happy moment when, following the nasty accident, Sheila would collect the insurance money. Of that they had no doubt, because, with their own eyes, they had seen the flaming car roll at increasing speed, then plunge over the edge of the cliff, bursting into a fireball as it landed. Sheila was certain—her two enemies were dead.

Now, two years later, here I was, walking up the path and knocking at a door that was opened a few moments later by Pauline. Ivor, climbing down a ladder from the attic, where he had been doing maintenance work, came forward to greet me. The marks of that terrible night were still on them. Pauline wore a headscarf to cover bare patches where some of her hair had been burned away. "I had lovely hair," she told me wistfully. Ivor's scarred arms were still swathed in pressure bandages, and the side of his face was a livid red. I shook hands carefully—his hands, after many skin grafts, were still fragile.

Ivor led me into their cozy living room, pointing out on the wall a framed engagement portrait of them taken three weeks before the crime at Barrow Wake. In the picture, they are a handsome couple. Ivor is young, successful-looking, while Pauline is lively and animated. It's not hard to see how she attracted a man ten years younger than she was.

"At the drop of a hat," Ivor told me, "we both knew immediately we were right for each other. We were very similar people, easygoing types."

We talked about the events leading up to the crime: the real estate deal that suddenly turned ugly—over horses; the night that started so innocuously with drinks at the Air Balloon. And they told me the details of the crime itself, and how they had felt as the true extent of their peril became clear. Finally, they filled me in on their miraculous escape.

As the burning car began rolling toward the edge of the cliff,

Pauline screamed that they were on fire. "I was screaming too," said Ivor. He had his hands over his face, trying to ward off the flames. "The pain was indescribable. I was burning alive. All I could think of was getting Pauline out of there."

One thing their tormentors had forgotten was that the six-foot-two Ivor had had the driver's seat way back from the steering wheel. The passenger seat, where five-foot-two Pauline had been sitting, on the other hand, was well forward. Their positioning gave Ivor his chance.

Carefully, he got down on the rug in front of the fireplace to show me what had happened. Even with the flames around him, "I worked out that there was enough room for me to kick across in front of her. I lowered myself down in the seat, like this," he said, squirming sideways. "Then I braced myself against the door pillar and kicked out. My feet being tied together, I suppose they acted like a battering ram."

If someone is going to push you over a cliff in a car, you'd better hope the car is an ancient Vauxhall Viva. No one ever called it a quality automobile. "Flimsy" would have been a good word for Ivor's vehicle. "The window broke, and then the door flew open. The locks weren't very strong," he said.

Still holding his hands in front of his face, he was not sure whether Pauline had escaped. But he knew he had to get his door open too. As he pulled his hands away, the flames savaged his face. But he managed to flip the lock, pull the handle of the door and roll out. He watched the car bounce down the hill and launch into the air, describing an arc before slamming down on its roof in a fireball. He dragged himself to the edge of the cliff. "I could feel the heat," he said. "I thought Pauline was in the car, but I couldn't get down to her."

Pauline, rolling out of the car, had felt the blessed relief of the cool, dew-soaked grass. To her horror, though, she saw that her clothes were still burning; her nylon bra was actually melting into her skin. She rolled on the wet grass to quench the fire. Pauline, too, thought her partner had gone over the cliff in the car. "I had to get to Ivor," she said. "I tried to get down to where the car was burning, but there was the sheer drop."

Neither of them aware the other had survived, they cowered in the grass in case their attackers had seen them escape. Finally, Ivor, painfully pulling at the reins around his legs with burned hands, staggered back up the hill, where a young couple stood beside a car. Seeing this strange apparition emerge from the darkness and mist, they ignored Ivor's calls for help and drove off, perhaps telling their friends they had seen the ghost of Barrow Wake. Luckily, another driver had seen the car explode and had called the police emergency number.

The first police officers to arrive still have difficulty describing the scene. They were met by Ivor, smoke still rising from his clothes, a red haze of heat surrounding him like a halo from hell, crying, "Help, please help! My girlfriend's been murdered. She's in the car."

"It was like something from a horror film," was how Constable David Spencer described Pauline's emergence from the mist, shaking and moaning.

Ivor's thoughts were still on Pauline as they lifted him into an ambulance. "It's okay, lad, we've got her in the car," a policeman told him.

The murder plan might yet have succeeded had Pauline and Ivor not pulled through. "The expectation of them living was not very high," Detective Inspector Trevor Gladding told me. "Especially

Ivor—he had a fractured skull." His lungs were also badly damaged from smoke and gas inhalation.

Because they might die, it was all the more urgent for police to get evidence against their attackers. Two short interviews were conducted with Ivor and Pauline at the burn unit at Frenchay Hospital, in Bristol, that night. "Ivor had a tube down his throat," Gladding remembered. "He was at death's door."

The three killers must have been satisfied with their night's work. Everything had gone just as it did in the movie. Almost. Sheila and Mark dropped Norman White at Matson, a large public housing community on the outskirts of Gloucester, where he said he had relatives with whom he could stay. Before getting out, though, he warned the other two that, if the police came calling, they'd better not bring his name into it or there would be trouble. "You," he said to Sheila, "You'd better get rid of this pickup or have the damage [from shoving the little car] seen to. And I mean right away!"

By now, Sheila must have realized that you can't simply remove people from your life and expect not to hear from the police. And shortly after she dropped Mark off at the bungalow, the police arrived. Finding only Mark at home, they arrested him.

Sheila, meanwhile, was driving around, intent on destroying evidence. She dumped the tonneau cover and the hard plastic box liner from the truck in a field. They were both turned over to police later by a member of her family. The liner had been washed, but forensic scientists found traces of blood.

In the early morning, she phoned her sister. "I've had an accident with the pickup, hit some black ice," she said. "I don't have the money to pay the garage." Her sister agreed to meet her at the repair shop.

The owner, Geoff Billett, after giving her an estimate to repair the broken headlight and dented bar at the front of the truck, noticed that Sheila seemed agitated. Perhaps she had read morning papers. "Lovers' Terror," the *Daily Mirror* headlined its report on Ivor and Pauline's remarkable survival.

Knowing the police would be looking for her, Sheila arrived at the nearby Cheltenham police station that afternoon, still driving the white Toyota and accompanied by her stepfather.

"She was a hard, cold, calculating woman," Inspector Gladding told me. At first, Sheila and Mark, obviously by pre-arrangement, denied the whole thing. Then, when Ivor and Pauline's initial statements made that position untenable, they claimed they had only intended to give Pauline and Ivor a fright. It had just got out of hand, they said, when the black fellow, whose identity was still unknown to police, had gone berserk. Who was he? They were too frightened to tell police. Only when the recording machine was turned off did they gave a name: Norman White.

The police knew White by reputation. The man whose own lawyer would call him "a violent brute" had been sent to prison three times for attacking his girlfriend, Joy Foster. On the last occasion, after being stabbed by White, Foster had required thirteen stitches.

But White had gone to ground, using all his underworld cunning. It was only after several weeks, and after negotiating with his lawyer, that police officers were able to interview him. And they got little out of him. White simply denied he was there the night of the attack. "I was home watching telly," he said. "I fell asleep."

"We couldn't place him at the scene," said Gladding. There were no incriminating fingerprints, Pauline and Ivor were not yet well enough to identify him, and even if they had been, their assailant had worn a mask.

Gladding said it was one of the most galling moments of his career when he watched White cockily walk out of the police station on bail.

In January 1993, though, Gladding's luck turned. He learned that White had once again been sent to jail, this time for assaulting another girlfriend, Rae Smith. Not only did Gladding now know where to find White, but Rae Smith, who had been nearly killed by her boyfriend, was willing to cooperate. She remembered that White had received many phone calls from Sheila Stroud, and he had even told Rae that Sheila had offered him $72,000 "to kill some guy off." One day he arrived home very pleased with himself and driving a white BMW. Sheila and Mark had provided it for him so he could trail the guy around, he told her.

Rae's evidence, especially about the occasions when she went along with Norman to meet Sheila and Mark, was good. Norman was even supposed to meet her the night of the attack, but phoned her to call it off. But Gladding was hoping Ivor and Pauline would soon be well enough to identify Norman.

Early one morning, Gladding was at the gates of Shepton Mallet Prison to arrest Norman White as he was released at the end of his sentence. That evening, Ivor and Pauline, still very weak, attended an identification parade in Bristol. After studying the faces, they admitted they could not pick out their attacker.

"It was a bit demoralizing," said Gladding. "But it had been six to eight months since they had seen him, and even then they had never seen him clearly." The police, though, felt confident enough with Rae's evidence alone, and Norman White was charged with two counts of attempted murder.

Apart from Pauline and Ivor, it was Rae Smith for whom the public felt the most sympathy. Norman had been sure she would be too frightened to testify against him. With the accused man glaring at her, she broke down several times while giving evidence. But her word was enough. White and his two co-accused were found guilty, and each received a sentence of eighteen years.

Ivor and Pauline will never get back the lives they once had. While they were suffering terrible pain in the hospital, Pauline told me, Ivor would send her a note every day. It was always the same: "I love you."

Pain still plagued their lives when I met them. The simplest task could be excruciating. But they are slowly recovering and learning to move on, and they appreciate every triumph that comes as they heal. "When it first happened," Pauline told me, "my biggest dread was that I wouldn't be able to pick up my baby grandchildren and cuddle them again. But I've healed enough to do that now, and it's great to be able to hold them close. You start to live your life again," she said. "We will accept what we've got."

They can still laugh, too: "Joan Collins paid a hundred grand for the kind of face-lift I've had for nothing," said Pauline, smiling. "Any wrinkles I had have gone."

A couple of months after we spoke, Ivor and Pauline wrote to say they had just married. A storybook ending in a storybook village.

Murder in the Fourth World

I had a hunch that Juliet Hulme and Pauline Rieper would make something of their lives. When I wrote in the early 1990s about the giddy pair of teenagers whose self-delusion had led to murder, I suggested it was likely that one or both had become schoolteachers after they were released from prison. I had no idea that soon afterwards, with the arrival of a movie about their case, *Heavenly Creatures*, Juliet's cover would be blown and she would be revealed as a famous mystery writer.

They were an odd pair, unlike each other in just about every way. Juliet was the pretty, utterly domineering daughter of Dr. Henry Rainsford Hulme, a physicist who arrived from London in 1948 to serve as rector of Canterbury University College in Christchurch, New Zealand. Pauline, on the other hand, was dumpy, unattractive and the daughter of a fishmonger.

Illness would be a theme in their relationship. Juliet, like many famous writers, had a sickly childhood. She was only a toddler when the blast from an exploding bomb in wartime London left her shocked and with nightmares for weeks. After the war, doctors told Hulme and his wife, Hilda, that Juliet had weakened lungs and was in danger of contracting tuberculosis. It would be best to take her to a healthier climate. An offer to work on Britain's atomic energy program was dangled in front of Hume, but he rejected it in favor of the New Zealand job for the sake of his daughter's health.

At first, the sacrifice seemed in vain: Juliet's lung problems returned, and she spent four months in a sanatorium. But by 1953, when she was fifteen, Juliet was stronger and was doing well at school, where her artistic temperament showed itself in story-writing, working with clay and an aptitude for memorizing chunks of the great poets. Her parents felt confident enough to leave her at home while they took an overseas trip during the New Zealand winter. It was during this period, with Juliet free to wander the family's sixteen-room mansion, Ilam, that she became close to Pauline, a classmate at Christchurch Girls' High School.

It was not so unlikely: attractive and brilliant young women often attract plainer best friends who offer admiration and little competition, and when they arrived home, the Hulmes were pleased by the new friendship. Especially because, when Juliet was confined to bed, Pauline would be there, reading to her and talking endlessly.

If Juliet's life was in a mansion on the hill, Pauline's was decidedly lower down the social scale. Her father, Herbert Rieper, pipe-smoking and amiable, owned a small wholesale fish business, and the family lived in the ground-floor apartment of a white-painted house not far from Ilam. Only when she was arrested and charged under the unfamiliar name Pauline Parker would the girl discover that her father and mother, Honora, were not, in fact, married.

Like Juliet, Pauline had known ill health. At the age of five she developed a bone disorder, osteomyelitis, which called for operations and long periods in bed. For Honora and Herbert, it was yet another burden: of the four children born to them, one was mentally handicapped and in an institution, another died soon after birth, and only the eldest, Wendy, was healthy, with a sunny, outgoing temperament.

The contrast between life at Ilam and the modest apartment may have made Pauline even more embittered; at home she was a difficult teen, refusing to speak to her parents except when she had to. Juliet did not make things easier: she called on Pauline riding her new pony, Snowball. Suddenly, owning a pony was the most important thing to Pauline. She would be part of the smart set, she could join the Horse and Pony Club with Juliet, and on horseback no one would ever notice her silly old limp. But Herbert and Honora could not even think of it. Pauline stormed out and spent more and more time at Juliet's house, staying there nearly every weekend.

It was as if Pauline and Juliet were living on their own planet. There was no room for anyone else. They loved each other passionately, although platonically: while it would be hinted in court, in a book about the case and in a subsequent movie, *Heavenly Creatures*, that they were lesbians, Juliet has said in recent years that there was no physical element to their relationship.

For the Hulmes, the girls' friendship was a godsend: they were free to lead busy lives with many social engagements while the girls sprawled on the lawn or in the house, talking innocently of their favorite Hollywood stars or writing stories together. Well, perhaps not so innocently. Because bit by bit they constructed a full-blown fantasy world. The stories became more and more real. They invented characters and wrote to each other assuming guises such as Charles, Emperor of Moravia, and Deborah, his mistress. Gradually, the subject matter of their stories took on a darker hue. Psychiatrist Dr. Reginald Mendicott, who gave evidence of their possible insanity at their trial, noted that "sudden death, suicide and murder assumed extravagant proportions. They were preoccupied with ideas of great power, especially to murder without reprisal, and vicious characters were greatly respected."

They were geniuses, they told each other, just waiting for the world to recognize them. But how could they ever be discovered in a backwater like Christchurch? New York was the place to be. The mounting pile of school exercise books containing their bizarre stories would snapped up by any New York publisher. And from there—Hollywood! Their stories would be made into movies. Movies in which they would be the stars. They even planned to send their pictures to Hollywood.

But how would they raise the money to go to America? "I'll sell Snowball," Juliet said one day. Her parents were surprised when they learned she wanted to sell the horse she doted on, which she had only recently acquired. A few days later, though, Juliet told her friend, "I sold Snowball. Mr. Perry gave me £50 for her."

Walter Perry, a rugged and engaging Englishman, had recently arrived in Christchurch. When the Hulmes, who met him on the social circuit, learned he was looking for accommodation, they offered him the empty maid's apartment at Ilam. He moved in at Christmas, 1953.

The Hulmes were becoming worried at the intensity of the girls' relationship, and Dr. Hulme went to see the Riepers for a talk. "I don't know what's got into them," said Honora. "Pauline's marks have been awful this term. We're thinking of taking her to see our doctor to see if anything's wrong."

The family physician, Dr. Francis O. Bennett, found nothing physically wrong with Pauline. He said nothing to the parents about his suspicions that the girls might be in a lesbian relationship, but suggested it might be a good idea for Pauline to change schools, to separate her from Juliet.

The Riepers expected a terrible scene when they made this suggestion, but were surprised when Pauline made no objection. The girls had gone underground. Pauline wrote in her diary for February 13, 1954: "Why could not Mother die? Dozens of people, thousands of people, are dying every day. So why not Mother and Father too? Life is very hard."

Her unsuspecting parents were not worried when the newly meek Pauline asked if she could spend the weekend at Ilam. The relationship, they thought, would soon wane when the girls were separated.

Juliet, meanwhile, had her own difficulties at home. Her mother had surprised her by throwing a fit because Juliet had borrowed a gramophone record from Mr. Perry's room. Then, coming home from school one day, she had found her mother and Mr. Perry sprawled in the living room in an embrace. It was terrible. What would her father do if he found out?

It was not so bad, Pauline said, after absorbing the scandalous news. It could even be helpful. Why didn't Juliet ask Mr. Perry for a loan of, say, £100? It would give them the money to flee. When Juliet asked why on earth Mr. Perry would loan them that amount of money, Pauline explained, "So you don't snitch on him to your father."

The blackmail plan fizzled, and in April, Juliet came to Pauline with devastating news. Her parents, she said, were separating.

"Deborah [Pauline's fantasy name for Juliet] and I are sticking to one thing," Pauline wrote in her diary the next day. "We sink or swim together."

Honora Rieper seems to have been no different from any mother with a stubborn, rebellious teenage daughter. Perhaps other young girls make the kind of entries in their secret diaries that Pauline did a few days later: "Anger against Mother boiled up inside me. It is she who is one of the main obstacles in my path. Suddenly a means of ridding myself of the obstacle occurred to me. If she were to die!"

For just about any other teenage girl, these would be empty words of anger, soon forgotten. But Pauline was serious. On April 29, she wrote, "I did not tell Deborah of my plans for removing Mother. The last fate I would wish to meet is one in Borstal [the institution for young offenders]. I am trying to think of some other way. I want it to appear either a natural or an accidental death."

Meanwhile, their plans to run away to America continued. In May, the girls began shoplifting, selling makeup items to girls at school to raise funds for their trip. On May 27, in the early hours of the morning, Pauline walked all the way to her father's business with the intention of robbing the till. The sight of a policeman on patrol put her off.

Pauline's thoughts of murder might have faded away, but a new domestic crisis at Ilam suddenly pitted the girls against their parents. Dr. Hulme came to tell the Riepers they would not need to send Pauline to another school after all. With his marriage ending, he was resigning from his college post and, on July 3, returning to England to take up the position originally offered to him with the atomic research team.

His son, Jonathan, would come to England with him, but he judged Juliet's health too fragile for the English fog and cold. She would go with them as far as South Africa, and would stay with family friends there before returning to New Zealand. The trip would have the double advantage of separating the two girls and, although he did not mention this to the Riepers, getting

Juliet out of the way while Hilda and Walter Perry sorted out their affairs.

It was the perfect solution. The Riepers were profoundly relieved. But the two girls had other ideas. "I won't go unless Pauline comes with me!" Juliet declared. It was out of the question; Pauline's parents would not allow it, Dr. Hulme explained.

Even when Juliet joined Pauline's pleas to the Riepers, they were adamant. "Put it out of your mind," Honora told Pauline.

"Deborah, dear," Pauline whispered to her friend later, "there's only one answer. We must moider Mother." Saying it with a Bronx gangster accent made it sound a little less real.

"But how will that help?"

"Just think about it," said Pauline excitedly. The devastating scene. Poor Mother murdered! Her daughter inconsolable. "Oh, Daddy," she cried, improvising the scene. "I'll never get over losing poor Mummy...perhaps it would help a little bit if I went with Juliet and her father to South Africa."

The conspirators went into peels of laughter.

"But how would we do it?" said Juliet at last.

"I know just the way. I've thought it all out," said Pauline.

That night, Pauline wrote in her diary, "We are both mad. We are both stark, staring, raving mad. There is no doubt about it and we are thrilled by the thought."

On June 12, she wrote, "Eventually we enacted how each saint [movie star] would make love in bed. We felt exhausted, but very satisfied."

By June 19, they had almost finished writing the books they thought would bring them fame and fortune in New York. Mostly, though, they had talked about how to "moider" Honora. "We have worked it out carefully and are both thrilled by the idea. Naturally we feel a trifle nervous, but the pleasure of anticipation is great."

Once again, Honora and her husband could only wonder at their daughter's swift mood changes. The South Africa crisis seemed to be in the past, and Pauline was now a cooperative young woman. "I rose late and helped Mother vigorously this morning," Pauline recorded on June 21. "Deborah called and we discussed the moider fully. I feel very keyed up, as if I was planning a surprise party. Mother has fallen in with everything beautifully and the happy event is to take place tomorrow afternoon. So next time I write in my diary Mother will be dead. How odd—yet how pleasing. I washed my hair and came to bed at quarter to nine."

She was apparently unable to wait until after the murder to record her thoughts again. The next morning, in an entry headed "The Day of the Happy Event," she wrote, "I am writing a little of this up on the morning before the death. I felt very excited and 'morning-before-Christmasish' last night. I didn't have pleasant dreams though."

A few days earlier, the sunny new Pauline had asked her mother if they could have Juliet over for a farewell lunch, followed by a walk in Victoria Park. With all the packing the Hulmes were doing, there might not be time for it later. Honora agreed with the plan, reassured that her daughter was accepting the inevitable.

When Juliet joined the Riepers for lunch that Monday, Herbert was surprised at the girls' high spirits, seeing as they were to be parted in two weeks. It was an overcast, chilly winter day, but the girls insisted on their walk. There were few people around as Juliet, Pauline and Honora stopped for tea at a refreshment stand in Victoria Park, in the Cashmere Hills above the city of Christchurch. After tea, they walked briskly along the labyrinth paths between laurels and rhododendrons, the girls in their gabardine school raincoats, Honora in her winter coat. As they turned back toward the park gates, Juliet went on ahead—presumably to keep watch. "What's that?" said Pauline, pointing out a pink pebble to her mother. "Oh, pretty," said Honora, bending to pick it up.

Pauline's hand slid out of her shoulder bag, her fingers twisted around the top of a woman's stocking. In the foot was a half-brick. As her mother bent over, she swung the weight and brought it down on the back of her head. With a groan, Honora fell to the ground. It had been ridiculously easy, exactly as they had foreseen. Birds continued to sing in the bushes. No one had seen them. The plan now was to call for help, explaining that Honora had had a nasty fall, hitting her head on a rock.

The only trouble was, Honora was moving. She wasn't dead. Pauline brought the weight down on her head again. And again. Juliet ran back up the path, took the stocking from her, and battered the struggling form on the ground. The stocking was soaked in blood. "Why won't she die?" screamed Juliet. Finally, she dropped the stocking. They looked at each other. There was now no way they could claim the death was accidental. Honora's battered head and face and the blood splattered over their hands and faces told another story. But there was no turning back. With no alternative story that could possibly account for the death, they had to follow through on the original plan as best they could.

Agnes Ritchie was washing teacups at the back of the refreshment stand a few minutes later when the two girls ran in. "It's Mummy," Pauline cried. "She's terribly hurt. Please come."

"She's all covered in blood. It's terrible," sobbed Juliet.

Even in that moment, Mrs. Ritchie noticed that they, too, were covered in blood. And Pauline saw her notice. "We tried to lift her," she explained, "but she was too heavy."

When asked what had happened, Pauline said, "She fell and hit her head on a plank. And then she kept falling and banging her head."

Even to their ears it must have sounded implausible.

"I'll never forget it," Juliet said, trying to bolster the story, "the way her head kept banging."

"Don't make us go down there again!" Pauline pleaded.

Agnes said she would fetch her husband. As she left, the girls were washing their hands. She thought she heard them laughing.

When Ken Ritchie found Honora lying dead on a bed of pine needles, he knew right away that this was no accident. The terrible damage to her face and skull was evidence of a furious attack. The brick in the bloodstained stocking lying nearby confirmed his suspicions. The pathologist would estimate that Honora had received forty-five blows.

At first, the police did not believe Juliet was present at the killing. "You're the one we suspect of killing your mother," Senior Detective Macdonald Brown said, when he interviewed Pauline soon after. "Do you want to make a statement?"

"No, ask me questions."

"Okay, who assaulted your mother?"

"I did."

"Why?"

"If you don't mind, I won't answer that question."

"When did you make up your mind to kill your mother?"

"A few days ago."

"Did you tell anyone you were going to do it?"

"No. My friend did not know anything about it. She was out of sight at the time. She had gone ahead."

"What did you use?"

"A half-brick inside the foot of a stocking. I had the brick in my shoulder bag."

Pauline was sitting on a police station bench shortly thereafter, when Detective Brown noticed her trying to conceal a piece of paper, which he grabbed. On it, Pauline had written, "I am taking the blame for everything."

The girls were well brought up and polite. At first, Juliet tried to spin the yarn about Honora having fallen and hit her head. The next day, she apologized to Detective Brown for misleading him. She admitted she had brought the half-brick from Ilam, wrapped in newspaper. It was she, too, who had found the pretty pink pebble the day before and had dropped it so that Honora would bend down to pick it up.

"I heard noises behind me," she said in her confused statement. "It was a loud conversation and anger. I saw Mrs. Rieper in a sort of squatting position. I saw Pauline hit Mrs. Rieper with the brick in the stocking. I took the stocking and hit her too. I was terrified. I thought that one of them had to die. I wanted to help Pauline. It was terrible. Mrs. Rieper moved convulsively. We both held her."

Juliet claimed that, when they went to the park, the girls had hoped Honora would change her mind and allow Pauline to go to South Africa. "But after the first blow was struck," she said, "I knew it would be necessary for us to kill her."

New Zealanders in those postwar years—and even today, to a lesser degree—were strangers to serious crime. The verdant land has been content to remain one of the world's more attractive backwaters (a position now threatened by its modern fame as the locale for the sumptuous *Lord of the Rings* movies). So it was hard for people in Christchurch to accept that two girls from good families attending a smart school had attacked and murdered an innocent woman with a fury beyond belief. Here, indeed, dwelt monsters.

In seeking an explanation, the defense naturally looked to insanity, and the girls' behavior lent credence to that position. A photograph shows them grinning as they leave the magistrate's court, as if they are enjoying a huge joke. Dr. Mendicott, a key defense witness, said that Pauline had called him an irritating fool, as well as ugly, while Juliet, forced to submit to a medical examination, had screamed, "I hope you break your flaming neck."

The girls, sitting with a wardress between them, never testified, but Pauline's bound diary and the stories in the exercise books told a great deal about the girls' state of mind leading up to the murder. One diary entry reads: "Today Juliet and I found a being of the Fourth World. We saw a gateway through the clouds... We then realized we had the key. We had an extra part to the brain which can appreciate the Fourth World."

The girls, said Dr. Mendicott, showed "a gross reversal of moral sense. They admired those things which are evil and condemned those things the community considers good."

Juliet and Pauline had even refused to attend the first visit to Christchurch by the new, young queen, proof, indeed, to patriotic New Zealanders of a disturbed outlook.

Juliet's father had already sailed for England. Hilda Hulme sat in court beside Walter Perry, whose last name she would soon assume by deed poll, while a forlorn Herbert Rieper sat with his elder daughter, Wendy. The parents could only cringe at the girls' behavior in court, with Juliet trying to outstare reporters in the press box and showing no emotion at all as the pathologist testified to Honora's horrific wounds.

Juliet became upset only when Mendicott related that Pauline had told him she'd had sexual intercourse with a boy staying at the Rieper home. Juliet leaned across and whispered furiously.

The psychiatrist was confident that the girls were mentally ill, that they were paranoiacs who reinforced each other's insanity—a condition known as folie à deux.

Juliet told one doctor that she quite believed Honora knew, on that day in the park, what was going to happen, "and did not bear any grudge." Another time, she said, "I don't wish to place myself above the law: I am apart from it. You see, we believe we are geniuses."

Dr. Bennett, the family physician who had known both girls, agreed with his colleague's diagnosis of paranoia. "They had delusions of grandeur, formed a society of their own and lived in it," he testified. "There came the threat of separation. Anything that threatens the paranoiac makes him dangerous. They thought that by removing Pauline's mother, the way would be clear... Neither will admit contrition or regret. Pauline told me she would still feel justified in killing her mother if she were a threat to them being together. [Juliet] not only considers the murder justified, but also that other murders might be justified."

Both girls, despite their skewed view of the world, had impressed their questioners with their intelligence.

Despite the psychological testimony issuing from the defense, the prosecutor, A.W. Brown, insisted that this was "a callously planned and premeditated murder, committed by two highly intelligent and perfectly sane but precocious and dirty-minded girls." In conclusion, he pronounced, "They are not incurably insane; they are incurably bad."

"Bad" may sound a quaint, old-fashioned word, but it seemed appropriate enough as the girls laughed and joked while the jury returned to give its verdict. Both were found guilty of murder and were sentenced to five years in prison.

The girls were separated at last. Pauline was sent to Mount Eden, an austere prison near Auckland, while Juliet was consigned to Arohata Borstal Institution, near Wellington.

Their behavior before, during and after the crime indeed suggested mental illness. Some might have predicted a future on the back wards of mental institutions for the pair. But after investigating and writing about a number of murders by teenage girls, I believed otherwise. Case after case can be cited where apparently normal, even intelligent girls have ganged up, usually on one of their peers, and killed them. Teenage boys usually kill singly; girls kill in packs or pairs, reinforcing each other's violence. In that regard, Juliet and Pauline were not so different.

Because of their intelligence and writing abilities, I speculated that the two young women, who had disappeared from public view once they were released from prison, had likely moved to Australia or England and become English teachers. But Juliet's rehabilitation was even more successful than that. In July 1994, while *Heavenly Creatures* was playing at film festivals, Juliet, then fifty-five, was discovered in a Scottish fishing village, tending her garden, walking her dogs and publishing murder mystery bestsellers under the name Anne Perry.

Both girls were released upon completion of their sentences. Pauline left New Zealand but, according to one report, has since returned and is now working in a bookshop in Auckland. She is said to be a devout Roman Catholic.

Juliet went to England to join her mother, who had married Walter Perry. She worked as a flight attendant, a buyer for a department store and a property underwriter before moving to California for five years. There was, however, "never anything I seriously wished to do except write," she says. She began by writing about Jack the Ripper, at the suggestion of her stepfather, then moved on to write Victorian murder mysteries; the first was published in 1973, and she has since sold more than ten million copies of her books.

She told an interviewer, "Once you have admitted you are at fault, have said, 'I'm sorry, I'm utterly totally sorry,' without excuses, and paid your price, then you have to put it behind you." She had not been in touch with Pauline.

In a New Zealand television interview, she explained, "Pauline was very distressed [before the murder] and she desperately wanted to come with us [to South Africa]. I felt that I was running out on a person who helped me when I was in trouble [when she was ill in the hospital] and that I was betraying her by just leaving and doing nothing. I really believed that if I didn't take her with us, she would take her own life and I made a very, very wrong decision." She added, "I didn't have the strength to say no, this is wrong, no matter what, and to just walk away."

Her first-hand experience of murder has played no part in her stories, she says. "You'll find that none of the crimes [in the books] are described in any detail, none of them inflict more pain than is necessary."

Saintly Billy

This was really rather wonderful. I was standing on Market Street in Rugeley, Staffordshire, in front of the hideous video parlor that then occupied Dr. William Palmer's Tudor house, while two history buffs argued fiercely over whether, 135 years earlier, the good doctor had, in fact, poisoned all those people.

"Of course," said historian John Godwin that day in 1990 when I visited Rugeley, "there were all those illegitimate babies of his. He was alleged to have done away with all of them."

"Fooey!" exclaimed Edwina Morgan, a retired teacher who was chairman of the local history society. "Everything was put on Palmer, but I rather like him. It's dreadful, but I do."

That was always the way with Billy Palmer: he was a scamp, a rascal, a cheat and quite possibly one of the most prolific murderers in British history. But you couldn't help liking him.

While a sinister aura surrounds the other notable medical poisoners of the nineteenth century—men like Dr. Neill Cream—Dr. Palmer, to whom sixteen murders are commonly ascribed, went about his deadly business with such cheerful élan that it was hard for some people, even in his own day, to take him seriously. Part of the explanation, I suspect, is that Billy Palmer was a sport, a follower of the turf. His crimes, for the most part, were committed not in gloomy gas-lit rented rooms or dark back streets, but at the racetrack and in the boisterous taverns favored by the touts, bookies and nobblers who followed the race meets.

Only a sport like Billy, on hearing the death sentence passed on him, could say, "When the jury returned to court and I saw the cocked-up nose of the perky little foreman, I knew it was a gooser for me!"

The ladies could never resist Billy. Fourteen bastards were born to various young women during the five years he was doing his medical training. As to what happened to all those babies, it's better not to ask. But some thought it more than coincidence that whenever Billy gave them a cuddle, they went into convulsions.

Even Billy's old mother couldn't resist his charm, although he had forged her name to the tune of thousands of pounds. "I'm Dr. Palmer's mother, and not ashamed of it, neither," she told an artist she came across sitting beside the canal painting scenes of Rugeley to feed the insatiable public appetite for books and pictures detailing the life of the notorious doctor. "Yes," she added with a regretful sigh, "they hanged my saintly Billy."

So on a chill, foggy day in early summer, I've come to Rugeley, a market town not far from the famous Staffordshire potteries, to learn more about Saintly Billy and the passions he still arouses.

Here on Market Street, as Edwina, John and I stand chatting, I can almost hear Billy's loud laugh off in the mist. Behind the windows of the video store, where they're advertising Hollywood's cheap thrills, Billy served the finest port to his racing cronies—sixty-seven dozen bottles were still left to auction when they took him off to be hanged. Billy, a chubby, bland-faced little fellow, must have passed right where we're standing as he went fussing back and forth to the Talbot Arms Hotel—now renamed the Shrewsbury Arms, or "the Shrew" to locals—where his friend, John Parsons Cook, lay ill in room 10. It was Cook's death, on November 20, 1855, that created all the fuss.

"This is where his garden was," Edwina is telling me. "He was very fond of his garden." Odd, I can't imagine Billy bending down to sniff the pinks and wallflowers. "But it's a shame what's been done," says Edwina. Like many another town linked with a notorious murderer whose misdeeds have long since become the stuff of legend, Rugeley has tried to obliterate every reminder. Billy's house has been gutted and visually destroyed, and not the teeniest plaque informs visitors of Rugeley's main claim to fame.

"The dislike for him, it's still there," says Edwina. When we get to St. Augustine's Church, where Billy sang in the choir, she points out the tombstone on Cook's grave that helps keep the resentment alive. Sacred, it says, to the memory of John Parsons Cook, "whose life was taken away from him on the night of 20 November 1855 in the 29th year of his age. Amiable and affectionate in his disposition and generous in his conduct, he was sincerely beloved and will long be lamented by his kindred and friends." But, says Edwina, when she was a girl, there was a very old lady who actually remembered Palmer, "and she said he was a very nice man."

Nice? I don't suppose even Billy would have made that claim.

He was born across the road in a fine old Georgian house once known as the Yard because of the timber yard out back where his father, old Joe Palmer, was said to have grown rich on timber stolen from the estate of a local nobleman. The Palmer children were a mixed bag: Tom became a clergyman, while

Walter was a hopeless drunk. Billy, on leaving the Rugeley Free Grammar School at seventeen, had been apprenticed to a Liverpool druggist.

When old Joe keeled over with a heart attack, leaving an unsigned will, the eldest boy, Joseph, allowed his mother the use of the property, providing she didn't remarry. It was a mean thing to do, but she got around it easily: she simply took as her lover a lawyer, Jeremiah Smith, many years her junior. So Mrs. Palmer was, you might say, broad-minded, and she didn't seem a bit surprised when Billy was caught stealing money from the mails. Especially when he explained to her that he needed the money to pay off his landlord's daughter, who was pregnant by him and demanding money for an abortion. Mrs. Palmer simply made good the money stolen and set him up in a new career, apprenticing him to a surgeon.

It was while he was furthering his medical studies at the Stafford Infirmary that Billy first came under suspicion of wrongdoing more serious than drugging his mates' drinks to make them throw up or pee green. He challenged a shoemaker named Abley to a brandy-drinking contest. After downing the second tumbler, Abley, feeling ill, went out to the inn yard, where he was found groaning in pain an hour later. He died that night. His widow, an attractive young woman who had caught Billy's eye at the infirmary, was said to be quite consolable.

In October 1847, Billy, his student scrapes behind him, came home from London's St. Bartholomew's Hospital a fully qualified surgeon. He married (over her guardian's serious reservations) Annie Brookes, his longtime sweetheart, and set up in practice in the old house on Market Street. He was popular and able, and he quickly made his mark. But Rugeley was a horse town (the horse fair is still one of its annual highlights), and just before the birth of their first child, a boy they named William, the doctor, using money he had inherited from his father's estate, leased stables and a paddock and became a horse breeder.

It was his downfall. Billy was a great judge of horseflesh, but a mug when it came to business. After his first horse, Goldfinder, won the Tradesmen's Plate at the Chester meeting and netted him nearly £3,000, Palmer, who had by then abandoned medicine, thought breeding winners was as easy as tumbling a girl in the hay. He got deeper and deeper into debt, and finally resorted to having Annie forge his mother's name on loan guarantees.

Then began a most unfortunate series of deaths, each taking place while Billy Palmer was close at hand. Annie's mother, an alcoholic, came to stay, and died within two weeks. Dr. Bamford, an elderly friend of Billy's, put down apoplexy as the cause of death. A punter named Leonard Bladon, to whom Palmer reportedly owed £600, stayed the night at the Palmers' with several hundred pounds in his moneybelt, and left feet first and with no sign of his money. On the death certificate, Dr. Bamford put it down to a stable accident of a few weeks before.

And then Annie herself caught a chill and, despite having survived five pregnancies (although four of the children died), succumbed soon after. Others in her family had committed suicide, and there was talk of her having taken mysterious powders. For once, Billy was distraught. "Saw the last of my beloved wife for ever. How desolate life is," he wrote in his diary.

Nevertheless, there was a £13,000 policy on her life that enabled Billy to pay off some of his debts.

The coincidences continued. To improve his stock and, he hoped, his income, Palmer bought two top-ranked horses, The Chicken and Nettle, for several thousand pounds. The loan sharks were quickly at his door again, in particular one Thomas Pratt, a

London solicitor with a pug nose and billowing mutton chop whiskers who charged eager clients sixty percent interest per annum.

To pay off Pratt, Palmer's eye settled this time on his brother Walter, who, having separated from his wife and being in the later stages of alcoholism, seemed a likely bet to die quite soon. A better bet, anyway, than some of the horses Billy was putting his money on. Billy's plan, eagerly embraced by Walter, was to insure Walter's life for a substantial amount and give him a cash advance of £400 against future profits when he died. The £400, of course, would be spent by Walter on booze, which would likely hasten his death. Although several insurance companies wisely turned down applications made in Pratt's name, the Prince of Wales fund, which had already been stung in the Annie Palmer episode, amazingly went for a £14,000 policy.

Billy spent Wednesday, August 14, 1855, in Stafford with Walter, who was drinking hard. Receiving a solid tip on a race just as his brother was expiring, the doctor fired off a telegram placing £50 on the horse. It lost, Walter died, and the insurance company, suspicious this time, refused to pay.

Rumors were going around, but Billy met them with a laugh. "Here comes the poisoner," he would announce, entering a bar, and then, with a wink, "What's your poison, boys?" It is still a cry heard in the pubs of Staffordshire.

Why, then, we must ask ourselves, didn't young John Parsons Cook shun Billy Palmer like the plague? Why did Cook—a solicitor three years Billy's junior who, after inheriting £12,000, had given up his profession for the pleasures of the racetrack— carouse with Billy, bet with him and get into no end of drunken scrapes with the man everyone said was as dangerous as a viper? The answer, as with the girls who believed Billy's stories about marrying them, was that he was an awfully plausible scoundrel. And a desperate one at that.

By November 6, Billy's house of cards, built largely on fraud, was about to collapse. On that day, two writs for £4,000 were issued, one against Billy and one against his mother, who was unaware her name had been forged on promises to pay. Pratt was delaying service of the writs, but with another £1,500 due in three days, time was running out fast.

On November 14, a new opportunity opened up to Billy. Cook's horse, Polestar, won the Shrewsbury Handicap, netting Cook, through bets he had with others, about £2,500. Billy, on the other hand, had bet heavily on his own horse, The Chicken, at the Shrewsbury meet, and was in an even worse financial position when it lost.

At the Raven Hotel in Shrewsbury that night, Billy issued a familiar challenge. When Cook asked him if he'd take a glass of brandy, he replied, "Not until you down yours. You must play fair, old cock—drink for drink." Cook downed his glass at a gulp, then complained that it tasted strange and that his throat was burning. Billy sipped the little remaining in the bottom of the glass, and declared there was nothing wrong with it. By midnight, a doctor was in attendance on Cook, who complained of violent stomach pains and a burning throat. By the following day, though, Cook was well enough to return with Billy to Rugeley, where he put up at the Talbot Arms, across the road from Billy Palmer's house. The doctor insisted that Cook take his meals at his place, and on two occasions when Cook, not feeling well, was unable to leave his room, Billy sent him over bowls of reviving broth.

With the bills now coming due, Billy left his friend in Rugeley and made a dash for London, where, pretending to be Cook's partner, he collected £1,000 of Cook's winnings at Tattersall's, the betting house, and then forged a check in Cook's name, using the money to pay down some of his debts.

Cook had been well enough to go for walks, but following Billy's return to Rugeley, he took a turn for the worse. With Billy and another physician, Dr. Jones, in attendance, he went into violent convulsions, his back arching like a bow, and died.

The helpful Dr. Bamford, in his eighties and doddery, suggested apoplexy when called in for the customary death certificate. Dr. Jones at first thought tetanus might be the cause of death, but later put it down to convulsions caused by the overexcitement of having his horse win.

A housemaid at the Talbot Arms would report seeing Billy going through Cook's belongings; afterwards, no sign was found of the £600 in banknotes Cook had had with him.

Then William Stevens arrived. Stevens, an irascible elderly relative of Cook's, demanded to see Cook's betting book, in which he had recorded all his transactions. But no trace could be found of that, either. How much had been owed to Cook? He was sorry to say, said Billy, straight-faced, that Cook actually owed *him* £4,000, which he'd be pleased to receive out of the dead man's estate. Stevens' response was to demand an autopsy.

As a physician and friend of the deceased, Billy insisted on being present as Cook's body was opened up. We should not be surprised to learn that the doctor performing the job had his arm mysteriously jogged, causing him to spill some of the stomach contents, that the sealed jar containing the contents had a slash in the top after Billy handled it, and that the messenger assigned to deliver the jar to an analyst in London was bribed by Billy to shake the bottle along the way. Even so, Billy was in a state of anxiety as he waited for the autopsy results. He got another of his cronies, Francis Cheshire, the postmaster at Rugeley, to promise he would steam open the report to the authorities when it arrived so that, if the results were not encouraging, Billy could make his escape. A few days later, Cheshire contacted Billy with the best news possible: neither strychnine nor prussic acid, the two suspected poisons, had been found. To be on the safe side, Billy dispatched a gift hamper containing a twenty-pound turkey, a brace of pheasants, a cod and a barrel of oysters to the Stafford coroner, William Webb Ward, along with a note that mentioned the autopsy finding (which Billy wasn't supposed to know about). The note ended, "I hope the verdict tomorrow [at the inquest] will be that Cook died of natural causes."

This time, Billy had been a bit too brazen: Ward handed the note to the police. Cheshire was jailed for tampering with the mail, and two police officers arrived at the Palmer house to arrest the good doctor for forgery, pending more serious charges. When Jeremiah Smith, his friend and sometime collaborator, and his mother's lover, saw the fix Billy was in, he cried, "William, oh William, how is this?" Billy didn't answer, but his cheeks glistened with tears.

Billy was eventually charged with murdering Cook with strychnine. Such hostility, such booing, such spitting greeted Billy Palmer's every appearance while in custody that a special act of parliament was quickly passed allowing him to be tried at the Old Bailey in London rather than in the atmosphere of hatred that prevailed in Staffordshire.

Immediately, the moneylenders closed in, and Billy's effects, as well as his horses, were auctioned. (Prince Albert, the Queen's husband, bought one of the horses, Trickstress, for 230 guineas.) As a final indignity, a photographer offered to take photographs of "ladies, gentry and inhabitants" posed at the rear of the notorious Palmer house, something guaranteed to thrill and chill their loved ones.

Billy may have forged her signature on his promises to pay, but for Mrs. Palmer, only the best lawyer would do for "my roguish Billy." When his trial opened on May 14, 1856, Billy was represented by Serjeant Shee, a brilliant Irish attorney, while the prosecution was in the hands of the Attorney General, Sir Alexander Cockburn.

This was the first of the great Victorian poison trials involving medical men, and it attracted great public interest. The *Illustrated Times*, for example, published a special Rugeley edition that sold an unprecedented 400,000 copies. Readers got their money's worth. As Cockburn paraded no fewer than sixty-six witnesses into the box, a tale of fraud and deceit was uncovered the likes of which had rarely been heard, even at the Old Bailey.

But the charge was not fraud, but murder, and Billy, who sat bland and unmoved for the whole twelve days of the trial, was quite confident it would not stick. There was one good reason for his optimism: the twenty-four scientists and doctors called by both sides were in total disagreement over whether John Parsons Cook had been poisoned. Dr. John Glaister, a professor of forensic medicine at the University of Glasgow, suggests in his book, *The Power of Poison*, that knowledge and testing were simply not advanced enough at the time for anyone to be sure of the cause of Cook's death.

So it was a shock when the jury, after an absence of only one hour and seventeen minutes, returned with a guilty verdict. It was not so much a decision on how Cook had died as it was a final judgment on the doctor's whole scandalous course of conduct. Billy's proven purchases of strychnine and prussic acid may have been intended for poisoning rivals' horses, but that made him an even greater villain in the eyes of the racing public than if, as the prosecution contended, the poisons were intended for humans.

Perhaps it was just as well for Billy to get the thing over with: the authorities, after exhuming the bodies of his wife and his brother Walter, stood ready with two more murder charges if the first failed.

Billy Palmer, at thirty-one a rotund and balding junior Mr. Pickwick, paled for only an instant when the verdict was announced, then recovered his composure. His only comment, a racing man's tribute to the Attorney General's masterful performance, was: "It was the riding that did it."

The three judges who tried Billy ordered that he should be hanged at Stafford in his own county as an example to local people, and when he arrived home, he was greeted by a jeering mob. Within a few days, though, opinions began to change. Doctors and scientists disputed the verdict in letters to the *Times*, and in London a crowd packed a hall in Longacre to protest the verdict. Instead of inferring the criminal from the crime, declared the motion passed at the meeting, the jury and the judges had inferred the crime from the criminal.

There was at that time no criminal appeal procedure. It was, as Billy so aptly observed, the gooser for him. On June 14, 1856, after a sleep of only a couple of hours, he was awakened by the prison chaplain, and the preparations began. Shaved, washed and breakfasted, he emerged at eight o'clock to face the vast throng that had been gathering in Stafford for days prior to the execution. "Murderer! Poisoner!" they shouted.

The common expectation at public executions was for a confession, or at the very least a speech. Billy made as if to speak, and the crowd went silent. Then he turned, and a moment later he was dangling from the end of the rope with hardly a twitch.

Did Billy Palmer poison Cook? We had completed our walk around Rugeley and were sitting opposite the Penny Bank, a building Billy would have known. "Well, you know what he said while he was in prison," said Edwina Morgan. "He said, 'I never gave Cook strychnine.' I think he just doped him up to keep Cook out of the way long enough to get his money, and things got out of hand. But the joke is"—I could see Edwina was enjoying herself—"the town council of Rugeley was so upset with the town's name being associated with Palmer that they actually went to London and petitioned the prime minister of the day to change its name. He told them they could only change it if they named it after him. And you know what his name was?" I shook my head. "Palmerston!" Several people looked around in surprise as we sat laughing on the bench.

Hot for Teacher

She arrived home from the school district meeting around ten o'clock, parked her nifty little silver Honda CRX—the one with the "Halen" vanity plate, named for her favorite rock group—then let herself into their rented townhouse at number 4E Misty Morning Drive. Greg, still wearing the business suit he'd worn to the Metropolitan Life sales meeting earlier in the evening, lay dead in the hallway, the blood drying from the single bullet wound in the back of his head.

Pam Smart must have stood for a moment, watching to make sure he wasn't still breathing. So this was it. It was finally done. She noted the disconnected stereo speakers standing by the door, just as if they'd been left there by the fleeing burglars, and the drawers and furniture strewn around to support the idea of a robbery. She wouldn't have been human if she hadn't allowed herself one small moment of triumph. Then she took a deep breath and prepared to go next door to raise the alarm.

Patrol officer Jerry Scaccia arrived at the cream-colored townhouse complex, a few steps from the giant Hood Commons shopping mall, at 10:10 P.M. By then, Pam Smart was at the neighbor's. Officers, guns drawn, quickly established that the killers were no longer in the house. Entry had been made, apparently, through a back door leading to the basement that had been carelessly left unlocked. A CD player and jewelry worth about $300 were among the few and paltry items stolen.

Greg must have blundered right into the robbery scene, Pam, petite, cute and twenty-two, told the police. As an ambulance took away the body of her twenty-four-year-old husband, the officers watched and listened and said little. Something, they knew, wasn't right.

"From the start we didn't think it was a burglary," Captain Loring Jackson, the man put in charge of the investigation, told me later. Burglaries in Derry, a New Hampshire town of 31,000 some forty miles north of Boston, happen during the day, when people are out working, not in the evening, when everyone is home, he said. "And this was a high-density condominium complex with lots of people around."

Even putting aside the odd circumstance of Greg Smart having been shot from the rear with the gun held to his head, execution-style, rather than from the front, as he would have been if confronting an armed robber, the whole gun business didn't make sense, said Jackson. "A burglar's whole instinct is to run if he hears someone coming. And in this state, burglars don't carry guns, because if they're armed, there's a mandatory additional sentence tacked on."

The next day, May 2, 1990, Jackson interviewed the attractive young teacher. She told him she was the media coordinator at Winnacunnet High School in Hampton, thirty miles from Derry, in charge of videos and other visual aids. She also taught courses on self-esteem and on the perils of drug and alcohol abuse.

Did Greg have any enemies? Did anyone have it in for him? She was surprised at the question. It didn't make sense. This was just a burglary gone wrong, a mindless thing, almost like a traffic accident. Greg just happened to come in the door at the wrong time. Jackson explained his reasons for believing this was anything but a burglary, but she still looked skeptical. Who would want to kill Greg, a guy everyone liked? It was especially tragic, she told him, because they would have celebrated their first wedding anniversary the following week. "He planned a big party. He was taking me down to Florida." There was a double reason to celebrate: Greg, who had joined Metropolitan Life the year before to sell life insurance like his dad, had just been named regional sales rookie of the year.

Pam Smart, Jackson noted, shed a few tears, but seemed subdued, reserved. You'd never have thought her husband had just been brutally slain. "But people react very differently to grief," he said.

In the days and weeks that followed, no clues turned up to suggest the identity of the killer. There were no telltale fingerprints at the crime scene, and local underworld sources could throw no light on the crime. Meanwhile, Pam Smart was putting the heat on the cops. Why hadn't they found Greg's killer, and why did they persist in believing it was not a robbery? On what would have been her wedding anniversary, she called the Manchester television station, WMUR (where she had earlier applied for a reporting job and been turned down), to offer to go on-air about Greg's death. When asked how she was coping, she said, with an easy composure, "I can't figure out where the strength is coming from. But it seems like it's coming from inside. Maybe it's a part of Greg that's helping me go on with everything." She told a newspaper reporter that the killing was undoubtedly the work of "some jerk, some drug addict person looking for a quick ten bucks."

A month went by with the murder still unsolved. Then a man named Vance Lattime Senior arrived at the Derry police station with a .38 caliber Charter Arms revolver. It was his gun, he said, but he believed it had been used by his seventeen-year-old son, Vance "JR" Junior, in the Greg Smart killing. Lattime Senior had wrestled with his conscience for twenty-four hours after Ralph Welch, also seventeen and one of his son's best friends, had told him that JR and another friend, Patrick "Pete" Randall, sixteen, had confessed to killing Smart.

Ballistic tests would show that the gun was, indeed, the one used to fire a particularly lethal hollow-tipped bullet into Greg Smart's skull. And Welch, who had accompanied Lattime Senior to the station, proved only too eager to cooperate with the police—he now feared for his life at the hands of his friends. He'd heard rumors that Randall and Lattime, as well as a third friend, William "Bill" Flynn, sixteen—all of them students at Winnacunnet High—had carried out the killing. One day at the Lattime home, he just came out and asked Vance and Pete if it was true.

"Who told you that?" one of them asked. His cousin, Ray Fowler, he replied. Was it true?

Pete and JR's answer was to slam the bedroom door on Ralph, for a conference of war. Undeterred, Ralph crept to the door and pressed his ear against it. "Bill's going to be pissed," he heard one of them say, referring to Bill Flynn's likely reaction on hearing the secret was out. "And you know who's going to be next." Ralph took that to mean they might kill Ray Fowler for telling. As he burst in through the door, it didn't occur to him they could have meant him.

117

"I can't believe you guys actually killed someone," he said.

Pete Randall told him to sit down and cool it. Then, in a monotone, he related the details of the murder.

"But to kill someone!" Ralph exclaimed at the end.

"That's what they do in the Army. They do it every day," said Pete coolly. And, full of bravado now: "Yeah, big deal. I figure I'll be a hired assassin some day. Good money."

"I couldn't believe it didn't even bother them," Ralph told the cops. "I couldn't believe my best friends actually killed someone. Pete told me they even said some prayers before doing it. Like that made it okay."

After listening to Ralph's story, the cops were all set to arrest the three youths and write finis to another sordid little juvenile crime. Except that Ralph Welch had one more fact to impart, a fact that would bring reporters scurrying to New Hampshire from around the world, set off a feeding frenzy among New York book publishers and literary agents, and light up the conference lines in Hollywood. His three friends, Ralph said, had been put up to killing the young insurance salesman by his wife, Pam. She had seduced Bill Flynn when he was only fifteen, and then had immediately started pressuring him to dispose of Greg.

It is, of course, the dream of every bored high-school kid. What else is there to think about during those mind-numbing English classes? What if! What if Ms. Hotpants got up from behind her desk at the front, came sauntering down the aisle and undid more than just the top button of her blouse? Whew! What if, just as you were leaving class, Mrs. Puckerlips said, "Randy, would you mind coming round to my place after school? I've got something that needs fixing." Wow!

Pam Smart's favorite group, Van Halen, even has a song about it: "Hot for Teacher." Maybe that's where she got the idea. But maybe not, because sexual tensions between students and teachers are one of the great unmentioned constants in schools everywhere. And, according to Victor Ross, a Colorado school superintendent and author of *The Forbidden Apple*, a book on the subject, the fantasies are played out in real life far more often than people realize. It can start with a well-muscled school football hero standing just a bit too close to a female teacher not much older than himself. Or with a male teacher who finds it necessary to lean over and help that particularly attractive co-ed in the third row. In most cases, people try to ignore it. Sometimes that's impossible, and in many teaching jurisdictions where such contact is forbidden—including New Hampshire—teachers regularly have their certificates revoked.

However it started, Billy Flynn was to have his fantasies realized to an extent he couldn't imagine. A tall, skinny kid with fair hair down over his collar, he had never been to bed with a girl when he reported for Project Self-Esteem, a mandatory program for Winnacunnet freshmen for which Smart was an adult leader. She was something—beautiful, full of zip—and he was smitten. Then Flynn, a guitar player himself, found out she was a heavy metal fan who liked Van Halen and his ultimate favorite, Mötley Crüe. He and JR soon found themselves student counselors in the program, and one day Smart invited Billy over to her office and showed him perhaps her dearest possession: a photograph of herself with guitarist Eddie Van Halen, taken backstage at a concert at the Tampa Stadium.

Bill was hopelessly, haplessly flattered and in love. He dreamed of nothing but Pam Smart. But, of course, she was a teacher. In real life, nothing could happen.

He was in her office on February 5, 1990, when she said the words he'd never expected to hear. "Do you ever think of me when I'm not around?" Had he heard right? She was looking at him in kind of a soft way. He turned a deep red. Yeah, he stammered. Yeah, he did a whole lot. Thought about her. A whole lot. She reached her hand across the desk toward him: "Because I think about you all the time."

To all outward appearances, Pamela Ann Wojas Smart was the daughter every American mother dreams of from the moment the doctor tells her, "It's a girl." Ambitious, pretty and smart as her name, she was aiming at a career as a television reporter, and didn't hesitate to tell people she planned to be "the next Barbara Walters," referring to the reigning queen of the network interviewers.

She lived and worked in New England, but her style and outlook owed more to Florida, where she spent her early years. Her parents were John Wojas, a Delta Airlines pilot, and his wife, Linda. The couple lived in Miami—not in the seething Latino capital of the headlines and movies, but in an anonymous middle-class suburb called Pinecrest-Palmetto thirteen miles south of the city center, where the water sprinklers hissed all night long and aquamarine backyard pools winked up at planes passing overhead.

In an atmosphere where family breakup was common and teen drugs a nagging problem, the Wojas family, in their stucco rancher, seemed almost old-fashioned. The three kids were well behaved, there were no spats, and Pamela in particular was seen as bright, clever and involved, making her way through public school and junior high without a ripple.

John Wojas, though, became increasingly concerned about crime impinging on the neighborhood, and when Pam was in eighth grade, he moved his family to a $225,000 house in Windham, a golf-and-country-club community north of Boston. Pamela, the good little trouper, adjusted well to the move and, after a year at Windham Center School, sailed through Pinkerton Academy in nearby Derry an honor roll student four years in a row. Energetic, nearly always with a smile, it was almost as if she was ticking off items for some future job résumé: homeroom rep, football cheerleader, Winter Carnival organizer, activist in Students Against Drunk Driving. And if Pam Wojas sometimes seemed a little, well, manipulative in getting what she wanted and in projecting the right image—dating the co-captain of the football team, for example—that only confirmed the feelings of those around her that she was headed for big things in life.

At heart, she was still a Florida girl, and in 1985, with several of her friends from Pinkerton, she enrolled at Florida State University at Tallahassee, where she studied media performance in preparation for a career in TV. At that point, there were two preoccupations in Pam's life: becoming another Barbara Walters, and giving her undying allegiance to the Van Halen heavy metal rock group. Those two themes came together nicely when she proposed to the university radio station, WVFS-FM, that she host a two-hour weekly late-night heavy metal show called "Metal Madness." It was a high point of the week for her when she went on-air with her familiar sign-on: "You're listening to the Maiden of Metal on Metal Madness."

Returning home to New Hampshire at Christmas during her junior year, she found a third preoccupation in Greg Smart, who had an unglamorous job as an assembler of truck booms in a local plant, but who, with his long hair, bore a passable resemblance to the rock performer Jon Bon Jovi. At first, Pam flew home frequently to spend time with Greg, courtesy of her father's airline privileges. But it got to be a drag. "Why don't you give up that dumb job and come down to Florida?" she'd urge him. Greg didn't need much persuading. With his parents, Bill and Judy, tagging along in their little Toyota—just to make sure he didn't run into trouble—Greg drove his Mercury Cougar south, with his belongings piled in back, and the couple set up house in a refurbished motel unit.

Those were busy times. In addition to her studies, Pam was working part-time as a news intern at a local TV station, WCTV, and also had a job as an errand girl in a government office. Greg got a job on a landscaping crew while he studied for the life insurance industry exams. There was still time to attend rock concerts, and at the Monsters of Rock show at Tampa Stadium in June 1988, Pam, using her rock show pull, managed to get backstage and have the picture taken with Eddie Van Halen that was to have its uses later.

Beneath the long hair, Greg was an old-fashioned boy. He told their friends he was saving up to buy Pam a diamond solitaire. In January 1988, they became engaged, and now Greg had another priority: to get Pam back to New Hampshire. He couldn't stand the Florida heat, and while other northerners lapped up the Florida sunshine, Greg dreamed of skiing. Pam graduated a few months later, having completed the four-year course in three years. For graduation, Greg presented her with a cuddly and very expensive brown-and-white Shih Tzu puppy. His name? Halen, of course.

The couple returned to New Hampshire on a high. Greg had passed his exams and was going to work with his dad. Pam didn't get the TV job she wanted, but settled for the media coordinator post at Winnacunnet High. A few months later, a Florida television station phoned and offered her a job as a starter reporter. Pam bit her lip and said no. After all, in May 1989, she and Greg were going to have a big wedding at Sacred Heart Church in Lowell. Every girl owes herself a decent wedding once in her life.

Perhaps it was turning down the TV job to marry Greg that rankled later. And maybe she quickly realized that a superficial resemblance to her favorite rock star was a long way from the real thing. Being married to a journeyman insurance agent fell far short of the glamorous life she had envisioned for herself. Most young people getting married eventually reconcile themselves to the realities of their humdrum lives. But Pam was not one to compromise. She still had big dreams. Soon there were bitter quarrels, talk of divorce and Pam was looking for someone to kill Greg.

What was it that Pam Smart saw in lanky Bill Flynn? When the three boys eventually appeared in court, it was Pete Randall, stocky and handsome, who seemed the likeliest candidate for romance. JR Lattime had a murky complexion and thick glasses, while Flynn, Tammi Plyler, a reporter in court that day, told me, "had kind of a gentle face, an air of vulnerability."

Perhaps Smart saw in him a youth who could be easily swayed, especially because Bill Flynn and his two friends were seen at Winnacunnet High as outsiders. While most of the kids at the school came from swanky Hampton, Hampton Falls and North Hampton, the three friends came from Seabrook, a tacky, depressed onetime fishing village (the model for cartoonist Al Capp's Dogpatch, the fictional locale of the "Li'l Abner" strip) that exists today under the shadow of a nuclear power station. At Winnacunnet High, Seabrook kids simply didn't cut it.

That didn't make Bill, JR and Pete punks. Bill's dad had been killed in a car crash in 1987, shortly after the family moved from California, and his mother told Bob Hohler of the *Boston Globe* that it was Pete and JR who drew Bill out in the bad year that followed. JR used to help his grandmother serve a Thanksgiving meal for the poor, and the boys were known as the Three Musketeers for their willingness to shovel snow for the elderly in Seabrook. But there was another side to them: although none had criminal records, they had been involved in minor drug and burglary incidents.

Pam Smart had to find a way to give the romance some momentum. Teachers don't simply hang around in the school yard smooching with students. So she went to Bill's house. An orange juice commercial they were making for a contest (first prize: a trip to Disney World) was excuse enough, and while Bill's mom was working in the kitchen, she joined him in his bedroom, where he put on Mötley Crüe's "Starry Eyes."

"Are you going to kiss me?" she asked, as he lay on the bed, hands behind his head.

"Yeah."

"Well, do I have to come over there and make you?"

He was bold now: "Yeah."

So she did.

It was her husband, Greg, who was the big problem, she told him. He was mean to her, had even hit her. And he was seeing someone else. She seemed close to tears. "One night, he locked me out of the house. In winter, too, and all I had on was my nightclothes."

One day at school, she had good news for Bill. Greg was going to be away overnight. Why didn't he spend the night with her? She drove him to the video store, where they picked up three videos, including the Kim Basinger–Mickey Rourke steamer *9½ Weeks*.

Bill swallowed hard as, nestling on the leather couch, they watched Basinger snapping off a pointy little pepper between her even, white teeth, popping strawberries suggestively between her lips, and spilling a glass of milk down her chin while Rourke massaged syrup into her thighs. "I always wanted to dance like that for someone," Pam murmured in his ear, as Basinger did a bump and grind for Rourke to Joe Cocker's throaty "You Can Leave Your Hat On (Take Off Your Dress)." "But there was never anybody I could do it for."

The movie over, she left him for a few moments, then he heard her voice calling him. Van Halen's "Black and Blue" was thumping on the stereo. She had on only a filmy turquoise negligee, through which he could see her nipples. Billy's mouth felt parched. "Come here," she said.

Later, he would say, she told him to fetch some ice cubes from the kitchen. The trick was to hold them in your hand until they melted, just the way Mickey Rourke did in the movie, then allow the water to fall drip by icy drip onto her neck, between her breasts, around her nipples, until it pooled in her navel, then ran in rivulets down her stomach.

The next morning, Bill was like a guy who'd won the lottery. Wait till the guys heard this! This was the kind of stuff you read about in those books on the top shelf at the milk store. Bill was still too young even to get into movies where they showed this sort of thing.

But as she drove him the thirty miles to school, Pam seemed sad. He thought he detected a tear. "What's up? What's the matter?" he asked, figuring she regretted the whole thing.

"Oh, Bill, I do love you. I love you truly," she said, gripping the wheel and staring straight ahead.

"I..." The words sounded awkward in his mouth. "I love you too."

She turned toward him, and her eyes were moist. Then she shook her head. "No, I can't ask you that."

"Ask me what? I'll do anything, Pam, honest. Just ask me."

"It wouldn't be fair. No, I can't."

"Tell me, tell me what's bothering you."

"The thing is, Billy, we can't go on seeing each other like this."

"Can't?"

"Not while Greg's around. It's too dangerous."

"Well, why don't you divorce him? You don't love him."

She sighed. "I wish I could, pet, but I can't. You see, he'd get everything. The furniture, the dog, the car, everything. It's all in his name. I'd have to move back in with my mother."

"Why'd you marry him in the first place?"

"Back then," she said, as if referring to some time in history rather than a mere year before, "it was the thing to do." Billy nodded. "So, you see, there's no future for us while Greg's around."

"Whaddaya mean?"

"I mean, Greg's got to be gotten rid of."

"You mean...?"

"I mean killed."

Now he was way out of his depth. He nodded, as if she'd put forward an airtight argument for going out for burgers and fries. "Yeah, I see what you mean."

They were a couple of blocks from the school. "I better drop you here," she said, stopping the car.

"Pam, I..." he began.

She held his collar and pulled his face toward her. "Don't say anything, sweetheart. Just think about it, will you? Think about it. It won't be difficult."

She didn't mean it, he told himself as he walked toward school. She'd have forgotten it by tomorrow. She was just pissed off at Greg. It'd blow over. Meanwhile, wait till the guys heard what he had to tell them. Shee-it!

A few days later—in a tribute to those marvelous Japanese engineers and the amount of space they manage to build into a micro-car—Bill and Pam had sex in a state park in her little CRX. He'd barely zipped up when she returned to her theme. If she divorced Greg, he'd never give her any peace, she said. He'd be forever following them. Had Bill thought about how Greg could be disposed of?

"But I got no gun, no car, nothing," he protested.

"Billy, unless Greg is gotten out of the way, I can't see you again, and that's that."

"Don't say that, Pam." His years were telling. He was going to blubber like a baby any minute. "Please."

"There must be someone you know. What about your friends, Pete and JR?"

"Why would they do it?"

"I'd pay them, that's why. See, there's two policies on Greg's life. I checked. It's a total of $140,000. I'd be willing to pay, say, ten percent. Fourteen hundred dollars."

Finally, it was making sense. He felt his heart thumping in his chest. "I'll talk to them," he said.

JR and Pete didn't have to think about it very long. It appealed to their sense of self-esteem. To be hit men, well, that was quite a promotion from being petty thieves and joyriders. Bumping off a guy—think what that would do for their reputations. Who knew where it might lead? The nice thing was, they'd be doing their friend Bill a favor, ensuring that he held on to his piece of ass. And they'd get paid for it, to boot (although Pam later changed her offer to $500 each, and they never did see that, only a pair of lousy speakers from Greg's Toyota truck). Viewed from every angle, it was a neat deal.

So now there were four conspirators. But Pam knew she had to keep up the pressure so the boys would carry through. She didn't want it to be just a talkathon. She wanted action.

For his sixteenth birthday in March, she bought Billy a sub-scription to *Guitar* magazine. Where were they going to get the gun, she wanted to know. "I'll have to buy one. It'll cost maybe two hundred bucks," he told her. No way was she paying for that, she said. In the end, JR said he knew where he could lay hands on one. He didn't want to say it was his father's, in case Pam vetoed that idea. Pam came through with $30 for Bill to buy hol-low-point bullets, which he'd heard were "quick and painless."

Pam and Bill regularly performed Honda acrobatics in a fac-tory parking lot and in a wood behind the ballpark in Seabrook, among other places. But it was always the same theme after-wards: "He hits me, Bill. He grabs my hair and throws me down," she told him, showing him a bruise on her arm. To keep him at the boiling point, she sent him a steady stream of love letters, some of them quite explicit, which he was pleased to share with his friends in a class called Crime and Punishment. One day in her office, she turned the phone speaker on and called Greg, and the boys listened in while they argued. At the end, Greg said, "Well, if you want a divorce, that's fine with me." Pam turned to them. "Now you see why I have to have this done," she said.

By May 1, she had the Three Musketeers psyched up for the job. The plan was to drive to Haverhill, Massachusetts, to borrow JR's grandmother's car. Heading there in the CRX, JR took the wheel, and Pete sat in the passenger seat, while Pam and Bill lay in the back, their feet between the front seats. By now, she was feeling panicky. "How should I act when I find the body?" she asked them. Her voice was shaky. "Should I scream, or run out of the house, or call the cops?" Just act normal, they told her. Maybe she should go to a neighbor's.

Perhaps to shock her a little, they started talking about how they'd kill Greg. A knife would be quick and easy, less noise than the gun. "Oh, Christ, no," she said. "I don't want you to get blood all over my white leather couch." She thought suddenly of Halen, her little dog. "Put him down in the basement first," she instructed. "I don't want him traumatized." And they should be sure to wear dark clothes and gloves, she told them. Bill should tie back his hair, she said, so that he could not be as easily recognized.

Shortly before nine o'clock that evening, JR sat waiting in his grandmother's car in the shopping plaza around the corner from the Smarts' townhouse, stabbing plastic soda bottles with an exacto knife and singing to relieve his tension. Inside the house, Bill and Pete, waiting behind the door, argued about whether to stab Greg with a butcher knife they'd found in the kitchen or hit him over the head with a candlestick. Either method would be preferable to using the gun, which Bill now had, because the bullet might be traced back to its owner, JR's father.

The sound of Greg's truck pulling up put an end to the argument. Their hearts thumped as they heard him put the key in the lock. Greg had no time to react. Pete grabbed him by the hair as he came through the door and slammed him against the wall. Suddenly, Greg found himself on his knees, the knife held to his throat. "Gimme that ring," rasped Pete. Incredibly, Greg said, "No."

"Why not?"

"It's my wedding ring," he said. "My wife would kill me."

The remark broke Pete's nerve. The knife trembled. He couldn't do it. Bill pulled out the .38 and rammed it into the back of Greg's head. He, too, waited what seemed like minutes. He thought of the only thing that could make him do it—Pam. "God forgive me," he said, then pulled the trigger.

Back in the car, Bill was laughing. They decided to drive over to Hampton Beach to see if they could buy some cocaine with some gold chains they'd grabbed in the house. JR, at the wheel, was singing "Shoo-Fly Pie" at the top of his voice. "Shut up!" yelled Pete. "I hate that fucking song."

After hearing the boys' stories, Captain Jackson at the Derry police had a problem. If the boys went into the witness box and claimed that a teacher had put them up to murdering her husband, they'd be laughed out of court. It would look like a too-obvious attempt to shift blame. Was there anybody else who knew about the plot? Well, there was Cecelia Pierce, the boys told him. She was Pam's sixteen-year-old student assistant, and she had known about the scheme for maybe a month before Greg Smart got knocked off. She'd even come into the bedroom at the Derry townhouse one day when Pam and Bill were having sex on the floor.

After a talk with the police, Cecelia was a very frightened young girl. Knowing about the murder ahead of time—even if she hadn't thought they would go through with it—could land her in court, she now realized. Three days after that talk, Cecelia agreed to make phone calls to Pam, which would be taped, and—even scarier—to wear a body pack to record conversations with Pam.

Finally, Captain Jackson, sitting in a surveillance van thirty yards from the school parking lot, where Cecelia and Pam sat talking in the little Honda, heard the voice of Pam Smart saying things no jury would have believed if it had not been on tape.

"If Raymond [Fowler, who told Ralph Welch, and later police, about the murder plot] hadn't run his fucking mouth off, this would have been the perfect murder," Pam told Cecelia on this sunny day, July 13. "The problem is, my heart is like, shit, having a heart attack, like I can't even fucking believe this, because why would they tell Ralph? If they never would have told Ralph, you know…"

Then she looked into Cecelia's face. "I'm afraid one day you're gonna come in here, and you're gonna be wired by the fucking police, and I'm gonna be busted."

Cecelia reassured her that would never happen.

If the police did question her, Pam advised, "You're better off lying. If you tell the truth, you're gonna have to send Bill, you're gonna have to send Pete, you're gonna have to send JR, and you're gonna have to send me to the fucking slammer for the rest of our entire life."

Pam was still confident that she would never be convicted of helping to murder her husband. It would come down to who the jury believed; they had to choose between a person like herself, "with a professional reputation and a course that I teach, and a sixteen-year-old facing the rest of his life in the slammer. They are going to believe me." As for having sex with Bill, "Why would a twenty-two-year-old woman like me be having an affair with a sixteen-year-old high-school student! That's just ridiculous, and people will not believe that." And then there were moments of fear: "I don't know what to do, you know what I mean? I feel like shit. But it's not my fucking fault."

If Cecelia thought what she was doing was potentially dangerous, Pam gave her no reassurance. "What good is it going to do if you send me to the fucking slammer?" she asked the student. "Because if you think that's going to be the end of your problems..." (By that, Pam later explained in court, she meant that Cecelia's family would face heavy legal costs if she went to the police. But was that all Pam meant? After her conviction in the murder plot, a further charge against her of attempting to get a fellow prison inmate to murder Pierce was eventually dropped.)

Television satellite vans lined the parking lot of the Rockingham County Superior Court, some one hundred reporters from as far away as Japan were in attendance, and people had been lining up since 2:00 A.M. for the few public seats in the courtroom when Pam Smart went on trial as an accomplice to murder in March 1991. The proceedings were carried live on WMUR-TV, the station that had once turned down Pam Smart for a job. The case was featured on *Entertainment Tonight*, and Greg's father, Bill, said he was contemplating a movie contract, although he insisted he wanted to keep "creative control." Even before the trial began, Cecelia Pierce had received several thousands of dollars for TV appearances and signed a $100,000 movie contract with Once Upon a Time Films.

Asked in court if he thought it was okay to make money off the death of his best friend, Brian Washburn, who had been close to Greg, shrugged and said, "Everyone else is."

In January, Bill Flynn had pleaded guilty to second-degree murder, JR and Pete to being accomplices to murder. Facing life sentences with no possibility of bail, all three had agreed to testify against Pam in return for lighter sentences. Pete Randall's courtroom account of how Greg Smart had pleaded for his life before he was shot was so harrowing that Judge Douglas Gray called a recess so the dead man's mother could be taken sobbing from the courtroom. Greg's family members cried again when Bill Flynn, testifying, got down on his knees to show Greg's position before he was shot.

The one person who never showed a hint of emotion was Pam Smart, who, wearing feminine pinks and flowing skirts, sat in the dock quietly taking notes, "almost like a princess," one awed young male spectator told a *Boston Globe* reporter. In the witness box, she was insistent that she had played no part in the murder.

"They murdered Greg," she said, meaning the three youths. "They're the ones who broke into the house. They waited for him. And they're the ones who brought him to his knees and brought a knife to his throat. I didn't force anybody to murder Greg."

Of her affair with Bill, she said, "I loved him at one point." Yes, she had sent him two photographs of herself wearing a frilly bikini and striking provocative poses, but she claimed that a week before the murder, she had told Bill, "There's absolutely no way I could live with this any longer, and I was going to tell Greg." When she told her husband and said she was sorry, "He asked me if I loved him, and I told him I did. I loved him."

And the taped conversations with Cecelia Pierce? "When someone you love is murdered, you do things you maybe wouldn't have done beforehand," she said. "I was totally obsessed with finding out who had murdered my husband. In my mind, I thought I would play a game with her and pretend I knew more about the murder...to get information."

In his summation to the jury—an unusually well-qualified group headed by a nurse and including among the seven men and five women a software engineer, a graduate student from Harvard and a retired banker—defense lawyer Paul Twomey argued that the three youths were simply thrill killers who had blamed Pam Smart in order to reduce their sentences. "They have not a shred of moral decency in them. They came in here and lied to you," he said.

But Assistant Attorney General Paul Maggiotto had a convincing three-layer argument to offer. Even if the jury did not believe the three boys, he said, there was the word of Cecelia Pierce and, most importantly, the tapes. And even if they had doubts about Cecelia, he said, there was still Cindy Butt, another student with no connection to the plot, who had testified that a month before the murder, Cecelia had said she had a friend named Pam who wanted to have her husband murdered. "If anyone in the jury room talks about fabrication, talk about Cindy Butt," he advised the jurors.

Jury members would say later that it was the tapes that ultimately convinced them of Pam Smart's guilt.

After Smart was sentenced, on March 22, 1991, to spend the rest of her life in the New Hampshire State Prison for Women, without the possibility of parole, Greg's father announced that he and his wife were going to visit his son's grave. "We're going to tell him, by God, she did it," he said. His mother had felt there was something wrong from the moment Pam returned Greg's belongings to them in plastic bags—even his picture and his favorite houseplants—three days after the killing. "She got what she deserved," said Judy Smart.

Speaking from prison as she started her lifelong sentence, Pam Smart was admitting nothing. "I feel like I'm in Russia," she told the *Globe*'s Bob Hohler. As for the criticism that no one had ever seen her shed a tear for Greg, "I'm sorry if I reacted wrong, but nobody gave me the twenty-two-year-old widow's handbook."

Why did Pam Smart engineer the death of her husband of less than a year? The reasons put forward seem laughable: the disparity in their educations was causing friction; he had cut his hair and looked less like a rock star and more like the insurance salesman he really was; he preferred spending time with his buddies in the backwoods with his Toyota truck to going to concerts and gourmet restaurants with Pam. If these were reasons enough for murder, the graveyards would be full of young husbands.

The answer lies, rather, in Pam Smart herself. Like many of the murderers in this book, there was nothing in her middle-class upbringing to set her apart. But somewhere along the line, it was as if a gene went missing. Call it a morality gene, call it knowing right from wrong. It used to be fashionable to call such people "psychopaths," but no one is quite sure what that term means any more. Education, good breeding and important positions in life provide no immunity. There are people who will use any means at hand to achieve their ends and who seem curiously blind to consequences.

We will give Pam the last word. Speaking from prison, she said she was outraged at the media circus, the Pam Smart T-shirts and the jokes about the case going the rounds. (There would also be a 1995 movie, *To Die For*, based on the Pam Smart case.) "I don't know how anybody in the world could consider anything about this funny," she said. "People seem to have lost sight [of the fact] that someone is dead." Indeed.

Wherever He Has Gone,
I Have Gone

There is still another body buried somewhere on Saddleworth Moor. It's that of Keith Bennett, who was twelve when he disappeared one day in 1964. He'll probably never be found now, unless the moor disgorges his body the way it did that of ten-year-old Lesley Ann Downey. And that would not be so surprising because, as I scramble up the slope toward the Stonehenge-like stand of boulders that dominates this desolate landscape, the moor seems to be in a permanent state of upheaval. Water gurgles beneath the grass, and several times, as I jump the streams exposing the black peat beneath like open wounds, I trip and slide cursing into the gullies. Forget any notion of the romantic moors of the Brontës: Saddleworth Moor, just outside Manchester, is about as beautiful as an opencast mine. As Joe Mounsey, who saw more than enough of it when he was up here on the long body search, told me, "It's the surface of the bloody moon up there."

In that sense, Saddleworth Moor differs from most scenes of notorious murders, which often turn out to be banal: tacky suburban bungalows, tired and shabby rooming houses, neat backyards

136

with bodies planted behind the cabbages. Even if you didn't know what happened here, I suspect Saddleworth would inspire a prickle of fear, a sense that anything could happen here.

Ian Brady and Myra Hindley disposed of four of their five young victims in this moor. In terms of the number they killed, Hindley and Brady are not in the same league as the Ted Bundy type of serial killer that has emerged in the last three decades. But in terms of horror, their crimes are equal to the Manson murders in California (in which the mostly female followers of Charles Manson slaughtered the pregnant actress Sharon Tate and eight others) and the Bernardo/Homolka murders in Toronto (the story of which is told in the first chapter of this book). All three cases changed our ideas about what women are capable of. What aroused unprecedented loathing for Myra Hindley—and what kept her behind bars until her death in November 2002—was the repulsion people felt at the idea that an apparently ordinary young woman could participate in the violation and murder of children, helping to photograph and tape-record their death agonies.

When Hindley said of her partnership with Brady, "Wherever he has gone, I have gone, and he has never been anywhere without me," she was not just alluding to the fact that she drove the car when they were hunting prey or disposing of bodies. Hers is the disturbing and final assertion of female equality. Colin Wilson, in *A Criminal History of Mankind*, suggests, as others have done, that Hindley was "a devoted slave," a dupe of Brady's. I believe it went beyond that and that, like Karla Homolka, she took a savage joy in the torture and killings.

Brady had the kind of background you'd expect of a pathological child killer. His mother, single at the time, put an advertisement in a store window when he was three months old, "Working woman willing to have child adopted," and he was brought up by an older couple in Glasgow's rough Gorbals neighborhood. From early on, young Ian had a cruel streak: friends remembered him burying a cat alive in a graveyard. His persistent thievery put him in an institution for young offenders in his mid-teens.

But by his early twenties, after a few dead-end jobs and a few more brushes with the law, Brady decided to adopt at least a facade of respectability. He studied accounting and, in February 1959, got a job as a clerk with a small chemical and soap company in Gorton, part of Greater Manchester. But the clerk who impressed people with his haughty manner at work amused himself at night reading *Pleasures of the Torture Chamber* and *Those About to Die* and collecting Nazi memorabilia.

Hindley's upbringing, by contrast, you'd almost call sweet. Born into a cheerful working-class Manchester family, she was a stocky, determined little girl who spent as much time next door with her Gran, who doted on her, as she did with her parents. A girl with intelligence a little above average, she enjoyed a normal enough childhood—with one exception. When she was fifteen, Myra befriended a boy named Michael Higgins, two years younger than herself, and protected him against bullies. One hot June day, Michael asked Myra to go swimming at the reservoir, but she couldn't be bothered. He was not home by supper, and Myra was in the crowd that watched his body being pulled from the slimy water. If only she'd gone, it would never have happened, she told herself, and for a long time afterwards she was a different girl—silent, withdrawn, going about in black and blaming herself for Michael's death.

There were boyfriends, but she didn't sleep with them. People thought her a bit old-fashioned, saving herself for the right fellow.

Meanwhile, she enjoyed babysitting, imagining what it would be like to have kids of her own.

In January 1961, she started a new job as a typist with a small Gorton firm, and soon noticed the standoffish fellow with the Scottish accent who worked in his own office. His name was Ian Brady.

For months she watched him, waiting for him to make a move. Her diary for the period is almost schoolgirlish: "Aug. 2, Not sure if he likes me; Aug. 14, He has a cold and I would love to mother him; Aug. 29, I hope he loves me and will marry me some day." She spied on him, noting when he got phone calls in the office, discovering by October that he lived with his parents and rarely went out. It wasn't until just before Christmas that she noted triumphantly: "Out with Ian."

After seeing in the New Year at her parents' home with a bottle of whisky Brady had bought, they returned to her grandmother's house, where Hindley lived. The light upstairs was out. Gran had gone to bed.

She thought her great romance had finally begun. She was wrong. It was her education that was beginning. Brady called her Myra Hess, a neat amalgam of Myra Hess, the pianist, and Rudolf Hess, Hitler's deputy. He tried out his German on her, got her to pose while he tried to take porno pictures like the ones in the magazines he had, and introduced her to the pain-pleasure-pain world of the Marquis de Sade. He got her to buy two handguns, a shovel, ostensibly for digging peat on the moors, and on weekends they would rent a car—not the kind of sporty little car you'd expect of a courting couple, but, oddly, a little station wagon with a fold-down seat and doors in the back—which Hindley always drove.

By the summer of 1963, Myra's training was over and Brady judged her ready. Pauline Reade, sixteen, was on her way to a jive session at the British Railways social club on the evening of Friday, July 12, 1963. She had attended Peacock Street Primary (Myra's first school), and her path that evening took her past Eaton Street, where Myra's mother lived, and Bannock Street, where her grandmother lived. Much later, it would emerge that she had encountered Myra on her way to the dance. Myra had a story about having lost her glove on Saddleworth Moor, and wanted Pauline to come and help her find it. Pauline did not arrive at the dance. Years later, Myra would lead police to the spot where her body was buried on the moors. No one was ever charged with her murder. By the time the body—still clad in the gold party dress she had worn for that long-ago dance—was discovered, it was a moot point: both Myra and Brady were serving life sentences. Then, on November 23, 1963, the day the newspapers were full of the assassination of President John F. Kennedy in Dallas the day before, the couple were sitting in their rented car in Ashton Market, watching for an unaccompanied child. We can wonder: was Myra Hindley—the babysitter who loved children, the girl who had grieved for Michael Higgins and who was devastated by the death of Gran's dog—was that Myra Hindley already dead and gone?

When John Kilbride came walking by, they offered him a lift. The twelve-year-old, who had lingered too long at the market, knew he was late getting home for his tea and was likely to catch it, so he climbed in beside the kind lady and gentleman. His mother had never told him not to talk to kind ladies.

The hue and cry was huge: large headlines, posters appealing "Have you seen this child?" organized searches, false clues, dashed hopes. Then people gradually forgot about John Kilbride.

Of course, John Kilbride's mother could not, would not ever forget. Late the following year, when Detective Chief Inspector

Joe Mounsey was assigned to Ashton-under-Lyne, John was still listed as missing, and Mounsey went to see the boy's mother, who lived in the district. "It was a missing child!" explained Mounsey, sixty-four and retired when I went to see him. He'll never forget Sheila Kilbride. "She was a very gracious lady," he said, his face softening. Mounsey was the son of a policeman, but only joined the force, following wartime military service, "for something to do." There must have been more to it than that: he made inspector in his thirties.

I pressed him on why police work had become his obsession. His arms flailed at my question, his face reddened. "I recognized," he said at last, "that there are victims, too many damn victims. And many of the victims are physically weaker. It's true—the strong do oppress the weak." And as if to conceal the strength of his emotions, he made a show of scolding Bill, the Staffordshire bull terrier his colleagues had given him on retirement, picked, I suspect, because Bill's bulldog features resemble Mounsey's.

After the first time, Mounsey called regularly on the Kilbrides. He didn't have any news, but at least they would know he hadn't forgotten. It wasn't until two years later that Mounsey's phone rang and Superintendent Robert Talbot of the Cheshire County constabulary told him he had an exercise book in front of him that they'd found in the home of a couple named Ian Brady and Myra Hindley. Written in the book were the names of a number of film stars and such, but one of the names was John Kilbride.

The arrest of Hindley and Brady occurred following a scene only Dostoyevsky could have imagined. The couple had been apprenticing David Smith, Myra's teenage brother-in-law, married to her sister Maureen, introducing him to *Mein Kampf*, de Sade, and other literature of torture and sadism. Smith, who had been in trouble with the law in a minor way, seemed a likely candidate to join them in their satanic exploits.

At about 6:15 P.M. on October 6, 1965, Smith went to borrow some tea from Hindley and Brady at the new house they had recently moved into with Myra's grandmother on Wardle Brook Avenue in Hyde, another district of Manchester. The couple was just going out, and Smith would remember that Myra was smartly turned out in a leopard-print dress and white high heels, but that she was carrying a large, unwieldy handbag—in which, it turned out, she was carrying two guns. She was also holding a pair of binoculars—an odd item for someone not known to frequent the opera or the theater to be taking along on an evening out.

Smith returned to the flat around the corner that he shared with Maureen, and went back to reading *Fanny Hill*. At 11:40, he and Maureen were in bed reading when the lobby buzzer rang. It was Myra. Smith was pulling on some clothes when she came in. He noticed that her makeup was smudged, her hair was a mess, and she was wearing the sloppy skirt and sweater she would typically wear only at home on weekends. After chatting a bit, she asked her sister to tell their mother when she saw her that Myra would be over on Monday night to bleach her hair.

Smith thought it was odd. Was that all she'd come for so late at night? But then she asked if Dave would see her home through the houses: "It's dark, and I'm scared." She had walked over just a few minutes before on her own; nevertheless, Smith got on his jacket and took up the special stick he used when walking the dog. But Hindley said he shouldn't bring the dog, because he was sure to fight with hers.

Outside her house a few minutes later, Hindley asked him to

wait across the street, "in case Ian's doing something." She'd flick on the landing light if it was okay for him to come in. He waited a few minutes, and then the light was flicked twice. When he tapped on the front door, Brady opened it.

"Hello. Want to see those miniature bottles?" Brady said, referring to an earlier conversation they'd had and speaking in an unnaturally loud, cheerful voice, as if he wanted someone in the sitting room to hear. Brady went light-footedly up the stairs and returned in a moment with some small bottles of liqueur, which he set on the kitchen table before going into the living room, leaving the door ajar.

A few seconds passed, then Smith heard a scream from the other room and Myra shouting, "Dave, help him! Help him!" He grabbed his stick, which he'd brought with him after all, and ran into the room thinking Brady was being attacked. By the subdued light of the small lamp on the television set, he could just make out Brady smashing down the blunt side of an axe on an object on the floor. It must be a joke they were playing on him. His mouth formed a smile. What did they think he was—stupid? That thing on the floor must be a store dummy or something of the sort. It couldn't be human. But the screaming was coming from the object on the floor, and as Smith watched, the figure writhed in agony and cowered away from the blows. It was Edward Evans, a seventeen-year-old youth whom Brady had once seen in a gay bar and whom he had picked up at a railway buffet earlier in the evening.

Smith was traumatized. Running seemed out of the question. Fourteen times the axe came down on the helpless figure, who tried at first to crawl away. Then the screaming, the gurgling and the writhing stopped, and Brady said, "He's a goner. We'll have to get rid of him." As if this was a chore he was used to, he took

143

a cushion cover, pulled it over the pulped remains of Evans' head and drew a length of electric cord around his neck.

Smith visualized himself running like a mad thing out into the night and home to Maureen, but instead he stood glued to the floor, held by the look in Brady's hard, cold eyes. "Here, Dave," Brady said, handing him the axe, "Feel the weight of that." Smith, in a trance, took hold of the still-dripping axe, thereby implicating himself in the killing. Brady took it back from him and laid it on the body. "This was the messiest yet," he said, wiping his hands on a magazine. "It normally only takes one blow."

"Myra!" The voice came from upstairs, thin and querulous. Hindley went to the bottom of the stairs. "It was just the dog barking," she called up to her grandmother, who had been wakened by the noise.

"Get cleaning stuff and rags," Brady told her when she returned to the sitting room. While Brady and Hindley scrubbed the floor and walls, Smith, following Brady's instructions, carefully wiped all the drips of blood off the bars of the budgie cage. Nothing was said about the cadaver lying on the floor, and they cleaned around it. Then, briskly, like a duty nurse coping with a messy emergency, Hindley fetched a blanket, a sheet and a roll of semi-transparent plastic sheeting kept in the kitchen. Brady laid them on the floor and, with Smith holding the feet while he grabbed under the armpits, they placed the body on the sheet. Hindley returned with water to clean the spot where the head had been. There was one thing they'd forgotten, said Brady. They didn't have any string. The cord on Smith's dog stick would do. Smith cut it free and handed it over, not realizing that, again, he was implicating himself in the murder.

With the corpse parceled, Brady and Hindley considered their options. Getting it to the car would mean walking past three houses. That wouldn't do. They'd put it upstairs, and the following day, Smith could fetch a baby carriage from his grandfather's. They'd use that to get the body to the car before taking it up to the moors. While Hindley held the door of her grandmother's bedroom shut, the two men carried the unwieldy parcel up the stairs and down the hall to one of the other bedrooms.

With the night's work done, Hindley made them all a pot of tea. As she sat with her blood-stained slippers resting on the mantelpiece, she asked Brady if he remembered the time he'd been burying a body on the moors when a policeman, seeing her sitting in the car, had stopped and asked her, "What's the trouble?" And she'd told him she was just waiting for the spark plugs to dry, and he'd driven off. What a lark! For her and Brady, the intoxication of the killing just done had not yet worn off. "You could see the blow register in his eyes!" she said eagerly.

It was after three in the morning when they let Smith out the front door. Once outside, he ran—but he could not escape what he had witnessed. He could never escape it. To this day he wakes in cold sweats.

Once home, he went into the bathroom, splashed cold water on his face and was sick. He climbed into bed beside Maureen.

"What's the matter, love?" she asked. "Not feeling well?"

Stumbling and stuttering, the cigarette shaking in his hand, he told her the whole story. At first, she wondered what he had been drinking...or smoking. He must be mad. But then she began to believe him.

It was getting light when, like two small, frightened animals, they crept out of their apartment building. Smith carried a large screwdriver and a breadknife, which were somehow supposed to protect them, under his coat. At the street corner, Smith went into a red phone box. It was 6:07 A.M. He dialed 999 and asked for the police.

That was only the beginning. After the police arrived at the little house on Wardle Brook Avenue and discovered the obscene, plastic-wrapped parcel in the bedroom, Hindley and Brady weren't going to make it easy for anyone. Let the coppers find out what they bloody well could.

And they did. In the tiny station wagon the couple now owned, they found a neatly ruled plan in Brady's handwriting for abducting a man, murdering him and disposing of his body. Superintendent Talbot, riffling through mounds of junk and memorabilia from a wardrobe, found a list of names in an exercise book, some of them movie stars like Joan Crawford and Alec Guineas [sic]. One name stood out: John Kilbride. He called Joe Mounsey in Ashton-under-Lyne.

"I knew it would come," said Mounsey. "First thing in the morning? I'll be there."

Smith had told the police that Brady and Hindley had talked about killing people and burying them up on the moors. When he arrived in Manchester, Mounsey asked Brady about that. It was just talk to impress young Smith, Brady insisted. And John Kilbride? Mounsey showed Brady the list of names in the exercise book. It was just the name of someone he'd known in school, said Brady. Mounsey thought of Sheila Kilbride, waiting, hoping.

Hindley corroborated Brady's story, offering blank-faced denials. "She was a hard nut," remembers Mounsey.

Stacks of photographs had been seized at the house, some going back to when Brady and Hindley were kids. Mounsey was interested in the more recent ones, some taken on the moor. They showed Hindley and Brady in different settings, sometimes in front of rock formations, sometimes with the car. The chief inspector ordered blowups. Tomorrow, he said, they'd start digging.

Day after day, the buses climbed the steep hill to Saddleworth Moor, carrying the most dispirited, reluctant bunch of cops ever assembled. As if the slogging hard work of the digging wasn't enough, they had to contend with reporters with their smart-ass jokes and photographers taking pictures. One afternoon, when it was time to knock off, a rookie constable, only three days on the job and wondering if he'd joined the police force to be a ditch-digger, had a call of nature and asked to be let off the bus before they started for home. They all laughed as the bashful youngster ran up the hill to get out of sight. They didn't laugh when they saw the expression on his face as he returned. He had seen a bone sticking out of the ground. It belonged to Lesley Ann Downey, who was ten when she disappeared on her way home from a Christmas fair on Boxing Day, 1964.

For Mounsey, finding Lesley Ann Downey wasn't enough. His men kept digging while he pored over the enlarged snapshots, trying to place them in that wild and almost featureless land-scape. One in particular fascinated him. It showed Hindley crouching with her puppy nestled in her coat. Her half-smile seemed to be directed not at the dog or the camera but at the ground in front of her. The enlargement had brought into focus a distinctive group of rocks on the hilltop in the background.

Mounsey scanned the slope from every angle, but could never get the rocks properly framed. One day, he crossed the road that meandered across the moor, went farther down the pitted, uneven slope, then turned around and looked back. He realized that all along he should have been viewing the rocks from a great dis-tance. The next morning he was back with a police photographer, who set down his tripod and studied the scene through his viewfinder. Then he beckoned to Mounsey to take a look. It was uncanny. It was exactly like the snapshot. Only Hindley and the dog were missing. By late morning, an officer, poking a long, thin stick into the ground and then withdrawing it to sniff the end, suddenly stopped and sniffed again. They had found John Kilbride.

The morning after the body was found, Mounsey called on Sheila Kilbride to get her to identify a shoe they'd found in the grave. Then he helped her arrange a funeral mass for John.

The police hadn't given up on the house yet, either. Detective Chief Inspector Jock Tyrrell worried over the list of names in the exercise book, wondering if there might be another such list they'd overlooked. He went back to Wardle Brook Avenue, let himself in and began the tedious business of going over every cranny in the house once again. Among the sex books and thrillers, one book struck him as out of place—a prayer book. Inside it was inscribed, "To Myra from Auntie Kath and Uncle Bert, 16 Nov. 1958, souvenir of her first communion." Tyrrell bent back the covers and tipped it upside down, then noticed a slip of paper concealed in the spine of the book. It was a ticket from the left-luggage office at Central Station, Manchester.

"I can remember how upset you were the night John Kilbride was found," said Margaret Mounsey, who was also a police officer before she married Joe.

"It was police work," said Mounsey gruffly, rubbing Bill's throat. "Maybe that's our cop-out as human beings. It wouldn't do to cry too much—spoil the evidence."

As I talked to him so many years after these events, the old indignation came boiling out. He wanted to talk about the contents of the two suitcases they'd recovered from the left-luggage office. There were nine photographs of a little girl, clearly Lesley Ann Downey, her mouth gagged with a man's scarf, her thin little body naked except for her shoes and socks. They'd posed her this way and that, and from the look on her face, you could see that, in addition to being frightened, she was simply puzzled about what was going on.

Perhaps Myra Hindley could have claimed she wasn't there, didn't know what had happened, if it hadn't been for the tapes. There were two of them, and they were something new in the human experience—the recorded sound of killing. The tapes transfixed everyone who heard them at the trial of Brady and Hindley in Chester, and left some people weeping. Mounsey fetched me a transcript from the next room.

At first, it's just pathetic: "Don't undress me, will you?" a child's voice says. By the end, it's Hindley's voice we're listening to: "Shut up," she whispers urgently. "Shut up."

"Oh, please, help!" cried the child, in pain.

"Shut up," comes the woman's hard, flat voice. The child screams and chokes. "Shut up, or I'll forget myself and hit you one."

"Please, Mommy, please!" These are the child's last words.

The Mounsey living room in Preston, Lancashire, was silent for a moment. "I think that was a horrendous thing," said Margaret. "The fact that a woman would entice a child and not protect her."

Brady and Hindley escaped execution by only a few months. When they were found guilty at Chester Assizes in 1966—he of the murders of Evans, Downey and Kilbride, she of killing Evans and Downey, and also as an accessory to the murder of Kilbride—capital punishment had just been abolished in the United Kingdom. (It's interesting to speculate whether it would have been abolished if the Moors murders had been discovered earlier.) Both were given life sentences. Brady faded from the headlines, and is still locked up, now a hopeless mental case. Hindley would never be out of the headlines.

The late Lord Longford, the penal reformer whom the London tabloids delighted in calling "the potty peer," campaigned hard for her release and described her as "a very gentle person." In 1987, perhaps hoping to finally win her freedom after twenty-one years behind bars, Hindley responded to an anguished letter from the mother of Keith Bennett, who went missing in 1964, by admitting knowledge of his murder, as well as that of Pauline Reade. Hindley was brought to Saddleworth Moor by the police, and was able to point out the spot where Pauline was buried. But Keith Bennett's body remains unfound.

In the fall of 1989, in another obvious attempt to create a new image for her with the public, Longford and some of Hindley's supporters released to the media a photograph of her dressed in an academic gown after receiving an Open University degree she had earned while in prison. It did little good: the response in the media was generally negative.

Who was Myra Hindley? The passing years make the question no easier to answer. In later years, she was certainly no longer the brazen blonde who laughed and joked with Brady in the prisoners' dock and, in a flat, emotionless voice, denied any knowledge of the killings. On the contrary, a *Sunday Times* interviewer in 1982 found her a soft-spoken, warmly engaging woman with dark, close-cropped hair and arresting blue eyes, a woman who, in spite of having spent a quarter of a century behind bars, was very much up with social issues and trends. She had been helped, she told the interviewer, by "the love of my friends and my love of life. I have a lot of friends." Sometimes, though, she said, "I feel I just want to lie down and die. I know I am hated, but for every thousand who hate me, there is one who loves me."

She spoke only the truth. A remarkable coterie of people—public figures, prison psychologists, lawyers, doctors and even a prison governor—fell under her thrall, sometimes to their later regret. In 1972, the governor of Holloway Prison, where Hindley was held at the time, was rebuked in parliament for taking Hindley for a walk on London's Hampstead Heath.

Hindley related her memories of that day to the interviewer from the *Sunday Times*: "The minute I stepped outside those gates, it was as though I had never been inside. Everything came back to me. It was the smells—of grass and trees, and throwing a ball for the governor's dog. There were children playing."

A year later, Pat Cairns, a former nun who had become a prison officer, was given a six-year sentence for helping Hindley in a futile and ill-conceived escape attempt.

But others still believed in her. A Quaker welfare worker sent her flowers twice a month; a prison psychologist kept a woolly toy Hindley had given her on her dressing table. Her friends spoke of her intelligence, the ability she had to make each of them feel important in her life—as no doubt they were. Only when pressed would they admit the one small reservation they still had about her: she still denied having had any hand in the murders of the young people; she still blamed it all on Brady.

Myra never tasted freedom again. A heavy smoker, she died of respiratory failure brought on by hypertension and coronary heart disease on November 15, 2002. She was sixty.

❌

On Saddleworth Moor, a raw February afternoon was drawing to a close. The last of the families out for a Sunday drive had departed. I scrambled up on the rocks that had pointed Joe Mounsey to the body of John Kilbride and looked down at the bleak and tortured landscape, questions tumbling through my mind. Was Myra Hindley a chameleon, soaking up the ideas, the lives of those around her and throwing them back—now a bleached zombie who took part in unspeakable acts, now the warm-hearted university graduate, all empathy and sensitivity? And, the more troubling question, how many of us, given the conditioning, could be Myra Hindleys?

Back in Preston, Joe Mounsey had been at a loss for answers to these questions. "She was more than a willing pupil of Brady," he said, shaking his head in consternation. "Maybe there are words to explain it all... Or maybe..." He walked to the window and looked out. "Maybe it's just the evidence of human inconsistency, that we are all different."

Coming down the slope from the top of the moor, leaping from rock to rock, sliding on the black peat, I could only feel grateful that human inconsistency throws up more Joe Mounseys than Myra Hindleys.

Dr. Waite's Curious Germs

A lfred Hitchcock had a special affection for New York's Grand Central Station. In *Spellbound* (1945) and again in *North by Northwest* (1959), his heroes, played respectively by Gregory Peck and Cary Grant, were pursued by police through the station's magnificent great hall and labyrinth corridors. Our drama also begins in that great monument to the age of steam travel.

It began, to be precise, on March 18, 1915, with a young man, handsome and dashing enough to be played by Cary Grant, leaning out the window of one of the first-class cars of the *Wolverine*, a crack express, as it drew sighing into the station from the wintry cold of Detroit and Grand Rapids. Not even waiting for the train to stop, he leaped down, a newspaper clutched under his arm, and hit the ground running. Bounding up the stairs three at a time, he dashed to a pay phone on the upper concourse. The number he dialed was that of the Plaza Hotel.

"Mrs. Walters, room 1105, please," he told the operator. "Margaret," he said when the phone was answered, "Arthur. Pay your bills and pack your bags and get out. I'll explain later." Without waiting for her reply, he put down the phone.

On the hotel switchboard, a private detective made careful note of the one-sided conversation and, with a satisfied smile, put down his earpiece. This scene, too, had its genesis in Grand Central Station, where, several days earlier, a young New Jersey schoolteacher, looking visibly agitated, had got off a suburban train and made her way to the telegraph office. The message she wrote on the telegraph form consisted of only five words: "Suspicions aroused. Demand an autopsy." Then, flustered for a moment about how to sign it, she remembered the name of a girlfriend, an ordinary enough name, and signed it "K. Adams." "Yes," she told the clerk, "It's to go to Mr. Percy F. Peck in Grand Rapids."

The arrival in Grand Rapids some twelve months earlier of Dr. Arthur Warren Waite had not gone unnoticed by the mothers of that city with daughters of a marriageable age. Indeed, Waite, who was twenty-eight, made sure he was not overlooked by arranging an interview with the local newspaper in which he described his exploits and accomplishments. The mothers would have been impressed not only by the fact that he was a dentist, trained at the University of Michigan and the University of Glasgow, but also that he was the son of a respected local merchant and his wife, and had just returned from several years of dental practice in South Africa.

Their daughters were struck more by Dr. Waite's matinee-idol good looks: his mane of dark brown hair, which he would throw back as he spoke, his sun-bronzed complexion and his boundless vitality. He made his winter-pallid Michigan rivals look pale indeed.

No one thought to mention that when Waite was growing up in

Grand Rapids, he was known as a nasty little boy who enjoyed drowning kittens.

After his travels abroad, Waite showed no immediate enthusiasm for returning to dental practice. "Doc," as he liked his friends to call him, was on a prolonged vacation. He filled his idle hours making inquiries about the financial status of various young women around town. When he settled on Clara Louise, the only daughter of an elderly millionaire drug manufacturer, John E. Peck, Waite decided to mount his main assault not on the daughter, but on her mother, Mrs. Hannah Peck.

"It was through mother that he gained consent to marry me," Clara would recall. "He paid little attention to me. His time was all for mother. He sat with her and told her stories of his accomplishments, and he had her completely won over in a short time. She suggested the marriage, telling me that it would be an excellent match and that I would be pleasing her if I consented. I was averse at first because father and Percy, my brother, were not favorable to the idea. We used to talk it over frequently, and then father and Percy gave in to mother's wishes, even though they slyly insisted that I should investigate his past. After a time, he began to lavish his attention on me, and with mother's helping influence, he succeeded in winning me."

Clara Peck could not have investigated Dr. Waite's background very thoroughly, because if she had, it is unlikely that her marriage to him on September 3, 1915—the social event of the year in Grand Rapids—would ever have taken place.

After the wedding, Waite proposed that they set up house in New York City, where he would be able to establish a more lucrative dental practice. In fact, after the couple rented a seven-room apartment suite in the Coliseum, at 435 Riverside Drive, Waite showed little inclination to do much beyond improving his tennis game. To explain his inactivity, he was soon telling various stories. To some people he represented himself as a dentist trying to get his papers to practice in New York State, to others he was a medical doctor interested mainly in Wall Street speculations. He deluded even Clara into believing he had medical qualifications, leaving her parked one day outside a hospital while he went inside, he claimed, to perform an operation.

Before his marriage to Clara, Waite had ingratiated himself not only with her mother, but with her aunt, Miss Catherine Peck, a wealthy woman who lived in the Park Avenue Hotel. Now he dined with her frequently, impressed her with his beautiful hymn singing when he accompanied her to church, and convinced her of his business acumen. Soon Miss Peck was entrusting him not only with treasured items of family jewelry, but with $40,000, which he was to invest for her. She was also making it known that she planned to leave him a large bequest. Waite opened a $30,000 brokerage account and, reading in the Grand Rapids newspaper that his brother, Clyde, had resigned from the Bell Telephone Company, apparently under a cloud, sent him a check for $10,000 with this surprising assurance: "Don't worry, old man, there's lots more where it comes from."

When, from time to time, Miss Peck missed items of jewelry or fancied she had lost sums of cash, she did not connect it with her charming nephew by marriage. And when one day she tasted something gritty in her favorite marmalade, she simply returned the jar to the grocer.

At home, Waite played the affectionate husband and dutiful son-in-law, expressing pleasure when, in January, four months after the wedding, Mrs. Peck announced she was coming for a visit. When she fell ill soon after arriving, Waite was indefatigable in his attentions. He sat with her, read to her, brought her flowers every day and, when she complained of feeling cold, went out and bought her a foot warmer. On only one matter was he less than generous: when the doctor attending her suggested a night nurse, Waite said it really wasn't necessary. On Saturday, January 30, 1916, Waite returned from a few sets of indoor tennis to find that his mother-in-law's health had worsened. In the morning, when Clara went into her mother's bedroom, she found her dead.

With his wife in a state of shock, Waite insisted the body be sent to Grand Rapids immediately. A casket lined with lavender satin was procured, and by 5:00 P.M. on Sunday the couple were on their way to Grand Rapids, where Waite persuaded the family not only that cremation was the sensible, modern answer to disposing of the remains, but also that it had been Mrs. Peck's wish.

On their return to New York, Dr. Waite dedicated himself once more to tennis, dashing around town in his automobile (garnering several speeding citations) and adding to his collection of nearly one hundred suits. He also became a familiar figure in café society and a frequenter of the theater, which was where he first saw Margaret Horton, a twenty-four-year-old actress and singer more notable for her looks than for her voice.

Infatuated, he went to hear her day after day, arranged a meeting and signed up for drama lessons with her, at which, appropriately, he read the part of Romeo to her Juliet. Impressed by his urbane manners, Mrs. Horton, who was married to a man nearly twice her age, signed up with Waite for French and German lessons at the Berlitz School of Languages. His next step was to set her up in a studio suite at the Plaza Hotel that he reserved in the names of Dr. and Mrs. A.W. Walters. There, Margaret Horton would assure skeptical listeners, they passed their days platonically singing and, in the afternoons, practicing their French.

"Dr. Waite had an extraordinarily kind heart," Mrs. Horton would say. "He loved all the fine sentiments and beautiful things of life. He used to say to me, 'Margaret, when you sing, you make me weep because you make me think of beautiful things' He loved music. It was that love of music that drew us together." He painted her glowing pictures of his earlier life in London, England, where, he said, he had been in charge of a hospital. He had returned to the U.S. only because of the outbreak of the Great War. Perhaps, when the war was over, they would go together to London, he suggested.

He made no secret of Clara's existence. His wife, he assured her, was eager to meet her, although somehow the meeting never came about. When some Peck relatives—Elizabeth C. Hardwick, her uncle, Dr. Jacob Cornell, and her cousin, Arthur Swinton—happened to see Waite and Mrs. Horton dining together at the Plaza on February 22, he explained that he had just come from completing a major operation and was taking his tireless nurse, Mrs. Horton, out to dinner as a reward.

Waite told his young protégé he expected to come into a large fortune very soon. In fact, he was already viewing estates on the Hudson that might suit his new status. And her resources? Oh, she told him airily, she and her engineer-inventor husband had independent means. Both Waite and Horton were indulging in a dance of deception: about this time, her husband was filing for bankruptcy.

Also in February, the Waites invited Mr. Peck, now lonely and disconsolate over the loss of his wife, to New York. His son-in-law spared no effort to cheer the old man up, going out for walks with him and taking him for drives. When Mr. Peck fell ill, Waite insisted he had the very medicine to make him better. Around this time, the old man had a lucky escape when Clara, coming into his bedroom, found that someone had left the gas on. A servant was blamed.

On March 11, Mr. Peck experienced severe stomach pains, and Dr. A.A. Moore was called. Believing his patient was suffering only from a minor digestive disorder, he prescribed a soothing remedy. Dr. Cornell, paying a visit that same evening, found that Mr. Peck's condition gave no cause for concern. As he was leaving, Waite came into the bedroom carrying some medicine. Dr. Cornell had the impression he had been waiting outside the door. As he stood in the hall putting on his coat, Cornell believed he heard the old man groan, but thought nothing of it. So he was greatly surprised when he received a phone call from Clara early the following morning informing him her father had died.

Dr. Cornell hurried to the Waites' apartment with his nephew, Arthur Swinton, but when they rang the bell, Dr. Waite blocked their way. "What did you come for?" he asked with uncharacteristic brusqueness. "I thought my wife called you up and asked you not to." The two men insisted on entering, and learned that Waite had made arrangements for the body to be embalmed and dispatched that same day to Grand Rapids for burial. It would be noted later that both Mr. and Mrs. Peck had died on a Sunday, when the coroner's office was closed, and that the bodies were on their way to Grand Rapids before the office opened again Monday morning.

At this point, it's legitimate to ask why Cornell, Swinton or other family members did not call in the police. The remarkable coincidence of two elderly people dying under such similar circumstances, and Waite's suspicious behavior, should have set warning bells jangling. But murder is not something that is supposed to happen among respectable folk living on Riverside Drive, and if there were doubts, they were generally put to rest by Arthur Waite's persuasive charm.

In Grand Rapids, though, Clara's brother, Percy, refused to allow cremation this time, and after the funeral the body was placed in the family vault. But Percy took no further action—until he received the mysterious telegram from "K. Adams."

Even as the first wisps of suspicions began to curl around Waite, he could not resist taking the next step in his grand scheme. Clara had inherited half her father's fortune—$500,000—and in their room at the Pantlind Hotel in Grand Rapids, Waite suggested that for their mutual protection they should sign wills leaving each other their money in case anything happened. After all, the demise of her parents was a reminder of just how vulnerable we all are to fate. Clara, perhaps unsettled by her loss, began making out a list of bequests to her favorite charities. Oh dear me, sighed her husband, it wasn't necessary to be quite so generous. He pruned the total amount of her bequests to $18,000, with the balance going to himself. She copied the will out at her brother's house, signed it and, again at Waite's suggestion, sent it to a lawyer's office.

At the same time, Waite was telling old friends around town that his wife was not in the best of health and he did not expect her to live long. His forecast should have been taken seriously: he had made similar predictions regarding his parents-in-law.

Did Waite realize the game was almost up? Apparently not. With his father-in-law safely in the vault, he caught the *Wolverine* back to New York. It was only when he bought a newspaper on the train that he learned that an autopsy was to be performed on Mr. Peck. By then, alerted by the Peck family, Assistant District Attorney Francis C. Mancuso and pathologist Dr. Otto Schultze had already arrived in Grand Rapids from New York, and family members had hired a private detective, R.C. Schindler, to track Waite's movements when he returned to New York.

The autopsy revealed that Peck had died of arsenic poisoning. For Arthur Waite, the result was an admission of failure. He had had to resort to arsenic, the easily detected poison of choice of the bumbling amateur. He had planned to dispose of his relatives using sophisticated new techniques that would have defied the skills of the best pathologists.

Perhaps the idea occurred to him during some tedious lecture on hygiene at the University of Michigan, or maybe it came to him as he stood beside Clara Peck at the altar. At any rate, it was an elegant idea that anticipated the arrival of germ warfare later in the century: how, Waite asked himself, could murder be proved if he introduced the germs of potentially fatal diseases such as typhoid and pneumonia into the systems of his victims? Pretending to be a medical researcher with a special interest in bacteriology, Waite obtained germs for typhoid, anthrax, diphtheria, pneumonia and influenza from the Rockefeller Institute, the Willard Parker Hospital, Bellevue Hospital and Parke, Davis and Co. He also received germs from Dr. Percival L. de Nyce at the Flower Hospital, but complained that they were not virulent enough for his "experiments."

One person who followed the news of the autopsy results with keen interest was John S. Potter, the undertaker who had prepared Peck's body for transfer to Grand Rapids. If Waite was arrested, who would pay his bill? Potter presented himself at the Riverside apartment with a demand for payment. Wasn't it a bit early to be pressing for payment? "It's the custom with out-of-town cases," Potter lied blandly. Waite asked who had embalmed Mr. Peck. Eugene Kane, replied the undertaker. And had he used arsenic in the embalming fluid? Potter knew then that the bill for preparing the body might be a small matter compared with the sum Waite might be prepared to pay for other services. He would send Kane along to see him, he told Waite.

The next day, Kane, an embalmer of romantic inclination who had once been convicted of bigamy, found Waite in a nervous state. Could arsenic be used in embalming fluid? Yes, Kane replied, but it was illegal. If, when the police came to take a sample of his embalming fluid, arsenic could be detected, said Waite, he would give Kane enough money "to set you up for life." A figure of $25,000 was mentioned.

The following morning, with police detectives shadowing him, Waite slipped into Gustave Cimiotti's garage, where he regularly had his car serviced, and asked Cimiotti if he would cash a check for $9,300 at the Corn Exchange Bank branch next door. Puzzled, Cimiotti went to the bank, but an equally puzzled bank official insisted on coming to the garage and identifying Waite before cashing his check.

Shortly thereafter, still under surveillance, Waite entered one of two telephone booths in a cigar store on Fifty-ninth Street. "For God's sake, get the stuff into the sample," he whispered to Kane, who was waiting in the adjoining phone booth. He stuffed the money into Kane's pocket before hurrying away. Police would eventually recover the money buried in a can beneath a tree by a remote Long Island beach, where the cautious Kane had hidden it.

The inevitable could not long be postponed. On March 23, detectives covered the exits of the Coliseum apartment building. Inside, they found Arthur Waite in a coma after taking an overdose of drugs. He later denied that he had been attempting suicide. I am inclined to believe him: I don't think he would have missed out on enjoying his subsequent notoriety.

In the apartment, police found a small medical library,

including a book on poisons with a marker in the section on arsenic, as well as hundreds of microscope slides containing what turned out to be the germs for potentially fatal diseases. No arsenic was discovered, but a check with drugstores in the area turned up a poison book bearing Waite's signature for a purchase of arsenic, which, he had told the druggist, he needed to put down a cat.

Shown the signature as he recovered in Bellevue Hospital the following day, Waite, as usual, was not at a loss for an answer. "I'll tell you, but you won't believe me," he told the district attorney. "Mr. Peck was an old man, and he was very despondent because of the death of his wife. He told me that he wanted to end his life and asked me to get some poison for him. I returned to the apartment with it and delivered it to Mr. Peck unopened. I have no proof that he killed himself with the poison, but if they found arsenic in his body, I guess he did."

As the DA left, Waite signaled to Schindler, the private detective working in the Peck family interest, to remain behind. "I didn't poison the old man. I'm telling the truth," he said.

"That's all well and good," replied the detective, "but how do we know you're telling the truth?"

"That's the trouble," said Waite. "But there's Dora Hillier, our servant. If you could see her, you could tell her that I'll give her $1,000 if she will say she knows of her own knowledge that Mr. Peck wanted to commit suicide." True to his word, he wrote out a check payable to Dora Hillier on a page of Schindler's notebook.

It was Waite's bad luck that he had not been able to read any newspapers. If he had, he would have known that Dora had already testified before the grand jury that, two days before Mr. Peck died, her employer had come into the kitchen as she was ladling out the soup and had added some "medicine" to his father-in-law's bowl. When he didn't eat the soup, Waite had returned to the kitchen and added some more medicine to the old man's tea.

By the following day, Assistant District Attorney John T. Dooling was claiming there was evidence that Waite had planned to poison his wife, his brother-in-law, Percy Peck, his aunt by marriage, Catherine Peck, and his mistress, Margaret Horton, and her husband. "There seems to have been no limit," said Dooling.

The two women in Arthur Waite's life reacted very differently. In Grand Rapids, Clara said the news that her husband was living with another woman at the Plaza was the last straw, and that her love for him had turned to hatred. Not a penny of her newly acquired fortune would go to defend him, she said. Murdering her parents, apparently, was forgivable, but taking up with "that woman" went beyond the pale. In New York, Margaret Horton, quick to capitalize on her notoriety, organized a small concert, to which her lawyer invited friends and newspaper reporters. One critic described her voice as "militant contralto."

In Bellevue Hospital, Waite finally admitted to killing Mr. and Mrs. Peck, but insisted "the man from Egypt," a sort of dual personality inside him, had made him do it. If he was hoping to convince a jury that he was insane, he hurt his chances by writing to Margaret Horton that he expected to be in an insane asylum for a while, but then expected to recover his freedom. The letter found its way onto the DA's desk.

"My God, why can't I get this thing off my mind?" Waite ranted in his hospital room to a detective named John Cunniffe. "Who are you anyway?"

"I'm from the DA's office, and I want to help you," the detective replied ingenuously.

"You don't want to help me," cried Waite. "You, everybody

and the law are against me. I'm the worst scoundrel on the face of the earth!"

"Well," replied Cunniffe, "we all make mistakes."

Percy Peck was not prepared to take such a generous view. "My one wish is to see Waite meet his merited end," he said. "His stories of my father's wish to commit suicide are absolutely false. He lies when he says it. The electric chair is too easy a death for my brother-in-law. If he were tortured, it would be no more than fair."

At the trial of Dr. Arthur Warren Waite, which began on May 22, 1916, the identity of the mysterious "K. Adams," who had first pointed the finger of suspicion at Waite, was finally revealed. Taking the stand, Elizabeth Hardwick, Dr. Jacob Cornell's niece, said she had disliked Waite from the beginning, and when she saw him with Margaret Horton at the Plaza, she had no doubt from their behavior that he was lying when he said she was his nurse. When her uncle told her of the reception he had received at the Waite apartment following Mr. Peck's death, she was no longer in doubt about Waite's game: murder.

With Waite no longer making any attempt to deny his actions, the trial was remarkable for the complete reversal of roles between the defense and the prosecution. While the prosecution made every effort to make Waite appear sane and rational, the defense attorney, Walter R. Deuel, did everything in his power to portray his client as a devious and depraved monster in the hopes of getting him off on an insanity plea. In the witness box, Waite gave his attorney all the help he could, describing how, as a boy, he used to drown kittens, how in high school he had begun the practice of stealing exam papers, a technique that got him through many of the hard spots in his university career. He had lost his first five jobs through dishonesty, he admitted, and in South Africa the firm for which he worked as a dentist had fired him when it was discovered he had been stealing from them. He did not love his wife when he married her, he said, but was only interested in her father's fortune. But that did not stop him from stealing five dollars from his future mother-in-law's purse when he went on a trip down south with the family.

His first attempt at murder, he said, was directed against Catherine Peck. "Did you ever give ground glass to Miss Peck?" asked Deuel.

Waite smiled. "Yes, I put some in her marmalade."

"How did you give the marmalade to her?"

"Why, she had it there in the closet. I took it down from a shelf and put ground glass into it and left it there. She was fond of marmalade and ate it frequently."

When that failed, he introduced germ cultures into a can of fish and presented it to her. Sometimes, he said, Miss Peck left milk and other foods out to cool in a window in the dining room, and every day or so he would empty half a test tube of germs into it. The germs were evidently not strong enough to bring down the redoubtable Miss Peck, so he turned his attention to his mother-in-law.

When she came to visit, "I had everything ready for her before she arrived." At their first meal together, he said, he went into the dining room ahead of the others and put what he believed were typhoid and pneumonia germs into her soup and other dishes. "They acted on her immediately. She died within a week," said Waite. The morning she died, he got up early to check that she was dead, then returned to bed, leaving the body for his wife to discover later.

But when Waite used the same techniques on Mr. Peck, adding tuberculosis germs for good measure, they seemed to have no effect. Growing desperate, he gave the old man half a bottle of calomel at a time to make him sick, gave him pneumonia germs, took him riding in his car on cold days with the windows open, and dampened his sheets before he went to bed. Nothing worked. Then, said Waite, as one juryman finally gave way to laughter, "I read in the paper how the soldiers in France were killed by chlorine gas. The paper said it was very effective, so I got some chlorine of potash and put hydrochloric acid in it and placed it inside his door. I fixed the electric heater with some stuff so it would smell as if varnish was burning if he woke up. But," Waite shrugged, "it didn't hurt him at all."

"Did you give him anything else?" Deuel asked.

"Oh, yes, I gave him arsenic along about Thursday or Friday."

"How much?"

"All of it. A little at first, and then more until he had it all. I put it in food, oatmeal, rice pudding, hot milk, soup and anything it seemed proper to put it in."

The night Mr. Peck died, Waite had slept on the couch outside his room so that he could hear if anything happened. "I slept awhile and then I heard a groan. I went in and gave him chloroform." When he returned to the room a few minutes later, there was no pulse.

"I wanted them to die," Waite said in response to another question.

"Why?"

"Because I wanted money," he replied.

Was there any reason why he had killed Mrs. Peck before her husband?

Waite was silent for a moment. "No, only that she was the first to come and see us."

Several defense alienists, as psychiatrists were called then, claimed that Waite was a moral imbecile, in effect a psychopath who was not responsible for his actions. Mr. Justice Shearn, in his address to the jury, demolished that argument. "Moral depravity is not imbecility," he said.

At the conclusion of his five-day trial, Waite stood to hear the verdict with, as one observer noted, "a pleasantly expectant expression on his face, as if some honor were about to be conferred upon him." When he heard the verdict "guilty as charged," Waite did not give Percy Peck, sitting a few yards away, the satisfaction of seeing him crumple. His composure intact, he returned to his cell and ate a hearty dinner.

Sentenced shortly afterwards to the electric chair, Waite passed his days in Sing Sing's death row writing poetry and giving interviews. "I played the game and lost," he told one reporter. He left his own contribution to the limited genre of death row verse with this poem, entitled "Peace":

> And when the sunshine plays along
> The corridor to death,
> Its light and shadows are but song
> Unto my fleeting breath;
> For where they play I soon shall pass
> Down through the small death-door,
> And I shall leave my failure there,
> Forever more, forever more.

But after a medical panel ruled that he was sane, and the moment came to make that walk, Dr. Arthur Waite was finally at a loss for words. "Goodbye, boys," he said, waving to the other prisoners on death row. And that was all.

A Shooting in Hampstead

T hey long ago repaired the front wall of the Magdala Tavern, removing any signs of bullet damage. Wouldn't do to have that sort of thing in fashionable Hampstead! But the memory of Ruth Ellis is not so easily disposed of. And that is something of a puzzle.

Walking past the bluebells on Hampstead Green on a sunny spring morning on the anniversary of that Easter Sunday shooting, I ponder why it is that her memory refuses to die, why there have been at least two movies, a play, a TV drama starring the late Diana Dors and three books produced about a case that would be commonplace in any city in the world, let alone London, and that the police would almost routinely write off as "a domestic."

Rounding the corner at Hampstead Station and climbing the short rise to South Hill Park, I can see the spot in front of the Magdala where David Blakely, her shallow, twenty-five-year-old boyfriend, who concealed his weakness under the bravura front of a racecar driver, parked his small station wagon that night before going into the saloon bar with his friend Clive Gunnell to buy cigarettes and beers.

It was one of those evenings when Hampstead is at its best, the streets taking on an almost Parisian flair. People were relaxing, strolling, dropping in at the pub, knowing that the next day, Easter Monday, was a holiday. Blakely cashed a check for £5 with the landlord, had a drink at the bar, then bought three flagons of beer to take back to the intimate party he was attending and headed back to the car. Juggling the bottles and trying to reach for the keys to the gray-and-green two-tone Standard Vanguard, he didn't notice the slender peroxide blonde wearing dark-rimmed glasses who was walking down South Hill Park toward him.

He didn't even seem to notice when she called out, "David!" His face, the small chin, the narrow, almost feminine features, was directed toward opening the driver's door without dropping the bottles. And when he looked up, it was with an expression of surprise at seeing her standing beside him. There was no time to register shock. She opened her purse and took out the large Smith and Wesson .38 so quickly that the words—of greeting, or more likely excuses—died on his lips. In that frozen instant, the gun looked impossibly large in her small, pale hands. As he turned to run, she fired and then fired again. His momentum carried him to the back corner of the car. "Clive!" he screamed. Ruth Ellis, still holding the gun out in front of her, came after him.

"Get out of the way, Clive," she ordered him. The gun shook as she fired toward Blakely's back while he writhed bleeding on the ground, and one wild bullet hit a passerby, Gladys Kensington Yule, in the thumb. Blakely was bleeding from the mouth, his blood mixing with the beer now frothing into the gutter. The firing stopped. All six bullets were spent. Her main regret at that moment, she would say, was that she had meant to save the last bullet for herself.

The crowd poured out of the pub. "What have you done?" someone shouted. "You'll both die now."

A tall man who had been having a drink in the bar and who, shortly before, had noticed the blonde peering through the window, stepped forward with an air of authority. "Phone the police," Ruth Ellis told him. "I am a police officer," he said. Off-duty Constable Alan Thompson put out his hand and took the gun from her. She said nothing as they waited for police cars and an ambulance to arrive.

At the police station, they offered her a cup of tea and a cigarette. Then, perfectly in control, she said, "My name is Mrs. Ruth Ellis. I am a model. I am twenty-eight, and I live at 44 Egerton Gardens, that's Kensington."

There was nothing immortal, nothing elevating about the affair between Ruth Ellis and David Blakely. You couldn't even properly call it a romance. It was more a grasping for control, an out-of-sync affair in which first David and then Ruth would pursue the other possessively, obsessively, while both were shamelessly unfaithful. By the end, when this dreary, often violent relationship between two selfish people had run its course, she loved him just enough to shoot him, but not enough to let him go.

So why has the story of Ruth Ellis continued to fascinate people? Why does the name of this part-time prostitute and night-club hostess win immediate recognition years after her body was doused in quicklime and buried in the yard at Holloway Prison?

There are many answers. In 1955, the murder took the lid off the new, sleazy postwar London of after-hours drinking clubs, underworld figures and sex for sale. Ruth Ellis, who consciously modeled herself on blonde sirens of the screen like Lana Turner and Marilyn Monroe, had resorted to a Hollywood solution to her problems: a six-shooter. From a British standpoint, it was also the eternal class struggle expressed in sexual terms—brassy blonde chases refined upper-middle-class ex-public-school boy.

But if we have to pare it down to one reason people would never forget Ruth Ellis, it was that she was the last woman in Britain to hang. The execution of a woman who, at worst, should have been convicted only of manslaughter, and who met her fate with such dignity, caused such a wave of disgust that the Ruth Ellis case played a significant role in Britain's abolishing the noose for good ten years later.

Even today, the Ellis case retains its relevance as a classic example of male injustice meted out to a woman. A court now, hearing that gently bred David Blakely had punched the pregnant Ellis in the stomach, causing a miscarriage, less than two weeks before the shooting, would likely free her, to the cheers of the public gallery.

For a young woman with a lot of verve and ambition, hers was a messy life. Born Ruth Neilson on October 9, 1927, in Rhyl, a North Wales seaside resort, she was the daughter of an unsuccessful musician who finally found work as a chauffeur and moved his family to London in 1941 in the midst of the Blitz. Ruth, the rebellious one of the four children, left school at fourteen and took a series of dead-end jobs that included waitressing and minding a machine in an Oxo meat extract factory.

Wartime London teemed with allied soldiers, and it wasn't long before Ruth was bringing home Clare, a French-Canadian serviceman whom the family liked and she adored. His paychecks, more generous than those of British troops, introduced her to a life of meals out and taxicabs home, and she began to think about how life would be as his wife in Canada after the war. When she became pregnant just before Christmas, 1944, Clare said it was no problem: they would get married right away. Ruth's mother cannily wrote to his commanding officer. That was when they discovered Clare had a wife and three children back in Canada.

Ruth had learned a hard lesson about trust. She cried for days, then got a job as a cashier, where she could sit down. She gave birth on September 15, 1944, to a son, Clare Andria, who during his short and tragic life would be known as Andy.

Her entrance into the glamorous world of London's West End came with an advertisement offering a pound (about £2) an hour for models willing to pose nude for members of a London camera club. Some members, it was said, had no film in their cameras. She would go out for drinks afterwards, and that was how she met Morrie Conley, who ran several after-hours clubs and who would later be identified in the press as a major vice boss.

Ruth was flattered when Conley spent the whole evening talking to her, and was even more impressed when he offered her work as a club hostess, a job that paid £5 a week, plus ten percent commission on drink and food sales, and free evening dresses. Soon she was taking home £20 a week, many times more than what she had earned performing menial jobs in factories and restaurants. There was even more money to be made by going to bed with the black marketeers and out-of-town businessmen who frequented the clubs.

When she met George Ellis, a Surrey dental surgeon, at the club, it seemed to Ruth she was finally ready to make that big jump to a fancy house and expensive lifestyle in the suburbs. Ellis, forty-one, was recently divorced, and couldn't get enough of Ruth. Marriage? Why not!

Their 1950 marriage was a disaster. Ellis, who would eventually hang himself with his own pajama cord in a hotel room, was an alcoholic. He beat Ruth up several times, and in 1952, expecting a baby, she left him and sued for divorce. With Andy and now the new baby, Georgina (who Ruth would put out for adoption), to look after, she turned to Conley again, and was soon back in the money, earning on one occasion a £400 tip from a satisfied customer with whom she had been on vacation.

One night, she met a snot-nosed public-school brat named David Blakely, who, typically, was getting his charges from insulting the hostesses, Ruth included. She didn't give him another thought until Conley promoted her to manager of the Little Club, one of his joints in Knightsbridge. Who should the first customer be but the brat Blakely? This time, she saw the other side of his character and found him charming and amusing. As he kept coming back to the club, it was Ruth's impression that he was playing hard to get. Not for long. Within a week, he was sharing her bed in the little two-room flat over the club that was one of the perks that came with her new job.

Ruth's sex life in those days was thoroughly complicated. In the afternoon, there were clients to be accommodated; Morrie Conley made his demands; and Desmond Cussen, an ex-bomber pilot who Ruth used as a doormat and a convenience, was another complicating factor. In the two years that remained before the shooting, Ruth would spend her time trying to earn a living while keeping the various men in her life apart, occasionally satisfied and minimally disgruntled. For the most part, she did not succeed.

David Blakely, three years younger than Ruth and the son of a Scottish doctor, was consumed with racing cars. This interest had been fostered by Humphrey Cook, a former racing car driver who his mother had married upon divorcing David's father. Never very successful at the track, David nevertheless introduced Ruth to the champagne and engine oil glamor of the weekend circuits. His dream was to manufacture a sports car called the Emperor that he and his friend Ant Findlater were developing. A former Guards officer who was supposed to be a hotel management trainee, David received an allowance from his stepfather, but with his flashy lifestyle and the money the sports car swallowed, he was always hard up and begging Ruth for money. A friend afterwards described him as "a dead unreliable bastard."

Ruth became pregnant by him in 1954, and claimed afterwards that David, who was engaged at the time to the daughter of a wealthy manufacturer, offered to marry her. "I was not really in love with him at the time," she said. She got an abortion one weekend when he was out of town. David's engagement ended soon after.

Adding to the tensions, David was ashamed to introduce Ruth Ellis to his family. One evening, he drove her to Penn, in Buckinghamshire, where his mother and stepfather lived, but when he learned his mother was in the pub, he refused to take her in, bringing a drink out to her in the car instead.

Before David Blakely came on the scene, Ruth had been proud of the job she was doing to make the Little Club hospitable and profitable, and she was always looking for ways to improve it. Now, David would frequently arrive drunk, make a scene over the presence of Desmond Cussen and take her up to the flat, where the sound of blows was clearly audible to the customers. Often, she said later, she was covered with bruises.

In June 1954, David went to the Le Mans racetrack in France to drive and didn't return when promised; an angry Ruth took Desmond as her lover. Of these two men in her life, she would say, "They hated each other."

By December, the club receipts were way down, and Conley fired her. With Andy, now ten, coming home from boarding school for the holidays, she had nowhere to live. David was furious when he discovered that she had moved with Andy into Desmond's large apartment. Almost immediately, she began sneaking out to spend nights with David at a hotel.

It couldn't go on. The men were bitterly jealous of each other. In February, Ruth made her choice: she left Desmond Cussen, and she and David rented a Kensington bed-sitter in the name of Mr. and Mrs. Ellis. It was a pathetic comedown for the girl who not long before had been earning big money, taking elocution lessons and aiming for a career in the movies. Then things got worse. The Emperor, on which David and Ant had been pinning their money and their hopes, blew up in a race. "It's all your fault," a bitterly disappointed David told her. "You jinxed me." And then Ruth discovered she was pregnant again. At her trial, Ruth would say, "He did thump me in the tummy." What she meant was that he first choked her, then punched her in the stomach, causing her to lose the baby.

It would be unfair to put the blame all on one side. On one occasion, following one of their violent encounters, friends noticed that David's back was a mass of bruises, and he admitted that Ruth had gone after him with a carving knife. She was drinking heavily and was subject to fits of extraordinary jealousy, especially in relation to David's friendship with Ant Findlater and his wife, Carole. Ruth knew that, some years before, David had had an affair with Carole. Now, whenever he was with the Findlaters, even though he often had to consult Ant about their car project, she interpreted it as an act of betrayal.

By now, they were so hard up that she sometimes didn't eat all day, and Desmond Cussen was helping with the rent. David was talking again about their getting married, but he was becoming increasingly reluctant to return every night to the depressing bed-sitter where young Andy, during the school holidays, slept on a camp bed alongside their double bed, and where the rows rarely stopped.

"I'm supposed to be calling for Ruth at eight tonight," he told the Findlaters at the start of the Easter weekend as they drank at the Magdala, "but I can't stand it any longer. I want to get away from her." Why didn't he leave her, asked Carole. "It's not as easy as all that," he replied. "You don't know her, you don't know what she's capable of." Carole suggested that David should stay the weekend with them.

At Egerton Gardens, the countdown to murder had begun. David was supposed to pick Ruth up at 8:00 P.M. By 9:30, he still wasn't there, and Ruth phoned the Findlaters. Ant, who answered, denied that David was there. Ruth called the one man she could rely on completely, Desmond Cussen, and asked him to drive her to Hampstead. Outside the Findlaters' Tanza Road flat, she saw David's station wagon. She rang the bell repeatedly, but there was no answer. When she phoned, the receiver was put down.

Deliberately, with icy fury, she took Desmond's flashlight and smashed in the rear windows of David's car. The police, who arrived shortly afterwards, took the lenient view and advised her to go home.

In the early hours of the morning, Ruth finally went home. Instead of sleeping, she sat smoking all night. "If only I had been able to speak to him and give vent to my feelings," she would write later, "I do not think any of this would have happened."

The next morning, the pattern repeated itself. She rang Tanza Road, but the receiver was put down. After lunch, she gave Andy money to go to the zoo and got Desmond to drive her to Hampstead again. She had somehow got it into her head that David was having an affair with the Findlaters' nanny. That evening, Saturday, there was a party at the Findlaters, and Ruth stood below listening to the laughter. Some of it, she was sure, was David's, as he chatted up a new woman. Around ten o'clock, she saw him emerge with his arm around a woman she assumed was the nanny.

Throughout Easter Sunday, Ruth later claimed, she stayed home drinking Pernod. At 7:30 she put Andy to bed. The idea had formed in her mind, she said, of killing David. At Tanza Road, not seeing the station wagon, she walked the short distance to the Magdala, assuming David might be there. He had arrived a few minutes earlier on an errand to buy Carole some cigarettes, as well as to get some beer.

Did he recognize her as she walked down the sidewalk toward him? Was he trying to ignore her and get into the car quickly before she arrived? By then, even if he had greeted her and spoken to her, it was probably too late. Ruth Ellis, as she opened her purse, had only one idea in her head.

Afterwards, she would write, "All I remember is the blood. I have never seen so much blood."

Awaiting trial in Holloway, a prison for women, Ruth Ellis, whom a jury member would describe as a "common little West End tart," turned out to be a lady after all. "Please try to believe me when I say how deeply sorry I am to have caused you this unpleasantness," she wrote David's mother, as if she was apologizing for a gaff at a tea party. When Melford Stevenson, her chief barrister, pressed her for details that might help her case, she told him, "Look, stop minding about me. I'm so sorry for you. It's such an awkward case, isn't it?"

To the frustration even of the prosecution, she would make no effort to save herself. "She was almost ludicrously offhand in her own defense," Jean Southworth, who assisted the prosecuting barrister, Christmas Humphreys, has said. "As if she didn't care." It was as if Ruth, who had modeled herself on those tough broads on the movie screen, was determined to play her last scene as if the cameras were rolling. The one favor she asked of Stevenson was that he get permission from the prison governor to have her hair, which was darkening at the roots, returned to its pristine shade of platinum blonde for her appearance at Number One Court at the Old Bailey. And, vindictive to the last, her main concern about the trial was that the Findlaters should be exposed as the people who turned David against her.

The trial was a scandal. It was the shortest murder trial on record, lasting just over a day. Ruth went into the witness box and told her story in that carefully modulated tone she'd learned at elocution classes, without ever betraying any emotion. Nothing was made of Ruth's "thump me in the tummy" remark, and any defense was effectively destroyed when Christmas Humphreys got to his feet and asked her a single question: "Mrs. Ellis, when you fired the revolver at close range into the body of David Blakely, what did you intend to do?" She replied, "It is obvious when I shot him I intended to kill him."

The jury took only twenty-three minutes to find her guilty, and a few minutes later she was on her way to back to Holloway and the death cell. "She wanted to die," her older sister, Muriel, has said. She refused to appeal. "Ruth had no patience with the people around her who were hoping to get her sentence commuted," Muriel said.

The one question that was not even examined at the trial was where Ruth got the gun. She had told the police an implausible story about acquiring it several years before from a club customer as security for a loan, and keeping it in her clothing drawer all those years. But the gun was properly oiled and showed no signs of neglect. And for someone who had never handled a gun before, Ruth had seemed surprisingly competent in the way she used it. The day before her execution, she finally told her parents and one of her solicitors, Victor Mishcon, that it was Desmond Cussen who had given her the gun, shown her how to fire it, and driven her to Hampstead the night of the shooting. Another of her lawyers said Desmond admitted as much to him only two days after the killing. Desmond, who now lives in Australia, denied the allegations in a television interview.

But even if this had been revealed at the time, it would likely not have affected the outcome. The particularly dimwitted Home Secretary of that era, Major Gwilym Lloyd George, the cabinet minister responsible for reviewing the case, said later, in defending his decision not to intervene, "We cannot have people shooting off firearms in the street. As long as I was Home Secretary I was determined to ensure that people could use the streets without fear of a bullet." In an era when guns were rare in Britain and gunfire in the streets rarer, the argument hardly held water. Giving further support to the fallacious argument, though, Gladys Kensington Yule, the banker's wife who had been struck in the thumb by a stray bullet, wrote to a newspaper, "If Ruth Ellis is reprieved, we may have other vindictive and jealous young women shooting their boyfriends in public."

In her cell, Ruth was torn by conflicting emotions. At one point, she threw herself on the bed, crying hysterically, "I don't want to die. I don't want to die." Another time, she asked her mother to smuggle a bottle of sleeping pills into prison for her. But as the July 13 execution date approached, she regained her composure. "Have you heard the big news?" she asked a friend visiting her. "I'm not going to be reprieved. Don't worry, it's like having a tooth out."

But there were others who did not accept her fate with such equanimity. Petitions were signed urging a reprieve, one by 50,000 people, and the largely dormant campaign against capital punishment sprang back into life. The morning Ruth was to die, Cassandra, the passionately abolitionist *Daily Mirror* columnist, wrote a column that would remain forever linked to Ruth Ellis in the memories of many. It began: "It's a fine day for hay-making. A fine day for fishing. A fine day for lolling in the sunshine. And if you feel that way—and I mourn to say that millions of you do—it's a fine day for a hanging."

Shortly before nine o'clock, Ruth was given a tot of brandy and she drained the glass. Outside the prison, a crowd of more than a thousand waited, some of them chanting anti-hanging slogans. She was led the few feet to the execution shed, where the final obscene rite was performed by Albert Pierrepoint, the state hangman. The executioner wrote Ruth's sister a letter afterwards saying she had gone to her death more bravely than most men.

A few years later, when changes were being made at Holloway, the body of Ruth Ellis, or what remained of it, was released to her family, and she was buried in a country graveyard at Amersham, Buckinghamshire—far from the lights of the West End. There was a gravestone, but her son, Andy, had it removed to discourage curiosity-seekers.

Andy led a disturbed life, committed suicide and is now buried with his mother. Ruth's daughter, Georgina, born just as she was divorcing George Ellis, was brought up by a well-to-do Cheshire couple and didn't realize who her mother was until she came across a pile of clippings in a drawer one day. Interviewed in

1983, Georgy, as she's known, had four children, had chosen a modeling career, and was living with her third husband.

In 1957, largely as a result of the Ruth Ellis case, the concept of diminished responsibility was introduced into British law, a measure that, given her state of mental anguish when she shot David Blakely, would have almost certainly have gotten Ruth off.

The Magdala Tavern was just opening for business, and the regulars were drifting in as I left for an appointment at the British Museum. I was to lunch there with Brian Lane, an author who had founded an organization called the Murder Club, which published regional guides to historic murders in Britain. But before that, Lane, who has since died, was an ardent abolitionist who campaigned for an end to the death penalty. His interest began, he told me, when he was fourteen years old and they hanged Ruth Ellis. It is hard now to realize what a shock went through Britain when that happened, he said. Like millions of young people who had grown up in the shadow of the Second World War, and in a world still governed by old leaders and old values, he suddenly saw that everything wasn't just black and white, that life wasn't as simple as an eye for an eye.

As for Ruth, she fulfilled a pledge she had made in a letter to David's mother: "I shall die loving your son. And you should feel content that his death has been repaid. Goodbye."

The House on
Rue Saint-Hubert

"Take a look at the shoes. They'll tell you something."

Detective Georges Farah-Lajoie of the Montreal Sûreté picked up one of the brown leather shoes sitting on the table beside the pile of clothing that, shortly before, had belonged to the cadaver Dr. Wilfred Dérome had just finished sewing up.

"Expensive," said the detective, running his fingers along the smooth upper. "And almost unworn," he noted, turning it over. "Certainly it was never worn outdoors. Look at the nails. They are not even rusty. So," he said, smiling at the doctor, who was washing his hands, "where are the overshoes?"

"You've got it," said Dérome. "No overshoes. And look at the topcoat. Not a mark on it. No bullet hole. Yet there was a hole right through the poor fellow's jacket."

"So he must have been shot elsewhere," said Farah-Lajoie, "and his body was carried somehow to the spot where it was found. But, of course, I knew that already, doctor."

"How's that?"

"The snow. Underneath the body. It was not melted at all. This was dead meat when it was put there."

The snow was not all that Farah-Lajoie had noticed that Monday morning, January 9, 1922. Chief Lepage had dispatched him to a piece of waste ground in Notre Dame de Grâce, a suburb of Montreal, where early on Saturday morning two workmen had discovered the body lying beside a tool shed. There was no sign of blood, either on the ground or on the shed, which had not been broken into, the snow showed no sign of a struggle having taken place, and people living nearby had heard nothing in the night.

Farah-Lajoie—called the Arab behind his back at the police station because he was born in Damascus—also learned from his colleagues that when the body was found, its hands were tied with a thin piece of string that would have been easy to snap, and the head was wrapped in a piece of quilting, while the tails of the overcoat had been pulled up and secured above the head with safety pins.

"Obviously," said the detective, after describing these details to Dérome, "someone wanted to be very careful not to spill the claret, eh, doctor?"

"Impossible, though," said Dérome, drying his hands. "I have never seen a messier job. A real amateur. It took six bullets to finish the poor boy. And the gun was put right to his head. My guess, if you want it…"

"Tell me, doctor."

"My guess is that when you find the place this was done, you'll find someone who has been doing an awful lot of scrubbing and cleaning."

Farah-Lajoie told Pigeon, who was driving, to stop across the street. Again the detective examined the envelope found in the pocket of the maroon pants the dead man had been wearing.

"Raoul Delorme, 190 rue Saint-Hubert, Montreal," read the address.

"Like a visiting card, eh," he said over his shoulder to Desgroseilliers in the back seat. "A bit obvious. Like it was put there to be found. This priest, what's he like?"

"He gives me the creeps," said Desgroseilliers, opening his door and shifting his ponderous weight across the seat.

"A real cold fish," added Pigeon. "I mean, you know, Georges, how people react when you bring them tragic news, but this guy..."

"We tell him we're from the police and ask him if Raoul Delorme lives there," said Desgroseilliers. "Yes, says he, he's my brother. And straight away he asks us if his brother is ill, because he was sleeping away from home the night before."

"So," said Pigeon, "I give him the usual story, tell him someone carrying identification in his brother's name is gravely injured, and he says, 'Where is he?' At the morgue, I tell him. 'Then he's dead,' he says, like he's telling us. We told him we wanted him to come with us and see if he could identify the body. Didn't turn a hair. 'Give me a few minutes so I can get dressed,' he says, 'and on no account tell my sisters, who live here with me.'"

"So how was he when he saw the body?" asked Farah-Lajoie.

Pigeon shook his head. "He just looks him up and down, like he was at the butcher's. 'Yes,' he says, 'That's certainly my brother.' No tears, nothing. Just gives him a quick benediction with his hand and turns away."

Opening the door on his side, Farah-Lajoie, careful not to slip, hoisted himself on top of the snowbank, holding on to the roof of the car to steady himself as he studied the tall yellow brick house across the street. Romanesque, he'd guess the style was; secretive was how he'd describe the overall impression. The three-storey building came right up to the sidewalk. Except for two bay windows above the front door, placed there, it seemed, more as lookout posts than for illumination, the windows were all disproportionately small, while the door itself was recessed and almost hidden at the top of a flight of five steps. The battlement-like decoration along the flat roof reinforced the fortress impression. The only other means of entry Farah-Lajoie could see was through a basement garage at the foot of a steep ramp. The very bulk of the house, situated near the corner of fashionable Dorchester Street, suggested people who had money, but you'd have to think they were very careful with it.

The priest himself, apparently cheerful, opened the door for them and, rubbing his hands, led them into his study. He was in his thirties, Farah-Lajoie judged, a little overweight, round-faced with a shock of dark hair and gray eyes that regarded them blandly from behind wire-rimmed glasses. L'abbé Adélard Delorme, Farah-Lajoie already knew, ministered to the poor as chaplain of a charitable institution, L'Assistance Publique, but looking around at the dark, expensive furniture and the priest's comfortable figure, he could see no sign that the priest shared any of his clients' hardships.

"Gentlemen—cigars?" The priest held out a box. Havanas, Farah-Lajoie noticed.

"No, thank you, Father. If you don't mind," Farah-Lajoie said, taking a packet from his side pocket, "I will stick with my Pall Malls."

"Go right ahead. Now, how can I help you?"

"If you don't mind," said the detective, "we would like to go over the facts again concerning your brother. I know it must be a nuisance to you, but, you see, sometimes something is forgotten, something important."

"Of course. No bother at all." The priest was all geniality. "As I told the officers before, Raoul—he is my half-brother, you know—Raoul left the house about three o'clock on Friday. He was going to the Princess Theatre. Then, at seven o'clock precisely, he telephoned me." Delorme indicated the telephone on his desk.

"Excuse me, Father. He called you on that phone, but may I ask what the other phone on the bureau there is for?"

"Ah, you are very observant, as a detective should be. That telephone is used only by my sisters. My sisters, Florence and Lily, and my half-sister, Rosa, they live here too, you see, and that is where they receive their incoming calls."

"And it was definitely to this phone on your desk that Raoul called?"

"I can't see that it matters, but yes, Detective, it was to this phone. He called to tell me he had met two old friends and they were going out together, I gather in some style. He told me he would probably not return home until the following morning."

"Names?"

"No, he didn't mention who they were."

"Where was he calling from?"

"He didn't say. He just said it was a pay phone. And then...it was most mysterious...the telephone in my bedroom rang three times during the night, at two o'clock, at three and then again at four."

"But there was no one on the line?"

"I don't know. Once I thought I heard groaning and sobbing. I was so annoyed the third time, Detective, I will admit I used a word quite unsuitable to my position, and then I called the operator to complain."

"There is a third telephone in your bedroom, Father?"

"For emergencies, yes. Sometimes I am called out to minister to some poor dying soul. It is an extension from this phone on my desk."

"Now, Raoul lived here with you, is that right?"

"Yes, except when he was away at university in Ottawa. He would have graduated this year, poor chap. He was just home for the Christmas holidays." The priest put his hand to his mouth and for the first time betrayed signs of emotion. "Only the day before, I had been out with him to buy him clothes to go back to college."

"You supported your brother, then?"

"You might say so. You see, gentlemen, my father, whose name was also Adélard like mine, was a building contractor. You may have heard of him. He had done rather well, and when he died six years ago, there was a good bit of property. Well, Raoul, who was only nineteen at the time, was too young to take responsibility, so naturally it fell to me as the eldest—I am thirty-seven now—to run things. My bishop very generously relieved me of my normal duties so that I would be free to administer the estate."

Farah-Lajoie noticed that the priest gestured a good deal with his left hand. His right hand remained inside his cassock. But now, as he began going into details about the rents he had to collect, the paperwork he had to cope with, he flourished that hand for a moment before concealing it again.

"Excuse me asking, Father, but you seem to have hurt your hand."

Farah-Lajoie watched for a hesitation, perhaps a slight flush. There was none. "Oh, that," he said, showing them the red mark on the wrist of his right hand, "Most painful. You see, I fell on the ice on the way to mass on Saturday morning. Mademoiselle Morache, our concierge, advised me to put iodine on it to avoid infection."

"Did you get along well with Raoul?" Just for an instant the priest looked rather sharply at Farah-Lajoie over his glasses.

"Our relations could not have been more cordial. I was like a father to him. Last summer, for example, we went on a long motor trip together in the United States. Of course," the priest smiled, "as a single young man, his interests were rather different from mine. During the holidays, he would go to the cinema nearly every day, and often to the theater. He would get up late every day, but then, isn't that the way with young people, Detective?"

"Did he have many friends?"

"To be honest with you, no. I have to say not a single friend came to the house during the Christmas vacation. That is why I was rather glad when he called me to say he was going out with friends on Friday night."

"Girls?"

The priest laughed. "I tried in my modest way to be a bit of a matchmaker. But when I mentioned certain young ladies who I thought were both pretty and virtuous, I am afraid he showed no interest."

"How was he doing at university?"

"He was not brilliant, I have to admit," replied the priest. "But his professor told me that last term his marks were quite improved. As a matter of fact, Raoul told me he was looking forward to getting back to college." The priest stood up, turned his back to them and looked out the window. "His trunk was packed. He was due to leave on Saturday." There was a small catch in his voice.

"Father," said Farah-Lajoie softly, "do you have a gun?"

For a moment it seemed the priest had not heard him. But he was smiling mildly when he turned. "Of course. It is an old revolver that used to belong to my father. I keep it in the car for protection."

"I see. Could I perhaps take a look at it?"

"Certainly. Why don't I show you over the house?" He looked over his glasses with an amused expression. "You were going to ask, weren't you, Detective?"

The priest led the way into the kitchen, produced two keys and unlocked a door opening onto a stairway leading down to the garage. "I am the only one who has access," he said, leading the way and switching on the light. "Here we are." From the glove compartment of the large Franklin sedan he produced a Bayard automatic pistol. It did not seem especially old to Farah-Lajoie.

"Have you ever fired it, Father?"

"Only once. When we were traveling in the States. A dog frightened Raoul, and I fired a shot to frighten it off."

"I see a box of bullets there too. Would you mind if we take them and the gun along for examination?"

Upstairs again, Farah-Lajoie asked for a description of Raoul's watch, which had been ripped from his waistcoat pocket, leaving only a piece of broken chain. "Oh, that was not his watch," the priest replied. "His was at the jeweler's being repaired. I loaned him my watch when he went out."

"And the overshoes, Father. I believe you mentioned earlier buying him a pair of overshoes to return to college. Could I see them?"

"Here they are," said the priest, opening the hall closet and producing a shiny new pair.

"I see an old pair there. Are they yours?"

"I expect so. I have several."

"Would you try them on for me, Father?"

The priest sat down obligingly on the hall bench and went to pull on one of the overshoes. After a great deal of tugging and going red in the face, he managed to get one on. "What's so important about overshoes?" he asked, with a trace of irritation.

"Just details, Father. We have to look at everything or we get in trouble with the chief back at the office."

When they returned to the sidewalk once again, the sun had come out, and the glare on the snow momentarily blinded the three officers. "A strange bird, our abbé," said Farah-Lajoie. "What kind of a priest would carry a gun?"

"Well," said Pigeon, climbing behind the wheel, "I don't think he liked you very much, either. When you went to the toilet—remember?—he said, 'I can read in that man's eyes, he is not a good Catholic, and he is also a flirt, a ladies' man. Isn't that so?'"

"Oh my," said Farah-Lajoie, stroking the points of his moustache, "I hope you agreed with him. I have my reputation to think of."

Back at the Sûreté office, the detective learned that a blood-stained cap answering the description of the one worn by Raoul Delorme had been found that morning in the street, not far from where the body was discovered. Beside it, the snow in the road was stained red. Several neighbors in the area, which was known for drinking, fights and prostitution, had come forward to say they had heard gunshots the night of the murder. But although a picture of Raoul was circulated widely throughout the city, no one in the following days reported having seen him at any local theater or restaurant the night of his disappearance, and none of his friends came forward.

Farah-Lajoie's investigations revealed that when Delorme Senior died in 1916, he had left a fortune worth $185,000, including twenty-one rental apartments or houses. The priest was the executor of the estate, but Raoul, who, unlike his brother, could be expected to produce children, would inherit the bulk of the estate when he reached twenty-five. The detective was also surprised to discover that, only a week before Raoul died, the priest had taken out a $25,000 life insurance policy on his brother's life and had split the sales commission with the agent. As to the priest's business methods, one large property owner told the police, "He has given us landlords a bad name."

Returning to the house on rue Saint-Hubert with more questions, Farah-Lajoie was surprised to find two uniformed officers posted at the door.

"Look, my friend," said the priest, after offering him the customary cigar. "Look at these terrible letters I have been receiving. They are accusing me of the vilest things, of killing my brother. I am afraid for my own life. That is why I asked your superiors for protection."

Had Raoul, Farah-Lajoie asked mildly, left a will? "I believe he wrote one last year when he had an operation for appendicitis," the priest replied vaguely.

"Could I see it?"

For once, the priest appeared flustered. "I don't know. I think it is still in Ottawa, at the college." He seemed more willing to talk about the grand preparations for Raoul's funeral the next day. "We are doing it with the greatest amount of pomp imaginable," he said. "You must come, Detective, and I am asking that for a special reason. Undoubtedly, there will be large crowds there, and I am quite sure Raoul's assassin will be among them. I implore you to watch carefully, because there might be an attack on my person."

The detective left, saying he would likely have to make a trip to Ottawa.

"I hope Raoul did not forget me in his will," said the priest, in what might have been a weak attempt at humor. "I was good to him."

Farah-Lajoie was glad afterwards that he had attended the funeral. It was, as the priest had promised, a sumptuous affair. There was no attack on the priest, and even though the Church of Saint-Jacques was packed, no suspicious characters were spotted. But what the detective noticed was the utter fervor with which l'abbé Delorme conducted the requiem mass, his voice sometimes choking. But afterwards, as he accepted condolences, the priest seemed quite himself again.

Less was learned on the trip to Ottawa. Raoul, said the Oblate Fathers at the university, had taken the will home with him at Christmas. But awaiting Farah-Lajoie in Montreal was more encouraging news. The owner of a gun store, Oscar Haynes, had volunteered the information that, on December 27, l'abbé Delorme had come to his store and exchanged an old Ivor Johnson revolver for a new Bayard automatic, and had bought two boxes of bullets for it. When Farah-Lajoie showed Haynes the priest's gun, he readily identified it as the one he had sold. The only difference, he said, was that when he sold it the gun was properly oiled, and now it was oiled excessively, as if by an amateur.

Back at his office that evening, Farah-Lajoie turned out the lights, lit a Pall Mall, put his feet on the desk and went over the facts as he had learned them. The following summer, Raoul would have been due to graduate and would have taken over the administration—and most of the profits—of the estate. Farah-Lajoie was certain now that the priest had lied about the gun and the will, and the bullets removed from Raoul's head had been identified as having been fired from the Bayard automatic.

The more the detective thought about events at the house on rue Saint-Hubert on the day of the murder, the more it seemed to him that, from start to finish, they had been orchestrated by l'abbé Delorme. The priest, who led a surprisingly active social life, had turned down several invitations that day. Considering it was the Day of Kings, a Quebec holiday, that was unusual. On the other hand, he had bought three theater tickets for a matinee performance for his sisters, and they had left the house after lunch. So the priest was the only one to see Raoul leave, if he did leave, at 2:30 P.M. Shortly after 5:00 P.M.—the time the pathologists estimated death had occurred—various people had seen the priest around the neighborhood, engaged on errands.

But what about the phone call the priest claimed to have received from Raoul at 7:00 sharp? Farah-Lajoie believed he knew the explanation for that. He had found a boyfriend of Florence's who said he had phoned Florence at that time. The priest answered the phone and told him she wasn't there and to call back in ten minutes or so. When he called back, the priest was all apologies. He had not realized it, but his sister was in the house all the time, he said. He would get her right away. It was after the first phone call, Farah-Lajoie conjectured, that the priest had put down the receiver and told his sisters in the other room that Raoul had called to say he wouldn't be home that night.

And the three phone calls in the night, which the sisters dimly remembered hearing? Farah-Lajoie had an explanation for those, too. It was possible, he had discovered, to use the sisters' telephone in the study to dial the priest's line so that the phone would ring in the bedroom upstairs. As for the priest's claim that he had complained to the telephone operator after the third call, none of the operators on duty that night could remember the complaint.

Suddenly it was daylight, and Farah-Lajoie's colleagues were coming noisily into the office. His ruminations, he discovered, had occupied him the whole night. "I didn't even have my breakfast coffee," he complained to Desgroseilliers. But he knew now what he had to do.

An inquest into the circumstances of Raoul's death had opened, but had then been adjourned to give the police more time to collect evidence. Now Farah-Lajoie went to the coroner, a man named McMahon, and laid out the facts as he knew them. They pointed, he said, to only one conclusion: that l'abbé Adélard Delorme should be arrested immediately for murder. McMahon, who had the power to issue the warrant, heard him out and then shook his head. "You know that you are dealing here with a priest. The evidence is only circumstantial. You'll need better proof than that."

The following day, l'abbé Delorme took the offensive. He announced to the press that he was offering a $10,000 reward for information leading to the arrest and conviction of his brother's murderer. He would even offer $25,000 if he thought it would help solve the case, he said. The priest assured reporters that he was offering the reward with the approval of the Sûreté, and that he was satisfied with the work of the detectives on the case. That didn't stop him from complaining privately to the reporters that he suspected Farah-Lajoie of stealing a coat from the house during the course of a search.

Two days later, as the case commanded more and more interest in newspapers throughout North America, the priest, in an interview published in *La Presse*, refuted rumors of his own involvement in his half-brother's death. "Is it reasonable I would have killed my brother when I have plenty of money?" he asked. "I want to see the killer caught and punished. I want revenge for the blood of my brother." Suddenly, the priest was seeing the police investigation as a plot against himself and the church.

"Let's arrest those dangerous people, those low people, the free-thinkers, the non-believers," he declared. But he was not surprised at the turn events had taken, he insisted. Jesus, who it was his privilege to represent, "suffered more than me."

L'affaire Delorme became the subject of a national debate, arousing fierce antipathies between Protestants and Catholics, and engaging the wits of private detectives, psychics and others claiming special knowledge. The priest did his best to stir the ferment by writing letters to the Minister of Justice in Ottawa, the Premier of Quebec and the newspapers, claiming that he was the victim of religious persecution.

Farah-Lajoie spent his days following up worthless tips and meaningless clues. The blood on the cap, which the priest had identified as belonging to his brother, was, in fact, human, but the "blood" on the road, to the amusement of newspaper readers, turned out to be horse urine. It was time for the detective and his colleagues to return to the house on rue Saint-Hubert, braving the priest's accusations.

They found him genial as ever, pressing his cigars on them and raising no objection when they asked to examine the automobile. This time, the officers found small, suspicious stains on two pillows in the back, as well as chicken feathers on the seat.

"Ah, those!" exclaimed the priest. "That was from the day I took a friend for a drive in the country and he bought some live chickens." The police took away the pillows and the feathers, which bore evidence of some sticky substance.

On a suitcase against the wall of the garage, Farah-Lajoie made a further discovery. Beneath a pile of dirty laundry, he found a small square of quilt material similar to the cloth found wrapped around Raoul's head. In the basement, he found string similar to that used to bind the dead man's hands.

Dr. Dérome's tests showed that the spots on the cushions were human blood, and the material and stitching of the quilt proved to be identical to the piece found with the body. The priest showed surprise when, the following day, Farah-Lajoie arrived at the house with Dr. Dérome, who said he wished to inspect the car personally. After finding suspicious spots on the upholstery, the doctor asked permission to take the seats away for tests—tests that would prove the further presence of human blood, although someone had tried to wash away the stains with soap.

"Every day you are taking something with you," said the priest, smiling as the car seats were carried away. "Eventually it will be my turn."

The priest's neighbors had all been away the day of the murder, but now Farah-Lajoie discovered a man who lived three doors away who remembered hearing the priest's car either entering or leaving the garage around nine o'clock and again around eleven o'clock that night. The priest had been quite definite in saying he hadn't used his car that day.

Now, finally, challenged by the coroner, l'abbé Delorme admitted that Raoul's will was lodged with a notary public in Montreal, although he objected to it being read out at the inquest because it would place him, he said, "in a peculiar position." The will, read nevertheless, named the priest as principal beneficiary.

Another part of the puzzle fell into place when a yellow envelope arrived at the office of the head of the provincial police. It contained the gold watch bearing the initials A.D. that the priest had loaned to Raoul the day he was killed. The watch was packed in a Pall Mall cigarette packet. The handwriting on the envelope, although disguised, was later identified as belonging to the priest.

As the coroner still hesitated over issuing a warrant, the Attorney General, the province's highest legal officer, finally intervened. But it was a reporter who arrived first at the priest's door with the news that he was about to be arrested.

"Are you crazy?" cried the priest wildly. "Don't they know this is a cassock and that as a priest I am protected?" Then he became coldly calm. "Let them come and arrest me," he said. "I had a gun in the car, yes, but I also have one here in the house. Believe me," he said confidentially to the journalist, "I have my agents, too, working for me. My boys are with me."

Alarmed, the reporter informed the authorities that the priest might be dangerous. To allay his suspicions, Chief Lepage of the Sûreté called the priest and invited him to his office, "to clear up a few questions." When he arrived, Lepage assured him it was a ploy to protect him from those who might attack him. The priest was calm as he was led into the final session of the coroner's inquest, which ended with a recommendation from the jury that the priest should be arrested for the murder of his half-brother. He merely gave a disgusted smile as he was led from the courtroom, flanked by police officers.

The next day, following a court appearance, it fell to Farah-Lajoie to drive the priest to the Bordeaux Jail, accompanied by Pigeon and another detective, Rioux. The priest was in mischievous mood. "Hey," he said to Rioux, "Didn't I see you on a certain evening recently with a woman, let's say, of some style. You know what I am talking about?" Rioux blushed beet red.

"So, Farah-Lajoie," he said, turning to the detective, "Here we are, you and me!" He gave the officer a thump on the back that suggested anger more than affection, then peered into his face. "Aren't you frightened?"

Farah-Lajoie gripped the wheel tightly. "No," he said, "I am not frightened."

The detective, after all, had won—hadn't he?

✖

When the trial opened on June 9, 1922, the defense made an immediate attempt to have the priest declared insane. The priest contributed to this impression by flourishing a bright silk handkerchief, laughing loudly at times and at others muttering to himself, "Bibi [his nickname for himself] has his cassock. Bibi has his cassock."

After a procession of psychiatrists trooped into the witness box to claim that the priest was unbalanced, the jury took only ten minutes to concur, and the priest was transferred from the Bordeaux Jail to the Asylum of Saint-Michael at Beauport.

And that would have been the end of the story—if not for the fact that, very soon afterwards, the priest made an application to the courts to regain control of the family estate, backing his demand with a certificate from the asylum's superintendent declaring that he was now sane. This was too much for the provincial government, and the priest was ordered to stand trial again for the murder of Raoul.

In court, he was jovial as ever and sucked pink-and-white peppermints throughout the proceedings. The evidence was damning: a witness had been found who claimed to have seen the priest returning home in his car at midnight on the night of the murder, and an examination of the estate books showed that $14,000 was missing. The chief justice of Quebec, Sir Francis Lemieux, who presided, delivered a powerful indictment of the accused. "All men are equal before the law. You must have courage," he told the jury. "Justice must be vindicated."

It was all in vain. The jury ended up hopelessly split, ten for conviction and two stubbornly against. A third trial ended with a similar result. It was clear that, in a heavily Catholic province, there would always be jurors unwilling to convict a priest, no matter how suggestive the evidence. By the time of the fourth and final trial, the provincial government had clearly given up any hope of convicting l'abbé Delorme, and after a token prosecution, he was this time found not guilty.

We need not be as squeamish. What really happened that night of January 7, 1922? If Raoul had survived only a few more months, his brother would have had to hand over their father's estate, and all the perquisites of wealth that went with it, and return to being a humble priest. But his brother's death would bring him, the police estimated, $180,000. He had plotted the murder for some time. The easiest thing, he had decided, would be to stage an apparent suicide. It was certainly not unheard of for a young student to blow his brains out in a fit of depression. And if it were suicide, there was no problem with using the priest's recently purchased Bayard automatic.

As Farah-Lajoie reconstructed the crime in a small memoir he wrote on the case, Raoul would have been sitting, likely smoking his pipe, in his study on the second floor, perhaps listening to gramophone music, as he often did. The priest came up behind him and, with a sudden movement, clamped an ether-soaked rag over his face. Almost in the same moment, he held the revolver to Raoul's temple and fired.

His scheme would have succeeded—except for one detail. The Bayard has a peculiarity in that the barrel is three-quarters of an inch below the line of sight. Instead of penetrating the brain, the bullet smashed into the jaw, where, in fact, two bullets were found.

Raoul grasped instinctively for the gun, and a desperate struggle ensued. The priest knew if he faltered he was lost. He fired wildly and repeatedly. Only after the sixth shot was Raoul still. But now the suicide plot was useless. Who ever killed himself with six bullets? The priest had to think quickly, had to somehow come up with a new scheme to account for his brother's death.

He saw immediately that the first requirement was that Raoul's body must be found elsewhere. He fetched his brother's overcoat, put it on him, then brought the quilting and bound up the profoundly bleeding head. He may have used the sheets from Raoul's bed to wrap the body or to clean up, because the sheets were found to be damp the next day after being washed. Undoubtedly, he tied Raoul's hands in the garage to make transportation of the body easier.

Now the priest attended to his alibi, making sure he was seen outside the house by several people shortly after 5:00 P.M. When the godsend call came from Florence's boyfriend at 7:00, the priest improvised brilliantly to convince his sisters that Raoul was alive and well at that time. By 8:45, when the sisters again went out, it was time for the priest to go to work.

Farah-Lajoie hypothesized that, to keep Raoul's blood from dripping onto the car's upholstery, the priest had propped up the body in the back seat with cushions and, garbed in his raccoon coat, had climbed into the front like any chauffeur driving his master. As an area where thieves and murderers operated freely, Notre Dame de Grâce was the ideal district to dump the body. He returned home around 11:00 P.M. and when his sisters arrived home, staged the clever telephone charade throughout the night to add a hint of mystery and intrigue to the story.

Considering how little time he had to concoct the scheme, and the panic any normal person would feel at the sight of the bloodied body lying on the carpet, the priest's performance was remarkable. Small wonder he forgot a few details, like the overshoes, the bullet through the overcoat and the fact that the body, having already chilled, would not melt the snow beneath it.

At any rate, he ultimately won his duel with Detective Farah-Lajoie. After being found not guilty, he was relieved of his religious duties and was assigned by his superiors to an institute for deaf-mutes. There, free at last from accusations and gossip—at least from his mute companions—he administered his substantial holdings, even adding to them by taking an insurance company to court and forcing it to pay up on the $25,000 insurance policy he had taken out on Raoul's life.

It would be nice to think that the priest felt at least a crumb of remorse every January as the anniversary of Raoul's death approached. Because on January 20, 1942, just past the twentieth anniversary of his brother's death, the priest, then fifty-seven, was found lying on the floor of his study, bleeding from the mouth after suffering a seizure. He died shortly thereafter.

And the house on rue Saint-Hubert? It stood in reduced circumstances until 1988, when, following a fire, it was demolished.

Murder at the Savoy

P.D. James, the grande dame of British mystery writing, believes that one body on the drawing-room floor is more horrible and a lot more interesting than a dozen bullet-ridden corpses down Raymond Chandler's mean city streets. What arouses our interest, she suggests, is the "contrast between order, normality, hierarchy and the dreadful and contaminating irruption of violent death."

Ms. James might have had in mind the shooting of Prince Ali Kemal Fahmy Bey, which occurred one sweltering summer night in 1923 in the Savoy Hotel in London, the British empire's high temple of order and decorum at that point in history. And for a heroine of the story, not even Ms. James could have imagined anyone more fascinating than Madame Fahmy, a French woman who proved to be so impressive in the witness box that she won a nation's heart and its approval for her act of homicide.

The suite where it happened—one of the hotel's most elegant, overlooking the River Thames—is still very much as it was then, although when I visited it I found no musty reminders of past misdeeds. Instead, as the door swung open, I was met by the springtime fragrance of an English cottage garden. The source was immediately obvious: in the entrance to this suite, where many of the world's wealthiest people and some of the biggest names in show business have stayed, stood a vast bunch of spring flowers, delicate narcissi dancing between tulips big as teacups.

In the early hours of July 10, 1923, another large bouquet, this time of pink roses, was framed by the tall windows to this honey-colored, paneled drawing room, and beyond was the panorama of the River Thames—coal black barges, busy tugboats and, above, a watercolor gray sky. From these windows that night in 1923, the view must have been stupendous. Following days of sweltering heat, London was experiencing the most frightening thunderstorm of a generation. Black thunderheads rolled down the river from the direction of Kingston, thunderclaps set the windows shaking, and again and again the sky was split by ghastly sheets of blue lightning.

But between the peals of thunder, John Beattie, a porter wheeling a cart of luggage down the plush-carpeted hall at 2:30 in the morning, heard unmistakably the sound of three gunshots. Dashing back down the corridor and coming around the corner, he came upon Prince Ali Kemal Fahmy Bey, slim, handsome, immensely rich and only twenty-two, dying of gunshot wounds outside the door of his suite. Standing over him in a shimmering white, low-cut evening dress, now splattered with blood, and holding a Browning .25 automatic pistol, was his French wife, Marguerite Fahmy.

"What have I done?" she cried repeatedly in French before throwing the gun down beside her expiring husband. And then, going down on her knees, "Speak to me, speak to me."

Only moments before, Beattie had come across the prince in a state of agitation in the hallway outside his door. "Look at my face! Look what she has done!" he told the startled porter, pointing to a slight pink mark on his cheek. At that point, his wife had come out of the suite and started berating her husband in French, pointing to her eyes. Beattie, as best he could, had urged them to be quiet and return to their suite before they wakened other guests. He had trundled his wagon only a few steps down the hall when he heard a whistle and, looking around, saw Prince Fahmy trying to coax their small dog, which had escaped through the open door, back into the suite.

If the murder had occurred in working-class Whitechapel, just across the river, it would have been written off as "a domestic" and dismissed in a few lines in the following day's newspapers. But this was a high-society murder with exotic foreign overtones. Better still, as the case unfolded, there were delicious hints of sexual depravity, and if that weren't enough, the British public found in Madame Fahmy a touching and attractive heroine, a woman the newspapers would call "The Tragic Princess."

Sir Edward Marshall Hall, one of England's most famous legal counselors, would capitalize on this natural sympathy to conduct a defense that, by the lights of that day, was considered brilliant, but that by modern standards has to be counted as the nastiest piece of racist demagoguery ever to disgrace a British courtroom. It prompted a protest from the Egyptian government of the day, although little satisfaction was gained. That's not to say that Prince Fahmy was an endearing character. He was a spoiled playboy who treated women with violence and contempt. But it's hard to avoid the conclusion that his wife had long intended to murder him and was only waiting for a suitable chance.

Prince Fahmy inherited a fortune of something like $5 million—

an unimaginable sum in those days—when his father, an Egyptian cotton magnate, died while the boy was still at school. The youngest of four children, with a Caucasian mother and three older sisters, Ali (who, in letters to friends, signed himself with the nickname boys at his English public school had given him: "Baba") had been spoiled rotten at home. After his mother died when he was seventeen, he was free to run wild, and was soon in the hands of blackmailers. Wiser heads in the family rescued him from embarrassment, persuaded him to set aside sizable chunks of his income for the education of the poor, and employed Said Enani, an official working with the Egyptian Ministry of the Interior, to be his secretary-keeper.

Marriage, his relations thought, might settle Ali down, but he was not interested in any of the demure and well-connected young women of Cairo that they had in mind. He was looking for someone more exotic, and at a reception in Cairo in January 1922, he met a French woman of obvious style and charm who was visiting the Egyptian capital. Marguerite Alibert, the woman he would marry, claimed afterwards that he had immediately offered to put on a Venetian fête for her, but that she had coldly turned him down before leaving a day or two later for Paris.

If she intended to catch him, she could not have baited the hook better. By July, when she was staying at her house by the sea in Deauville, Ali was in Paris, and this time his methods were more subtle. Marguerite found herself befriended by a woman from Morocco who, after they returned to Paris, phoned her to say there was a man she simply must meet. Intrigued, she agreed to meet her friend for tea at the Majestic Hotel—and found herself looking into Prince Ali's expressive brown eyes.

As they left together for the fashionable Château Madrid restaurant, Ali tried to impress her with a bit of princely showing off. Which car would she care to travel in, he asked, with an airy wave at the two automobiles parked at the curb, the Rolls Royce coupe or the sporty open Torpedo? Marguerite was not easily intimidated. She let him know that she owned her own lavish apartment on the avenue Henri Martin, had her own car, and employed two maids and a chauffeur.

It's easy to understand why Ali was infatuated with her, showered her with jewelry and even bought her a car she obviously did not need. Marguerite, tiny with huge dark eyes, represented to Ali the sophistication of Paris, and the fact that she was divorced and ten years older than him only made her appear that much more intriguing.

By the time she returned to Deauville in mid-August, Ali was making what she would call *"des advances furieuses."* Rejected once again, he got his secretary, Enani, a neat little man who wore Western suits, to pitch Marguerite the alluring song of Ali's immense fortune. She finally agreed to let Ali accompany her to Biarritz in September, not, she claimed, because of the diamonds from Cartier or the bracelet of coral and emeralds he lavished on her, but simply because she liked his smile, "which was like that of a child."

They dined in the best restaurants and went on excursions to Spain, but still Marguerite refused to commit herself, and Ali left for Italy, from which he bombarded her with passionate letters. When he got home to Cairo, he declared in a letter that she was "the torch of my life," and said his only thoughts were for "your bewitching charm, your exquisite delicacy, the beauty of your heart." He signed his letters "your faithful little Baba." She succumbed and agreed to meet him in Egypt only when he announced he had fallen ill. "I am dying," he declared. "Your name alone is on my lips."

When she arrived in Alexandria on November 22, the Ali who came bounding aboard the ship to meet her showed no signs of ill health. She, in turn, showed no surprise. In Cairo, he installed her in his palace, the interior a copy of Fontainebleau, her room specially designed for an earlier guest, the king of Serbia. There were so many gold cigarette cases lying around, she would write later, "that they got in the way." Her safety was assured by the presence of twelve black servants in uniforms bearing Ali's stylized monogram—servants she would soon view as her jailers.

For now, though, Marguerite felt as if she had wandered into the *Arabian Nights*. Her charm overcame the objections of Ali's sisters, and she finally agreed to marry him—but not without proper caution. She made a stipulation in the marriage contract that, although she would wear the black veil of a Moslem bride for the ceremony, there would be no purdah for this daughter of the Champs Élysée, and she secured Ali's agreement that, contrary to the usual Moslem custom, she would have the right to divorce him if the marriage did not work out.

The civil ceremony took place on December 26. But in the course of the religious ceremony that followed, Marguerite discovered that Ali had pulled a fast one and that she would not, after all, be granted the right to seek a divorce. The guests waited uncomfortably on their antique gilt chairs while the bride and groom and their respective advisers went into lengthy negotiations. After four hours, the deal was set. Marguerite would give up her right to divorce in return for a lavish gift and Ali's promise of undying fidelity. For her, it turned out to be a poor bargain.

Perhaps it was the note of acrimony that crept into the prenuptial negotiations, or perhaps it was the unconventional sexual demands Ali put on his bride, but never was a honeymoon so short-lived. After a banquet at Shepherd's Hotel, the couple boarded Ali's yacht, which had a crew of twenty-five, for a honeymoon cruise up the Nile to Luxor, where the world's attention was focused on the November 4 discovery by Lord Carnarvon of the burial chamber and treasure of King Tutankhamen.

Marguerite was making her own discoveries. No neophyte in sexual matters, she was still shocked when she found that Ali's interest in her was confined to acts of sodomy. It was a blow to her self-esteem. She, the sought-after darling of the Paris salons, realized that her husband saw her as no more desirable than the pretty youths he bantered with, and whose significance now became apparent.

Almost immediately, Marguerite and Ali were having furious arguments in public and slapping each others' faces. After one row, Ali forbade her to go ashore and left his uniformed guards to see she didn't escape.

It would not be long before photographs of Marguerite wearing the latest fashions would be emblazoned on front pages all over Europe and North America as the central figure in a notorious murder trial, but Ali had his own ideas about taking her picture. In the Valley of the Kings, he got her to climb into an ancient sarcophagus, close her eyes and cross her hands in the style, perhaps, of Cleopatra. The theme of entombment depicted in the photograph may have been more than symbolic: a few days later, Marguerite sent a document to her lawyer in Paris that, she instructed him, should only be opened in the case of her death or disappearance. In it, she declares: "I, Marie Marguerite Alibert, of full age, of sound mind and body, formally accuse in the case of my death by violence Ali Fahmy Bey of having contributed to my disappearance." The day before, January 21, 1923, he had sworn on the Koran to kill her, she claimed. The reason, she would explain later, was that she was refusing to return to him some of the jewelry he had given her earlier.

Around the same time, Ali, displaying his spiteful sense of humor, was writing to Marguerite's sister: "Ha, ha, ha, just now I am engaged in taming her. Yesterday, to begin, I did not come in to lunch or dinner, and I also left her at the theater. This will teach her, I hope, to respect my wishes. With women one must act with energy and be severe." His "energy" included punching his wife and dislocating her jaw when she returned from a solitary visit to the cinema.

However cynical Marguerite's reasons for marrying Ali may have been, she now faced a terrifying future. Subjected to violence by her husband, watched over by a new Algerian bodyguard she called the Black Hercules, and far from her friends, she was little more than a prisoner. And then, unexpectedly, the door of her prison opened. Ali, without telling his wife, had accepted a diplomatic post with the Egyptian embassy in Paris. Even as they boarded ship for Marseilles, he gave her no hint of their destination, and on board the conflict continued, with Ali at one point locking her in her cabin for twenty-four hours.

But once they were back in her beloved Paris, even with the bodyguard lurking nearby, Marguerite was free to see her friends again, go riding and attend the theater. Now here is the surprising thing: considering the treatment she had received, the death threat she claimed her husband had made against her, the most natural thing in the world would have been for Marguerite Fahmy to leave her husband and sue for divorce. It's hard to believe she did not, in fact, consult her lawyer and, discovering the difficulties in the way of getting a divorce and a decent settlement, set her mind to alternative ways out of her predicament.

On July 1, Prince Ali Fahmy Bey, exhausted with the diplomatic round in Paris, traveled with his wife and an entourage that included a valet, two maids and the ever-present Said Enani to

London, where he proposed to holiday at the Savoy Hotel. The journey must have been an uncomfortable one for Marguerite, because the first thing she did on arrival was have the hotel front desk summon Dr. Edward Gordon, who had his office across the Strand, to examine her for a painful and particularly unglamorous complaint: hemorrhoids, a condition she believed was connected to her husband's sexual demands.

Dr. Gordon, not one to neglect a wealthy patient, visited her every day for the next eight days, prescribing medications and finally bringing in a specialist, who, on the morning of July 9— Ali Fahmy's last full day alive—suggested she enter his nursing home for an operation.

It was to be a day full of tensions, mysteries and flare-ups. Sometime that morning, Marguerite received an anonymous note in French warning her not to return to Egypt lest she be poisoned or otherwise killed in what might appear to be an accident. "Remain in Paris with those who love you and will protect you," it concluded.

At lunch, Ali and Marguerite argued furiously over the proposed operation. Enani would say that Marguerite wanted to return to Paris to have the procedure performed, while her husband wanted her to enter an English nursing home as the specialist had suggested. Was Enani being entirely frank? In a note Marguerite wrote to Dr. Gordon after lunch, but for some reason did not send, she wrote, "Doctor, Things have come to a crisis. My husband refused to take the responsibility for my operation. I am therefore returning to my family—that is to say, tomorrow I leave for Paris." She concluded, "Will you please pay the specialist for his trouble? This account is a personal one."

Against this tense background, on that airless and humid evening, Prince Ali prepared to enjoy what he had planned as one of the highlights of his London visit: a box at Daly's Theatre in Leicester Square to see *The Merry Widow*. We can only imagine the effort it took Ali, Marguerite and the inevitable Enani to maintain their smiles and civilized small talk as they gazed down at the lesser mortals in the pit.

But as soon as they returned to the Savoy, open hostilities were resumed. Marguerite twice refused to dance with her husband in the Savoy Grill and was heard to threaten to smash a bottle of champagne over his head. When the obsequious orchestra conductor asked Madame if there was a piece of music she would like to hear, she replied in French that she was simply not in the mood for music because, "My husband is going to kill me tonight." With that tact for which the Savoy is famous, the conductor replied that he hoped to see Madame in the best of health tomorrow.

There is evidence that, as Marguerite went up to their fourth-floor suite, Ali took a cab to Soho. His purpose is unknown, but if he was in search of vice, there was no shortage in that colorful quarter of London. At any rate, he could not have stayed long, because when John Beattie saw him in the corridor it was 2:30 A.M., and at that time he was wearing mauve silk pajamas and backless green velvet slippers. Moments later, his blood was staining the Savoy's broadloom and, according to the evidence from the autopsy, bullets from his wife's revolver, one of a matched pair they kept beside their bed for security, had smashed through his upraised arms before penetrating his skull.

As lightning and thunder created a scene of Wagnerian drama, Marguerite sobbed to Arthur Mariani, the night manager, who had hurried to the scene, "I have been married six months and I have suffered terribly." Dr. Gordon, always nearby when comfort was needed for the comfortably off, would say that Madame Fahmy, in her agitated state, told him her husband had threatened to smash her head in and that, back at the suite, he had threatened her again and she had fired the pistol through the window to warn him off. When he later advanced on her again, she told the doctor, she had fired the gun at him, believing it was unloaded now and not realizing a fresh bullet would automatically drop into the firing chamber. When Ali slumped over, she thought he was shamming, lost her head and fired two more shots. Dr. Gordon noted that his patient had a scratch on the back of her neck that might have been made with a fingernail.

The trial of Madame Fahmy (she was not entitled to use the title Princess), which began at Number One Court at the Old Bailey on September 10, attracted worldwide attention. The accused was represented by three of the most expensive lawyers in England, led by the redoubtable Sir Edward Marshall Hall, while the Fahmy family interests were represented by several Egyptian lawyers. Women spectators, who made up a large part of the crowd in the public gallery, leaned forward eagerly as Madame Fahmy, a tiny figure in a black fur coat—the weather had long since turned cool—and a small cloche hat with a veil, asked how she pleaded, replied in a low voice, *"Non coupable"*—not guilty.

The defense had spent money unstintingly in digging into the prince's background, and as Said Enani took the witness stand for the prosecution, two very elegant young Egyptians, supposedly intimates of Ali's brought specially from Cairo, sat prominently at the defense table. They never testified, but the unspoken message conveyed to Enani was that if his testimony strayed too far from the facts, witnesses could be produced to straighten the record. Even so, Enani's memory of threats Ali was supposed to have made against his wife proved spotty. He did admit that his employer frequently quarreled with women and that Ali and Marguerite had come to blows.

After producing a cartoon from an Egyptian satirical magazine showing Enani in a romantic pose with his employer, Marshall Hall made this final statement to the witness: "I suggest that the association between yourself and Fahmy was notorious in Egypt!"

"That is not so," the secretary replied coolly.

The crowds that waited sometimes from two in the morning to gain admission were, of course, waiting to hear Madame Fahmy testify. On the day she was to take the stand, the prosecutor, Percival Clarke, with the jury absent, asked permission of the judge to question the accused woman about her past. "I want to prove," he said, "that she associated with men from an early age, and that she is a woman of the world in the widest sense. I submit that I am entitled to ask her how she treated other men. I do not want it to be thought that all the fault is on her husband's side." The public gallery that day was with Clarke to a man—or rather, a woman. But they were to be disappointed: the judge, Mr. Justice Rigby Swift, tersely refused permission for a prosecution fishing trip. Marguerite Fahmy, frail-looking and leaning on a wardress, then made her way to the witness box. Testifying in French, some of her words translated by a young woman barrister brought over from Paris by the defense, she told the unhappy story of her brief marriage, sobbing frequently. The last tragic night, she testified, "He said, 'I will kill you,' and crouched to spring. I lifted my arm, so... I did not know how many times the pistol went off. I did not know what had happened. I saw him on the floor and knelt down beside him. I caught hold of his hand and said, 'Sweetheart, it is nothing, speak to me!'" At that point, Madame Fahmy broke into helpless weeping.

Under Clarke's aggressive questioning, though, she showed no lack of mental adroitness.

"Can I correctly describe you as a woman of the world?" he asked, getting to his feet.

"I have had experience of it," she replied carefully.

"Did you go to Egypt with the idea of living with him or marrying him?"

The warm brown eyes looked suddenly helpless. "I had decided nothing. I loved him so very much and wished to be with him. I accepted to be his *amie*."

Why hadn't she left her abusive husband when she had a chance in Paris?

"Where would I have gone?" she asked.

"You had a flat in Paris."

"He would have fetched me back from there the minute he returned."

"Haven't you many friends in Paris of influence and wealth?"

"I did not want my friends to know my sorrow," she said softly.

Had she hated her husband?

Dangerous ground here. Madame Fahmy paused, and then gave the absolutely correct answer: "I did not hate him. I only hated the things he wanted me to do."

With a master stroke, Marshall Hall waited until re-examination before introducing the explosive letter Madame Fahmy had sent her lawyer from Egypt regarding the death threat allegedly sworn by her husband on the Koran. Marshall Hall's technique from his opening speech had been, in effect, to put Prince Ali on trial and thus divert attention from his client's possible failings. "Fahmy Bey," he had thundered at the start of the trial, "shortly before he was shot, attacked his wife like a raving, lustful beast because she would not agree to an outrageous suggestion he made—a suggestion which would fill every decent-minded person with utter revulsion. Almost throughout their miserably tragic life of six months, this treacherous Egyptian beast pursued his wife with this unspeakable request, and because she—immoral though she may have been—resisted him, he heaped cruelty and brutality on her until she was changed, by fear, from a charming, attractive woman to a poor, quaking creature, hovering on the brink of nervous ruin."

Strong stuff, but the great defender saved his worst vitriol for his summation, which one writer has called "the greatest defending speech of his life," but which appealed in the baldest terms to the racial prejudices of the English jury. Madame Fahmy, he said quietly, "made one great mistake—possibly the greatest mistake any woman of the West can make. She married an Oriental. I dare say," he went on, "the Egyptian civilization is one of the oldest and most wonderful in the world. I do not say that among the Egyptians there are not many magnificent and splendid men. But if you strip off the external civilization of the Oriental, you have the real Oriental underneath. And it is common knowledge that the Oriental's treatment of women does not fit in with the way the Western woman considers she should be treated by her husband."

Now Marshall Hall advanced on the jury box, inviting the jurors to picture that terrible thunderstorm the night of the murder. "Imagine its effect on a woman of nervous temperament who had been living such a life as she had lived for the last six months—outraged, abused, beaten, degraded. In sheer desperation, as he crouched for the last time"—and Marshall Hall matched his words by crouching with the revolver in his hand—"crouched like an animal, like an Oriental, retired for the last time to get a bound forward, she turned the pistol and put it to his face. And, to her horror—the thing went off!" With these words, the lawyer, defying every consideration of safety, swung the gun until it pointed at the jury and then, for maximum impact, dropped it clattering to the floor.

He concluded his astonishing performance by reminding the jury, which included two women, of a popular novel of the time, *Bella Donna* by Robert Hichens, in which the heroine marries a man of the desert. "You will remember the final scene, where the woman goes out of the gates of the garden into the dark night of the desert." At that moment, a shaft of sunlight pierced the gloomy courtroom. Marshall Hall, not one to ignore a godsend, held his hand up as if bathing in the light. "I ask you to open the gate and let this Western woman go back into the light of God's great Western sun," he cried.

It was useless for Percival Clarke to point out that the heroine of *Bella Donna* had tried to murder her husband, useless for him to remind the jury that it was Madame Fahmy who was on trial, not her late husband. It took the jury only an hour to arrive at the verdict: not guilty. The cheering was so unrestrained that the judge had to order the courtroom cleared of spectators before discharging the prisoner.

The verdict, of course, had little to do with the facts of the case. My feeling is that Marguerite Fahmy had decided some time before that she would never return to Egypt with her obnoxious husband. And, as a widow, she was much more likely to collect her winnings than she was as a divorcee.

The scenes in the Savoy Grill, the note to the doctor—only handed to him when he attended her after the shooting—and the timing of the shooting, with a porter conveniently near at hand to witness their last row, all suggest careful stage-managing. If

Fahmy was about to spring on her, how was it that he was shot in the corridor and not in the suite? And is it likely that a man whistling for his dog would, no more than a minute later, become a ravening monster who must be shot down?

What was the evidence about Marguerite Fahmy's past that Percival Clarke was prevented from introducing? In a London newspaper morgue, I came across galley proofs of an article entitled "Life of Mme. Fahmy," unpublished then perhaps for libel reasons. Marguerite Alibert was the daughter of a cab driver and a laundress. Strikingly beautiful, she was by the age of sixteen already a cocotte, earning her living from men, and soon became the mistress of a department store owner. He was the first of a series of lovers, many of them wealthy foreigners visiting Paris, who paid handsomely for her favors. She was married briefly to an Alsace businessman, Frederick Muller, and to another store owner named Laurent, and she had a daughter who, at the time of the trial, was attending boarding school in England. A young Mexican mining heir, a former Turkish ambassador with whom she lived in Cairo for three months, and an Egyptian general all figured in her life before she met Ali Fahmy Bey.

Following her acquittal, Marguerite returned to her flat on avenue Henri Martin, and she later starred in a movie in which she played the part of an Egyptian wife—this time wearing a Moslem veil. Meanwhile, her lawyers had commenced a lengthy battle in the Cairo courts over her widow's inheritance, which Fahmy's relatives were, understandably, contesting. At one point, Marguerite was involved in a crooked scheme cooked up by a Cairo businessman that would have seen her faking a pregnancy and supposedly having the child, which would afterwards be reported as having died. Under Egyptian law, her right to inherit would have been stronger if she could claim she had had a child by Fahmy.

In 1930, after a six-year court battle, Marguerite lost the last roll of the dice. The Cairo court ruled that, as she had shot her husband, she had no right to his fortune, which was then estimated at $7 million. It had all been for nothing.

Excuse Fingers

"Our bedroom, you see, was once the day nursery," Martin Beales explained. "And soon after we moved in here, I woke up one night with a start. I could hear a child crying, 'Daddy, Daddy!' And my eyes watered."

We were having lunch in the big, bright kitchen of Mayfield. The door of the larder, where Major Herbert Rowse Armstrong is supposed to have spread the arsenic on the scone, was open. The drawing room, where he is said to have handed the scone to fellow solicitor Oswald Martin with the immortal words "Excuse fingers" is almost unchanged. And climbing the wide staircase and entering the wing at the back of the house, where the nursery was, I too find myself listening for some echo of the inexpressible anguish the three Armstrong children must have felt when they discovered their father had been executed—the only British lawyer ever to hang—after being found guilty of poisoning their mother.

Murders sometimes cast their spell over us. They are events of such personal and particular violence that they seem to reach out to us, even generations after the crime. I have often felt this when visiting the scenes of notorious murders, but never in quite the way Martin Beales has.

When Beales moved to Hay-on-Wye, the little Welsh-English border town now famous for its second-hand bookstores, he had never heard of Major Herbert Rowse Armstrong, the killer who made the town's name familiar around the world in the early 1920s. So it meant nothing to Beales, when he articled to a Hay-on-Wye solicitor in January 1977, that the practice had once belonged to Major Armstrong. When Beales and his wife, Noelle, rented the renovated schoolhouse, they didn't realize it was the site of the inquest into the death of the major's wife, Katharine. And when, looking for a place with a paddock where their horse could graze, they bought Church Cottage, they didn't have a clue that it had witnessed one of the eeriest scenes in modern crime detection.

Beales became a junior partner in the practice and found himself assigned Armstrong's old swivel chair and glass-topped desk, both of which he was still using when I met him. By this time, he was familiar with the Armstrong case. Mayfield, the gloomy late-Victorian house that had belonged to Major Armstrong, had by then sunk into disrepair. The gate was always closed, the house was usually in darkness, and most people thought it was empty. Beales learned, though, from a British Broadcasting Corporation interviewer who had just come from the house, that the reclusive couple who lived there was thinking of selling. "We're bound to live there, then," said Beales flatly. How so? "It's fate," he said.

Beales let the couple know he was interested. Eighteen months later, the woman came to his office and said they wanted a smaller place. They'd like to swap Mayfield for Church Cottage, with a cash adjustment, of course. Beales, who had given up smoking, went into the next office and lit a cigarette. Noelle

Beales, with three small children, was not excited at the prospect—until she saw the house.

"This house embraced us," she told me, as she got lunch ready. "I think the spirit of the house has overcome anything that happened here. It was waiting for us to make it into a real family home again. It just seems to enjoy having the kids roller skating in the hall and sliding down the banisters."

Guests are sometimes hesitant about sleeping in the big front room where Katharine Armstrong died, but the children refer to it dismissively as "the dead woman's room," and aren't a bit intimidated. And the dandelions, which Major Armstrong tried to kill with arsenic, are as persistent as ever on what used to be the tennis court.

"But what's the purpose of it?" said Beales, who owns a strongbox filled with documents from the case. "Why has all this happened to us? Why? What are we supposed to do?" Beales answered his own question by writing a book, published in 1995 and titled *Dead Not Buried*, in which he challenged the guilty verdict delivered against the major.

If there is a starting point to the story, I suppose it occurred in May 1919, when Major Armstrong came marching home to Hay from the Great War (in which he had filled administrative jobs on the home front), ready to pick up the threads of his law practice and resume life with Katharine and their three children. Before he went away, Armstrong had led a dog's life, henpecked and abused by the forbidding Mrs. Armstrong, who, even in her wedding picture, looks like one of those stern Victorian missionaries sent out to cow the savages. "Bath night!" she had declared once at a tennis match, and poor Armstrong had gone home with his tail between his legs.

During the war, Armstrong had tasted a different life, which involved smoking—something he was allowed to do only in one room in the house—drinking in the mess, and even having an innocuous affair with a woman named Marion Gale. If he thought life would be different now, he was quickly disabused. "No wine for the major!" Katharine would bark down the table at dinner parties, and he accustomed himself once again to being told off in front of the servants.

If the major, a tiny, precise figure with waxed moustaches who walked everywhere through Hay's narrow ancient streets, seethed inwardly, he showed nothing of it. His behavior in public toward his wife was impeccable.

But the very month Armstrong came home, Katharine went to see Dr. Thomas Hincks, complaining of pain in her shoulder and right arm and numbness in her fingers. On August 20, 1920, Dr. Hincks was surprised to find her showing signs of mental deterioration. Her speech was affected, and she had delusions, blaming herself for being unkind to her children and cheating tradespeople. She was afraid she would be arrested.

Major Armstrong immediately wired her sister, Bessie Friend, and an old family friend, a solicitor named Arthur Chevalier, who both hurried to Hay. After another doctor gave a second opinion, it was decided to commit Katharine Armstrong to a private asylum, of which Dr. Arthur Townsend was medical superintendent. Doctors at the asylum were puzzled that Mrs. Armstrong, in addition to running a high temperature, was experiencing pain in her arms and legs. Finally, they gave her a tonic that contained minute amounts of arsenic for a month, and her condition, both mental and physical, steadily improved.

By January 1921, Armstrong, through Hincks, was urging that his wife should be allowed to return home. Townsend resisted, arguing that she wasn't yet well enough. He suggested she be allowed home on trial, so that she could be returned quickly if she had a relapse, but Armstrong insisted on a full discharge for his wife.

Katharine could not walk very well, but seemed pleased to be home. Then, a couple of days later, she asked the nurse Armstrong had retained whether throwing oneself from the attic window would be sufficient to cause death. On January 27, Major Armstrong sent for Eve Allen, an experienced mental-health nurse, who arrived the same night and remained with Mrs. Armstrong around the clock. By February 11, visitors reported that she was looking wasted and wan, and Dr. Hincks, calling that day, found that she had lost some of her coordination and that her peculiar high-stepping walking gait had returned. A few days later, after taking a Sunday lunch of mutton and vegetables with pudding and preserved gooseberries, she vomited and was put to bed.

By February 16, when Dr. Hincks called again, her condition was serious; she was running a high temperature, was complaining of abdominal pain and was unable to keep her food down. By the morning of February 22, she had lost consciousness, and Dr. Hincks, who had been making daily visits, told Armstrong she would not last the day. The major asked Hincks to give him a lift to the office, as he had a lot of work to do. Mrs. Armstrong died soon after nine that morning.

On the death certificate, Dr. Hincks listed gastritis, heart disease and nephritis as the causes of death, and Katharine Armstrong was buried in the churchyard at Cusop Church, where the major frequently read the lessons.

In 1917, while her husband was away on service, Mrs. Armstrong had carefully drawn up a will in which she left £50 each to her sister and Arthur Chevalier and a small annuity to

Emily Pearce, her elderly housekeeper. The major was to receive £50 a year until 1933, and thereafter £100 a year. The balance of her estate would go to her children when they came of age.

At the funeral, Armstrong mentioned to Chevalier that the previous summer, just before she was being committed to the asylum, Katharine had written a new will. Under its terms, the major would receive all her money. The earlier will was in Mrs. Armstrong's handwriting. The new one, when it was presented, was in the major's handwriting and had been witnessed by Emily Pearce and Lily Candy, a maid at the house.

Mrs. Armstrong's death aroused comment and gossip around town. John F. Davies, the town pharmacist, was particularly suspicious. Since 1913, he had been selling the major large amounts of arsenic to kill weeds in Mayfield's extensive garden. On January 11, 1921—the very day Armstrong had applied to have Katharine discharged from the asylum—Davies' assistant, John Hird, had sold the major a quarter of a pound of arsenic, to which he thoughtlessly neglected to add the distinctive dye that was required when the poison was sold as a weed killer. It was midwinter, an odd time to be buying weed killer.

Davies reported his suspicions to the authorities, but they decided to take no action. Major Armstrong, after all, was clerk to the local magistrates and a former Worshipful Master of the Hay Freemasons. You need more than idle gossip to go after a man like that.

With Katharine's tongue finally stilled, the major was free to cut loose. The following month he left for Italy and Malta, where dates with young women figure frequently in his diary. On his return to Hay, he became a frequent, if embarrassing, presence at local dances, where he often pestered young housemaids and farm girls. There was, he discovered, a price to be paid for his new freedom: Dr. Hincks was soon treating him for venereal disease.

If Armstrong thought his worries were at an end with Katharine gone, he was soon beset with difficulties in his law practice. Shortly before Armstrong returned from war duty, a younger solicitor, Oswald Martin, had become a partner in the only other law firm in town, that of Robert Griffiths, who practiced right across the street from Armstrong. When Griffiths died shortly thereafter, Martin took over the shop, and he and the major were in head-to-head competition.

There were inevitable tensions. Martin, injured during the war, had never risen above private, whereas Armstrong was an officer, even though he had never come under fire. Mrs. Armstrong had looked down on Martin as not quite a gentleman and expressed that opinion to the major frequently, particularly when, in June 1921, Martin married Constance Davies, the druggist's daughter. Especially mortifying, though, was that Armstrong's finances were a mess, and young Martin was taking business away from him.

Disagreements between the two solicitors came to a head over closing the sale of an estate in the nearby town of Brecon. Armstrong was holding a £500 deposit, but through delaying tactics managed to hold up the closing for over a year, despite appeals from Martin, who was acting for the purchaser. Finally, Martin wrote to say that the sale would fall through if the deal wasn't completed by October 20, 1921. The major stalled and won another week's delay. Then, surprisingly, he asked Martin to tea at Mayfield. After putting him off several times, Martin agreed to go on Wednesday, October 26, offering that morning to drive Armstrong out to the house in the afternoon. "No, thank you," the major replied, "I have something to do at the house, so must go there before you."

Martin expected it would be an awkward meeting, but was surprised when Armstrong, not even mentioning their problems, went out of his way to be cordial. The housekeeper, Emily Pearce, had put out her homemade currant scones, uncut and unbuttered, along with buttered plain and currant bread. Curiously, although there was no butter on the table, Armstrong handed Martin a buttered scone with the memorable words "Excuse fingers." As Martin was eating it, Armstrong went to turn on the gaslight and broke a globe in the process.

Arriving home at 6:30, Martin put in forty-five minutes of work with his clerk, Alan Preen, before his wife, Constance, announced supper. "I feel sick, I don't think I can eat anything," her husband told her. After picking at his food, Martin became violently ill, vomiting repeatedly. Mrs. Martin, a nurse, noticed that the vomit was dark and foul-smelling. When Dr. Hincks saw him early the next morning, Martin was recovering, and the doctor put his illness down to a bilious attack brought on by overwork and lack of exercise.

Armstrong called several times at Martin's office that day, asking for him and, when he learned Martin was ill, inquiring about his health. "It looks rather bad because he was up at my house to tea last night," he told Preen in what was taken as a joke. Meeting Martin on the street after he recovered, the major said, "It seems a queer thing to say, but you will be ill again soon." Queer, indeed!

His son-in-law's illness had not escaped the attention of John Davies. He expressed to Dr. Hincks his suspicion that young Martin had been poisoned. The doctor was startled by the suggestion, but after they had gone over Martin's eating patterns, they concluded that the only food he had eaten away from home—where no one else had fallen sick—was tea, taken with the major. Davies warned his daughter and son-in-law that they should be on their guard against any further possible attempts to poison them. That was when the Martins told Davies about the chocolates.

The previous month, they told him, a box of chocolates had arrived in the mail with no card and no return address. The couple ate a few, and handed them out when Martin's two brothers and their wives were visiting. One of the wives, Dorothy, suffered a bilious attack, a high temperature and a rapid heartbeat after eating some of the chocolates. When she recovered, her illness was put down to an untimely chill.

Examining the chocolates, Davies discovered that some appeared to have been tampered with. In Davies' mind, that resolved the matter; he had his son-in-law provide a urine sample and gave it, along with the remainder of the chocolates, to Dr. Hincks to send away for analysis. Days and weeks passed with no word of the result. Meanwhile, young Martin was in a high state of anxiety: nearly every day, Armstrong pressed him to come again to tea, either at Mayfield or at his office, and the younger solicitor was running out of excuses.

Dr. Hincks, too, was a worried man. If he had been wrong in diagnosing Martin's attack, he thought to himself one day as he rode across the hills to see a distant patient, then perhaps he had been wrong about Mrs. Armstrong too. He suddenly realized that the high-stepping gait, the vomiting and the discoloration of her skin were all symptoms of arsenic poisoning.

On New Year's Eve, 1921, in the doldrums between Christmas and New Year's when little legal work gets done, Major Armstrong, a tiny soldierly figure (he weighed only ninety-eight pounds) in riding breeches and an army greatcoat, walked down to his office to put in a couple of hours work. With his back to the window of his cozy second-floor office overlooking Broad Street, he did not notice three men enter the front office below. Giving instructions that Major Armstrong was not to be alerted, the three marched up the narrow staircase, knocked and entered Armstrong's office.

They introduced themselves as Superintendent Albert Weaver, deputy chief constable of Herefordshire, and Chief Inspector Alfred Crutchett and Sergeant Walter Sharp of Scotland Yard. Since he had been assigned to the case on December 10, Crutchett had been sneaking into town after dark to interview Davies, Martin, Hincks and others while swearing them to secrecy. He told Armstrong that arsenic had been found both in Martin's urine and in the mysterious box of chocolates, and invited him to make a statement.

"I will make a statement and tell you all I know," said Armstrong.

After dictating a statement, in which he denied giving poison to Martin or sending the chocolates, the solicitor was formally charged with administering arsenic to Martin. He was asked to empty his pockets, and the contents, which included several letters, were put on the desk. Armstrong was told to sit in the center of the room while they examined his desk, but when he asked if he could sit at his desk and read some business letters, this was allowed. A few minutes later, Crutchett noticed Armstrong going through the papers taken from his pockets. He ordered Armstrong away from the desk. Much later, the police, finally examining the material taken from Armstrong's pockets, would discover three love letters to "Marion" and a small white envelope containing a potentially fatal dose of arsenic.

Three days later, at dusk on January 2, 1922, policemen boarded up the windows of Church Cottage, where the Beales family would one day reside. Across the way, digging had gone on all afternoon as the coffin of Mrs. Armstrong, buried ten months before, was exposed. Later, by the light of a hurricane lamp, officials trundled the coffin across the lane and into the cottage, where, safely concealed from peeping toms, it was examined by Sir Bernard Spilsbury, the most famous pathologist of his generation. When the organs removed from the body by Sir Bernard were sent away for examination, they would yield a phenomenal three-and-a-half grains of arsenic. Two grains is enough to kill.

If the Black Mountains, in the lee of which Hay-on-Wye shelters, had disappeared one morning in a puff of green smoke, it could not have caused a bigger shock than the arrest of Major Herbert Rowse Armstrong on suspicion of poisoning his rival. People initially refused to believe that the major, a pillar of the local gentry and clerk to the magistrates, was locked up like some common thief in a cell at Hay police station. But then tongues began to wag. The death of his wife ten months before was the focus of most of the gossip, although every suspicious death for miles around was soon being laid at his door.

The little Hay courtroom was jammed on January 2 when the major, just as if it was any old morning and he was coming to perform his customary duties, marched in and gave the magistrates a polite bow. Perhaps forgetting himself, he leaned forward and took part in the discussion setting a time for the next hearing. Meanwhile, not far from Mayfield, spades were biting into the chilled ground as the exhumation of Katharine Armstrong got underway. On January 19, Armstrong was charged with the murder of his wife, and the issue of the tea party became secondary.

As an experienced solicitor, Armstrong realized that his arsenic purchases, his wife's peculiar death and the business of the will, not to mention Martin's illness, could be tied up into a very plausible package by an able prosecutor. Yet he had good reason for optimism. By one of those inexplicable coincidences, another rural solicitor in Wales, Harold Greenwood, had also been charged with poisoning his wife by putting arsenic in the dinner wine at their home in Kidwelly on June 16, 1919. Mrs. Greenwood had died early the following morning, and she had not long been in the grave when Greenwood, forty-four, set tongues wagging by marrying an attractive young woman. At his trial in November 1920, Greenwood was defended brilliantly and aggressively by the great defense counsel Edward Marshall Hall, who put Greenwood's daughter on the stand to swear she, too, had drunk the wine without any ill effects. A Hay woman traveling on the train with Armstrong right after Greenwood's acquittal would recall that the major could speak of nothing else that day.

But if Greenwood's acquittal made him confident of the result of his own trial, Armstrong was ignoring one thing: many of the prosecution lawyers, policemen and medical experts who had suffered a bruising loss in the Greenwood case would be on the team opposing him. And they didn't intend to lose again. In addition, instead of the terrier-like Marshall Hall (who was ill and unavailable), Armstrong chose as his leading barrister a much more placid counsel, Sir Henry Curtis Bennett, who was more used to prosecuting than defending. Certain remarks made by Bennett suggest that he did not believe in his client's innocence, and he clearly intended to win by legal maneuvering rather than with a down and dirty attack on the prosecution.

When the trial opened in Hereford on April 3, 1922, Curtis Bennett was gambling that the judge, Mr. Justice Charles Darling—who had tried Sir Roger Casement, Dr. Crippen and many other notable cases of the Edwardian era—would rule as inadmissible any evidence about the famous tea party as having no bearing on the main charge of murdering Mrs. Armstrong. Without the Martin incident, it would be immeasurably easier to defend the major, because no one had seen him administer poison to his wife. And if she did die of arsenic poisoning, who was to say it wasn't suicide?

But Bennett lost the gamble—and the case. Judge Darling, perhaps as determined as the prosecution that another lawyer "wouldn't get away with murder," was consistently hostile to the defense and asked mischievous questions of witnesses to put Armstrong in a bad light. Most damaging, he ruled the Martin incident admissible without giving any reasons. There was only one small bone thrown the defense's way: despite an exhaustive search, the police had not been able to trace the purchase of the chocolates, so these were not mentioned in the trial, although they had figured in the preliminary hearings, which had been exhaustively reported in the press.

For the prosecution, Sir Ernest Pollock, the Attorney General, built a devastating circumstantial case against Armstrong. Lily Candy, the maid who had signed the second will, said the major had instructed her to do so in his study, while the housekeeper, Emily Pearce, could not remember the circumstances under which she had signed it.

The indomitable Dr. Spilsbury was definite in saying that a fatal dose of arsenic must have been taken by Mrs. Armstrong in the twenty-four hours before she died, while Nurse Allen and Dr. Hincks were equally emphatic that the woman could not possibly have got out of bed to take arsenic herself in the last four days of her life.

The only real surprise was a piece of ambiguous evidence produced by Armstrong's solicitor, Tom Matthews, which still mystifies. After his initial interview with the police, Armstrong told Matthews he had forgotten to tell them that the residue of the white arsenic was in a packet in one of the desk drawers in his study. Matthews went to Mayfield and searched the desk, but did not find it. The arsenic did not appear on a police list of items seized at the house, so Matthews returned several weeks later, and this time found the arsenic, amounting to about half the amount purchased by the major, jammed in the back of the drawer. Was it planted by the defense? By the police? Or was it simply, as Matthews suggested, an oversight indicating that the police had been less than thorough. And what was its meaning? The judge chose to interpret it as an example of Armstrong's deviousness in his dealings with the police. Curtis Bennett said the discovery, because it showed where the balance of the arsenic had gone, might save Armstrong's life.

Armstrong's own explanation on the witness stand of the uses to which he had put the arsenic strained belief. Using one ounce of the white arsenic, he said, he had made up twenty lethal little packages, using nineteen of them to kill nineteen individual dandelions. The one packet remaining was in his pocket when he was arrested. He realized now, he said, that each packet contained a dose fatal for a human being.

After a stiff cross-examination from the Attorney General, Armstrong was about to step down when the judge intervened: "Do you tell the jury that you absolutely forgot about that white arsenic?"

"I do," Armstrong replied.

"Does it not occur to you it would have been a very, very bad case for you if you had to tell the police that you had got, not only [dyed] weed-killing arsenic but white arsenic in your possession?"

"But I did not remember it," the major said, floundering.

"That is not what I asked you," said the judge, boring in.

"It would have to be explained," Armstrong said weakly.

"Why make up twenty little packets, each a fatal dose for a human being, and put them in your pocket?"

"At the time it seemed to me the most convenient way of doing it."

As Armstrong stepped down after six hours in the witness box, it was his final unconvincing replies to the judge's questions that remained in the minds of the jury.

Even though Mr. Justice Darling's summation was devastating for the defense, Curtis Bennett, perhaps remembering Harold Greenwood, was so confident of an acquittal that he went for a walk in the country outside Hereford, expecting to meet a freed Armstrong on his way back. Stopping at a small post office, he was told by the woman behind the counter that her husband had just phoned to tell her the result: guilty.

Armstrong's first thought upon his arrest had been of Harold Greenwood; now, in the few weeks remaining before Armstrong's execution, Greenwood was thinking of him. In an article in *John Bull* magazine, Greenwood wrote, "I know what the prisoner felt. Helpless, trapped, overborne." For him, and probably for Armstrong, the judge's summing up was "more painful than can be described. For a trained legal mind can appreciate exactly the effect upon the jury. As minute by minute the cultured, measured voice flows on, hope seems to evaporate."

On May 31—Derby day—with the sun shining out of a cloudless sky, Major Herbert Rowse Armstrong, his appeal having failed, walked with erect military bearing to the scaffold set up in the yard at Gloucester Jail and declared to the governor, "I am innocent of the crime for which I have been condemned to die." He was so light that the hangman had to allow for an unusually long drop of eight feet, eight inches to ensure that Armstrong's neck snapped.

It is not unusual for men and women to go to their deaths proclaiming their innocence, even in the face of the most damning evidence. Armstrong might have wanted to provide his children, who were taken into the care of Arthur Chevalier, with a chance to believe in his innocence. In poisoning cases, the evidence is almost invariably circumstantial—what poisoner invites witnesses? In Armstrong's case, there was motive (the apparently forged will, the years of abuse from his wife), opportunity and a suggestive chain of evidence. But there is another version of the case, developed but never published by Thomas Kane, who was a schoolboy in Leatherhead, avidly reading newspaper reports of the trial when he first became convinced of Armstrong's innocence. He went on to a career as a tea planter in Sri Lanka, then Ceylon, but never forgot the case, and continued to research the background.

Kane, eighty-five when I spoke to him, finds the clue to the mystery in the underlying social currents that were never mentioned in court. Major Armstrong, he says, was gentry, whereas John Davies, the druggist, wasn't. Davies had a vested interest in seeing Armstrong arrested: his son-in-law, Martin, would gain a good deal of business. Davies had resigned from the Masons, apparently after a dispute, and may have borne a grudge against Armstrong, a strong lodge man.

Armstrong had another enemy in his sister-in-law, Bessie Friend, who, says Kane, disapproved of her sister's marriage and thought Armstrong "a horrid little man." It was under the influence of her sister, he argues, that Katharine wrote her 1917 will, leaving her money to her children, and it was only when her husband returned from the war that she began to worry that she had dealt unfairly with him and wrote a new will.

After extensive reading on the effects of arsenic and a close study of Mrs. Armstrong's symptoms, Kane suggests it is quite possible that the large dose that proved fatal was taken on February 17. A prying woman, she may have found the major's packet of arsenic in the cupboard in his study and, mistaking it for bicarbonate of soda, taken it as a remedy for the biliousness she was feeling at that time.

As for the tea party, Davies handled the urine sample and had the chance to tamper with it, and the purchase of the chocolates was never traced. Could Davies have bought and mailed the chocolates, injecting a non-fatal drug into some of them to cause a bilious attack and adding the arsenic only when the chocolates were to be sent away for analysis? It was this theory that Beales accepted in his book, *Dead Not Buried*.

There are holes in Kane's arguments, but Martin Beales' partner, Elizabeth Charles, told me she is certain of one thing: Armstrong did not get a fair trail. The newspapers were full of reports of the preliminary hearings, she said, so the chances of finding twelve jurors who had not made up their minds by the time of the trial were slim. The judge, she feels, was wrong to allow the tea party evidence to cloud the basic issue of whether Armstrong murdered his wife. "I certainly think," she said, as we drank afternoon tea just across the field from Mayfield, where that other famous tea party occurred, "that if he was being tried now, he would be acquitted simply because they were unable to connect him with administering the arsenic." But was he guilty? She took a while to answer: "I am not convinced either way," she said.

Lizzie, You'll Kill No More

L izzie Tilford reminds me of my great-aunt Ruth from Seven Sisters in Wales. Like Lizzie, Aunt Ruth told fortunes and, like Lizzie, she was an unforgettable mixture of the sacred and the profane, a larger-than-life woman who, seventy years after her death, is still the talk of my relations in Wales. Aunt Ruth, they will tell you after the second sherry, would entertain the minister in her bedroom on Sunday afternoons—and get her husband, who was a bit simple, to bring them tea in bed afterwards. But, unlike Lizzie, no one ever accused Aunt Ruth of giving her husband arsenic.

Lizzie married three times, once for love, she told people, once for spite and once for envy. She never did say which was which. By her account, she married her first husband, Fred Yates, in England when she was fifteen. "I did it more for a dare than anything else. The girls bet me five shillings I would not dare marry him. We only lived together for a week or so, then we separated, and I never saw him again."

Then, Lizzie would have us believe, she devoted her life to good causes, becoming in turn a Girl Guide leader, a Sunday

237

school superintendent, secretary of a branch of the Comrades of the Great War and a member of a choral society. She topped off this record of selfless service by marrying William Walker, a miner who was a Salvation Army sergeant major, and becoming a Salvationist herself.

In 1928, the couple arrived in Canada with their four children, and Walker made a futile attempt at farming before falling ill. He went blind and lingered for a few months before dying in Woodstock, Ontario—the very place where Lord Somerset was hanged a generation earlier (see "Lord Somerset's Clever Scheme")—on February 19, 1929. A brain tumor was listed as the cause of death.

Lizzie, ever resourceful, kept her family together by working at a galoshes factory and telling fortunes. A steady stream of Woodstock women—and a few men, too—found their way to her parlor to have their palms read or to learn the future from the bottom of their teacups.

She saw no conflict between these activities and going to church, and it was at the Baptist church that Tyrrell Tilford, a thirty-one-year-old teamster, noticed the large, pleasant-looking woman singing in the choir. When it came to showing a proper fervor, Lizzie, who claimed to be in her mid-forties at the time but was actually in her mid-fifties, did not believe in half-measures. Introduced to Tyrrell's elderly mother, she threw her two-hundred-pound bulk thunderously to her knees and began praying aloud. Perhaps this was considered a bit over the top, because when she and Tyrrell were married on November 10, 1930, his relations stayed home.

Nevertheless, the Tilfords allowed Tyrrell to build a small house on the corner of their lot on Cronyn Street (it was still there, a cheerful clapboard-and-shutters affair, when I visited the town in the late 1980s), though relations between Lizzie and the old folks were never cordial.

Early on the morning of Friday, March 29, 1935, Tyrrell's seventy-four-year-old father, James, heard a scratching noise at the back door. He thought it might be an animal or a child. But when he opened the door, he found his son on his knees trying to reach the latch. "He came bundling in, all doubled up. He was as black as a chimney sweep," Jim Tyrrell would say. Helped to the couch, he gasped, "I've come to tell you, Dad, I'm going to die." He had to stop to catch his breath. "I'm full of arsenic. Look at my tongue, Dad. It's all cut to ribbons." Lizzie and her two grown sons, he claimed, had been dosing him with arsenic, putting it into everything he ate or drank, giving him capsules of the white powder and even pouring it on his tongue.

Tyrrell told his father he'd seen Bill Blake, a friend of his wife's who was always around their place, ostensibly learning the fortune-telling business, peer at him around the curtain covering the bedroom doorway and heard him say, "My God, he's had enough poison to kill twenty people!"

When his frail mother came downstairs, Tyrrell urged her to phone Keith's Drug Store to find out if arsenic had been sent to his home. "Not for weeks and weeks" was the answer she got when she phoned.

"Mother, that's a lie, and a big lie," retorted Tyrrell when she told him what had been said.

Dr. Hugh Lindsay, who had already been treating Tyrrell, was called, but when he produced capsules containing headache powders similar to those he had prescribed earlier, his patient said weakly, "Them's different to what [Lizzie's] been making."

When he called again the following morning, Dr. Lindsay told

Tyrrell breezily, "You look better already. You'll be up and about by Tuesday."

"Why, you damned fool," said Jim Tilford, not one to mince words, "he's dying now."

Indeed, by Saturday night, Tyrrell was feeling worse. "I'm dying," he told one of his brothers. "You better fetch Lizzie."

When she arrived, Lizzie was all cooing concern. "You know, honey," she said, enveloping him in her arms, "you should not have come up here."

Tyrrell pushed her away. "You've been poisoning me, Lizzie, and you know it. I'm going to die."

When she tried to soothe him and make light of his fears, his father butted in: "You great cow, can't you see the lad's dying?"

"Honey, you're not going to die," she said, ignoring his father.

"Yes, I am," argued Tyrrell. "There's enough money in the insurance to bury me, and then you can have your man with the two farms, Bill Blake." Turning to his family, he said, "When I'm dead, have my stomach analyzed. They'll find arsenic. Lizzie, you've killed two, but you'll kill no more." Flushing with anger, his wife marched to the telephone, called Keith's Drug Store and demanded to know if arsenic had been sent to her house. Whatever the reply, she held out the phone to the hostile family and said, "I want you to bear witness to that."

Tyrrell—pale, panting for breath, and with a proper sense of drama—called his mother to his side. "I want to give you a last kiss, Mother," he said.

Not knowing what to do about their son's accusations, the old couple later went to bed, leaving Lizzie watching over Tyrrell. Hearing a sound in the middle of the night, Jim got up and went to the kitchen. There was no sign of Tyrrell or Lizzie. On previous occasions, Lizzie had been seen lifting her 155-pound husband and carrying him as if he were no more than a baby.

All through the next day, the old people fretted, but did nothing. Early on Monday morning, Tyrrell's mother thought she heard her boy shout. She hurried to the door, but everything was still. When she phoned across the yard, Lizzie reassured her, "He had ice cream, a wing steak and apricots and a smoke yesterday—and he kept them all down." Later that morning, Lizzie's sons told Tyrrell's mother that he had died at five that morning—before she had even spoken to Lizzie.

Dr. Lindsay, who had been away for the weekend, was in a quandary as to what to put down as the cause of death. After consulting the coroner and the Crown attorney, he listed influenza and a weak heart on the death certificate. At that time, talk of poison seemed only "street rumor," he would say later.

Lizzie was in a fever of anxiety that the Tilfords would call in the police. At the funeral home, she told a friend, "I had him out of the coffin myself to make sure he was all right." His organs, to her relief, had not been tampered with. "I made sure he had his underwear on," she added with a chuckle. "I had my first husband [she probably meant Walker, her second husband] out of the coffin too."

Even with Tyrrell safely underground, she still worried. Unable to sleep one night, she sent one of her grown boys to the cemetery to make sure no one had dug Tyrrell up. And when one of her late husband's brothers, Frank, came calling, she told him if his parents kept up their accusations, "I'll sue them for every penny they've got. I'll make them print an apology in every newspaper in Canada."

By now, local gossip had it that strychnine and arsenic had been delivered to the Tilford house for killing rats, and Tom, another of Tyrrell's brothers, decided to find out once and for all if there had been a call for rat poison. "By golly, Lizzie," he said one day as he came in the door, "You should do something about the rats around here. A twelve-inch one just jumped across my boot."

"Oh, Tom, there are no rats here. Never have been," she blurted out. And, she added, there wasn't any rat poison around the house, either. Anyway, she said, seeking to reassure or maybe distract Tom, she would soon be talking to his dead brother again.

"How do you figure that?" he said, intrigued.

"Oh, I see you don't believe in spiritualism," she said.

The Tilfords got no response when they tried to get the police to investigate Tyrrell's death, so they finally took their suspicions to the provincial Attorney General in Toronto. Only then, and by the light of lanterns in the middle of the night, did spades strike into the fresh earth of Tyrrell's grave. His dying wish was finally respected: his vital organs were removed for analysis, and his body was returned to the grave before daybreak. Professor Joselyn Rogers, the head of analytical chemistry at the University of Toronto and known to the public as "the chemical detective" for his involvement in many criminal investigations, was able to report shortly afterwards that he had found two grains of arsenic in the stomach—enough to kill.

A month after Tyrrell's death, the Tilfords finally got the inquest they'd been demanding, and Victor King, a scrawny nineteen-year-old who worked as an assistant at Keith's Drug Store, went into the witness box clutching the shop's poison book. He had delivered two ounces of arsenic to the Tilford home on March 20, he testified. Lizzie's sixteen-year-old daughter, Isabella, had signed for it, and there was her signature, plain to see, in the poison book.

Yes, agreed Isabella when it came her turn to testify, she had signed for the poison. "I was alone in the house with my brother William when the poison came," she said. "Between 2:00 and 2:30, I telephoned Keith's Drug Store for the arsenic because Dad [Tyrrell] had asked me to do so. He wanted it to kill rats in the barn."

Where was her mother?

"At a birthday party. She left home about 1:30," replied the girl.

"You know Mr. King?"

"Yes."

"You paid Mr. King?"

"Yes, two dimes. My father gave them to me out of his pocket."

"What did you do with the parcel?"

"Dad came in the back door, and I gave it to him, and he went over to the barn."

"Did you tell your mother?"

"No. My father told me if I told Mother about it, it would be the worse for me."

"When did your father commence to get sick?"

"The next day. Mother said to get Dr. Lindsay."

"Did you ever know your father to vomit like that before?"

"Yes, on Valentine's Day, when he ate too much ice cream."

"What did your mother do when Mr. Tilford was ill?"

"She babied him up."

"Did you ever tell your mother about this arsenic?"

"Yes, eleven days after Father was buried." At that point, Isabella burst into tears and was excused.

Hutchinson Keith, the druggist, had a different version to tell. He had known Mrs. Tilford for several years, and she frequently phoned him for goods, he said. At about 12:30 P.M. on March 20, she called him and said, "Is that Mr. Keith? Can I get some arsenic? Since my husband has been collecting waste paper and garbage, the whole place is overrun with rats." Keith said, "She told me to send two ounces." He knew it was Mrs. Tilford's voice; he recognized her English accent.

Victor King, recalled to the witness stand, said Mrs. Tilford called again a little later and asked him, "When are you bringing out that parcel? I've got to go out." King also remembered that a few days after Tilford's death, when he was making a non-toxic delivery to the house, Lizzie asked him, "Aren't you kind of shaky?" "No, why should I be?" he replied. "Well, you brought some poison out here," she said, with a significant smile.

On June 11, with clumsy Speed Graphic newspaper cameras flashing, Lizzie Tilford walked out her door between Provincial Police Inspector E.D.L. Hammond and Constable John Clark, on her way to be booked for murder and lodged in the Oxford County Jail.

Soon the midnight shovels were busy again, this time digging up what remained of Lizzie's second husband, William Walker. This time, no poison was found, but to this day some people in Woodstock are convinced he was murdered. Mrs. Lily Macdougall describes an encounter she had with Lizzie shortly before Walker died: when she complained to Lizzie that her husband was ill and giving her trouble, Lizzie gave her a folk remedy to deal with the problem. "That will fix him," Lizzie said. "You'll soon be rid of him."

For most of the trial, which began in September, Lizzie maintained a cool front, studiously taking notes as, day after day, the web of guilt was spun around her. Her composure cracked only when Tyrrell's sister Annie described the scene in the kitchen when Tyrrell had cried, "You've killed two and you will kill no more." "She has done nothing but tell lies," Lizzie shrieked as

Annie Tilford left the witness box. "I can't go on. May God have mercy on my kids." She collapsed and had to be helped from the courtroom.

The one thing lacking in the prosecution's case was motive. An insurance agent testified that she had called him several weeks before Tyrrell died to check how much he was insured for. It was only $300—about the same amount there had been on William Walker's life—barely enough to cover funeral expenses. Tyrrell brought in so little money that Lizzie and her son, William Walker Junior, had to contribute to the household expenses, and some welfare assistance was still needed for them to get by. Nevertheless, Agnes Allen, another of Tyrrell's legion of brothers and sisters, testified that when she and her husband visited shortly before Tyrrell died, Lizzie asked them to help her write out a will in which everything was left to her.

The druggist, Keith, had told of Lizzie coming into his store once and asking for empty capsules into which she would put a product she was using for slimming. Now Mrs. Allen recalled Lizzie coming out of Tyrrell's bedroom with a capsule that she said her husband hadn't been able to keep down. Lizzie opened the top of the wood stove and threw the contents into the fire.

Things looked bad enough for Lizzie, but then the prosecution produced a surprise witness. Mrs. Catherine Argent was the friend whose birthday party Lizzie had attended on the day the arsenic was delivered. Lizzie had brought an angel cake to the party, and no, said Mrs. Argent, no one had suffered any ill effects after the party. But while there, Lizzie had made a phone call— possibly to the drugstore to make sure the arsenic was delivered while she was away from home—and had also received a phone call, apparently from Isabella. "I ordered some arsenic," Lizzie told her friend, "and Bella is frightened to death to accept it." On the day Tyrrell died, she phoned Mrs. Argent. "Tyrrell's passed out,' she said. "You remember that arsenic?" And that was as much as she said. A month after Tyrrell's death, Isabella brought Mrs. Argent a note from her mother: "The provincial police have been to see Bella and she has told them I came to your house about one o'clock and left around five. Don't get mixed up in this. Burn." Instead of burning the note, Mrs. Argent put it carefully away.

A brilliant October sun was streaming through the courtroom windows as the all-male jury filed out to consider its verdict. The public gallery was packed with women, some knitting, some drinking from flasks of coffee, none willing to risk going outside for fear of losing their seats. No woman had been hanged in Ontario for sixty years. Juries bent over backwards to give female accused the benefit of the doubt. Most people expected that Lizzie Tilford, too, would be spared the gallows.

As the afternoon wore on, the muted cheers of a crowd watching a lawn-bowling tournament outside the courtroom wafted through the open windows. Finally, at 8:30 P.M., the jury filed back in and the foreman delivered the verdict: guilty. Lizzie slumped forward with a cry: "Oh!"

"...and thence be taken to a place of lawful execution..." intoned the judge.

"Oh my God, it is not right, not fair," Lizzie wailed. "Oh, your Lordship, I've been framed, framed! May God have mercy on the Tilfords' souls." She slumped in her seat.

"...and there be hanged by the neck until you are dead," concluded the judge, as women cried and moaned. "And may God have mercy on your soul."

In the Oxford County Jail, Lizzie, once she was over the initial shock, busied herself knitting small items such as baby booties, which were snapped up by souvenir hunters when they were put on sale at a charity bazaar, while the Woodstock Ministerial Association asked that her death sentence be commuted or at the very least postponed, since the December 17 execution would cast a gloom over the Christmas season.

On November 30, an enterprising reporter from the *Detroit Times*, Dorothy Williams, fooled the sheriff at the jail into believing she was from the office of Lizzie's defense lawyer and secured an interview with the condemned woman. She described Lizzie as a tall, poised woman with an attractive, fresh English complexion and short, graying blonde hair brushed straight back. The only softening touches in the vaulted whitewashed death cell were the rocking chair in which Lizzie sat and a pink begonia in a blue-and-white pot.

Lizzie, though she had forgone her chance to testify at her trial, still insisted she was innocent. "Gossip put me in this cell," she told Williams. "They said I wanted to get rid of my husband to marry William Blake. That's a lie. Blake was a friend of my son Norman [who was twenty-two]. He didn't mean anything to me. He always called me Mom. I read his fortune one day, and he discovered he could see into the future too."

Blake, forty-two, was by then calling himself Professor and was telling fortunes in Toronto. But Lizzie was showing signs of disillusionment with the occult. "I never saw this kind of death for myself in the tea leaves," she said, puzzled.

In a small town, neither life nor death are as anonymous as they are in a big city. Many of the people who gathered outside the jail on the night of December 17 had had their fortunes told by Lizzie Tilford or knew her from church. Mrs. Chris Clark, eighty-seven when I spoke to her, has memories as fresh as yesterday of the events following Lizzie's arrest by her husband,

Constable John Clark. Mrs. Clark worked several relief shifts guarding Lizzie in the death cell as a prison matron, and the hangman, a prison guard from Toronto who used the name Sam Edwards, stayed with her and her husband for several days while he prepared his equipment. He didn't seem at all upset at the prospect of hanging a woman, she said.

Others were more squeamish. A *Toronto Star* columnist argued that Lizzie should be spared on the odd grounds that, having attracted three husbands, she was not devoid of womanly qualities, and that her work for the Salvation Army indicated that there was a worthy Jekyll side to her character, "as well as a peculiarly atrocious element of Hyde." His final plea was "that she should be saved from this horrible death simply because she is a woman. This whole judicial machinery has been devised by men and is carried out by men; women have a very slight part in it; and the debt of men to women is so vast that to exempt women from the death penalty is a very slight expression of their obligation."

There was, in the event, no last-minute reprieve. Snow was falling as Lizzie, who had refused an injection of morphine, walked bareheaded across the prison yard to the scaffold. She was finally lost for words as the black hood was put over her head and her arms and feet were secured. Only forty-five seconds elapsed from the moment she emerged from the jail until the tell-tale thud of the rope.

But Lizzie Tilford was a character not easily forgotten. When I mentioned her name to Victor King, who delivered the arsenic and who had once had his fortune told by Lizzie, his hands shook violently. King, then sixty-five, was living in a senior citizens' home not two hundred yards from the cemetery where Lizzie is buried. "She was an uneducated, lower class of person," he spat out. "I guess I feel she got her just desserts."

And the Tilfords haven't changed their view. "Oh, she poisoned more than one husband, I'm sure of that," said one of the Tilford women guardedly from behind her screen door.

But there were still her children and a handful of friends left to gather by the light of car headlights and flashlights for the funeral in the Baptist cemetery shortly after the execution. The Reverend Stanley Baker, to whom Lizzie had left her Seth Parker Hymnal suitably inscribed as a token of gratitude, conducted the funeral service. Her coffin was lowered into the ground beside the recently disturbed remains of her second husband, William Walker, who, having died a natural death, had no reason to bear a grudge.

Or had he?

The Devil Said, Try
Chloroform

Y ou would have liked Dr. William Henry King, I'm sure.
Everybody did. Tall, charming, energetic, with a sensu-
ous mouth and a shock of dark hair from beneath which
he studied his patients with intense brown eyes, he was an overwhelming favorite with the ladies and, in turn, found it difficult
to resist their charms. "Women," he would write ruefully in his
prison cell, "have been my ruin."

Looking back on it later, it was difficult for people to see how
a man who embodied so many of the nineteenth-century virtues
could have gone so wrong.

At his very first school, when he was only five, his abilities
were so pronounced that his teacher would take him to other
schools on exhibition days to recite from the stage. When he was
eleven years old, his parents settled on a homestead in the rough
country of eastern Ontario, north of what is now Brighton. A few
years later, his father became ill. Young William, in his mid-
teens, took over the farm operation and built up wheat
production to a respectable 1,200 bushels. Mature in his manner,
he was remembered later by his younger brothers and sisters

more as a parent figure than as a sibling. His schooling during this period was restricted to two months in winter, and then often at the hands of incompetent teachers. After the harvest of 1851, when he was eighteen, his parents sent him to the Normal School in Toronto, where, after two years, he obtained a first-class teaching certificate.

King was a young man in a hurry. On New Year's Day, 1855, he married Sarah Ann Lawson, who was called Annie. She was a plain young woman, but she had her uses: her father, John M. Lawson, was a well-to-do farmer who might be expected to provide financial help for King's projected medical studies. When the young couple moved to Hamilton, at the west end of Lake Ontario, Annie took in boarders to help keep them afloat while King taught school and studied medicine. But already there were rumors that King was abusing his wife, and she went home to her parents. It was there, a year after their marriage, that their only child, a daughter, was born. King did not take to the baby, but did not have to put up with her for long. After a month, she died—apparently of natural causes.

The trouble with Annie, as far as King was concerned, was that she refused to shake off her country ways. Her conversation was still of the farm kitchen, her manners were clumsy, her small talk abysmal. What sort of wife was this for a smart, up-and-coming doctor? From Hamilton, he wrote her cruel letters, accusing her of infidelity, letters that she showed to her father. Later, he apologized, and the letters were returned to him through a friend, but John Lawson was careful to keep copies.

Whatever distress he had caused from afar, in person King was irresistible. He returned to Brighton, was reconciled with Annie, and even persuaded his father-in-law to give him some money before he set off for two years' study at the Homeopathic

Medical College of Pennsylvania in Philadelphia, where one of his professors would describe him as his ablest student. He received his diploma in March 1858, returned to Brighton and went into practice.

From the start, his services were in demand. "His whole exterior appearance," said a contemporary report, "was not only prepossessing, but showed that he was a man of strong, original intellect and determined perseverance." He was gentlemanly, a regular churchgoer, careful in his speech and dressed well. He was soon pulling in between $100 and $200 a week, a comfortable income for that time.

Beneath the genteel exterior, though, King seethed, ruing the day he had married frumpy Annie. Now he realized he could have married just about any one of the far more attractive young women flocking to his office. Or was he deluding himself? When he sent one of his Quaker patients, Miss Dorcas Garrett, a declaration of his affection, adding that his wife was likely to die within a year and suggesting that she should apply herself to learning the skills necessary for a doctor's wife, she was properly shocked. Miss Garrett demanded an apology and declared she would have nothing more to do with him.

Then, on September 23, 1858, only six months after King had gone into practice, Melinda Freeland Vandervoort, a coquettish twenty-year-old, came fluttering into his life like an exotic butterfly. On that day, Melinda took it into her head to pay a visit to Annie, whom she had known several years before. Soon, William and Melinda were ignoring Annie and impressing each other tremendously with their wit and sincerity. Time flew by, and it was nearly evening when Melinda said she had to be going because she was visiting Annie's parents too. "I'll get out the horse and we'll drive you over there," offered her host.

As they drove home later, leaving Melinda to stay the night at her parents', Annie said tartly, "Miss Vandervoort says she has fallen in love with you." King hunched over the reins and said nothing. "She loved you before she ever saw you."

"That would be most singular," he said.

"Oh, yes," said Annie, nodding. "She saw your likeness at my father's while you were away in Philadelphia, and she fell in love with you there and then." He was grateful that the darkness hid the flush that had come to his face.

The next day, Miss Vandervoort returned to the Kings'. In the evening, they gathered around the piano while she sang "Old Dog Tray" and "Kitty Clyde" and "Hazel Dell," and William swore that, while he had heard many young ladies sing in Philadelphia, she surpassed them all. "In fact," he would write later, without a trace of remorse, "her beautiful voice completely intoxicated me. What a desirable accomplishment in a companion, thought I to myself." He added, "Mrs. King had no tune at all, and I never knew her to sing a word. She had no taste for music, the very thing I was particularly fond of. I had urged her very strongly to try and cultivate a taste for and learn music, but it was quite impossible."

Miss Vandervoort stayed the night, and the next morning, as she and King took a lingering farewell, she promised she would send him her likeness. A few days later, it arrived at the post office with a note: "Dr.—Please inform me if you receive this. I arrived home safe and quite well. Truly yours, M.F. Van."

"Sweet little sugar lump of good nature," he began his reply the same day, October 10, "I long looked with prudent anxiety for the arrival of the object of my thoughts, but began to despair. Still I had too much perseverance, and I walked to the P.O. this morning and found the most precious thing (except the original) on earth. Better to me than all California. Could I indulge in the hope that those winning and genial smiles would ever be found in my possession, all troubles would then cease. It is a perfect infatuation to me. Can you keep from sacrificing yourself on the hymeneal altar for the next year? I wish so."

And why should Miss Vandervoort hold back from marrying anyone for the next year? Almost as an afterthought, King added, "[Annie] is very sick. Last night we thought she would die." At that point, Annie King was quite well. It was not until four days later that she fell ill.

In her reply of October 18, Miss Vandervoort pronounced herself overwhelmed and a little confused. "I hardly know in what manner to address you," she wrote. "As circumstances are with you, it appears almost in vain for me to think of you only as a friend. Yet something seems to whisper, 'still hope.' Since I first had the pleasure of an introduction, my heart is constantly with you and I am not contented for a moment. O! Could I for ever be with you; I think I should be happy." Then she added playfully, "Well now, Dr., don't you consider it very wrong of me to correspond with you? I'm afraid if known it would destroy Annie's happiness, and if I were in her position, I would much rather be in my grave than suffer the idea of your intimacy with another."

By then, Annie King had other worries. She was gravely ill, and her husband was assuring her she was not likely to recover.

Arriving at the young couple's door on the morning of October 14 in response to a summons, Mrs. Lawson found her daughter feeling a little better than she had been earlier. But after her husband gave her a spoonful of a white medicine mixed in a spoon, she began vomiting. "Keep it down, Annie," he told her. "She tried to do so, but she could not," Mrs. Lawson would say. "The vomiting continued fifteen or twenty minutes." Two hours later, he gave her another dose of the medicine, which Annie complained was fiery-tasting, with the same results. What was the matter with her? King spoke vaguely of a fall she had taken getting out of the buggy a few weeks before. She was also two months pregnant, and he announced that her womb was "cankered right through."

In the weeks that followed, Mrs. Lawson was never away from her daughter for more than an hour. One day, she found black spots on a nightdress of Annie's and showed it to her son-in-law. "Burn it," he said; when she didn't, he cut out the spots with a pair of scissors.

As Annie failed to improve, her father wanted to know why another physician was not called in. His suggestion only angered King. Finally, at John Lawson's insistence, Dr. A.E. Fife made several visits. Perhaps treading delicately where a fellow physician's wife was concerned, Fife did not examine Annie, but simply prescribed ipecacuanha and camphor for the vomiting, which he thought was due to her pregnancy. During his last visit, on November 3, Annie told him, "I feel much better than at any time since my illness began." Dr. Fife would say, "She did not look like a dying woman."

That evening, though, she was worse, and her husband brought her a mixture in a teacup. "Here's Dr. Fife's good medicine, Annie," he said. When she tasted it, said it burned and refused to drink any more, John Lawson was ready for a showdown. "William Henry, if God spares my life, I will have a jury of doctors in the morning," he declared.

"Who would you have?" asked King.

"Dr. Gross, for one," said Lawson.

"Gross is the greatest enemy I have. I know very well what he would prescribe."

"And what would that be?"

"Calomel and opium."

"Would it ease her?" Lawson asked.

"It might. Would you take it, Annie?" King asked his wife.

"If it will do me any good," she replied weakly.

King returned from his office a few moments later with something in a spoon. A moment later, Annie vomited. "Keep it down, Annie," he ordered, holding her down by her shoulders.

"Oh, oh, I cannot. I'm dying," she gasped.

"Now she's thrown it up!" said her husband, exasperated. "She must have some more."

"Give her very little," pleaded Lawson.

"I won't give her a quarter of what Dr. Gross would give her," said King grimly.

After a second dose, Annie went to sleep. The following day, at Lawson's insistence, Dr. Gross was called in, but there was little he could do. By evening, Annie had died.

Her husband was prostrate with grief, sobbing and throwing himself about. Finally, he had to be given a sedative. But when the Lawsons suggested an autopsy, he declared that Annie had been firmly against it.

On November 7, following Annie's instructions, the body of her baby was disinterred from the cemetery, and mother and daughter were buried together on the Lawson farm. At the funeral, King was again overcome with grief. The Lawsons were not convinced. Several days before her daughter's death, Mrs. Lawson, who had heard rumors about her son-in-law, had taken advantage of King's temporary absence from the sickroom to go through his jacket pockets. She found the likeness of Melinda Vandervoort, kept it and said nothing.

A pattern of suspicion was forming. A friend of Annie's

THE DEVIL SAID, TRY CHLOROFORM

reported that Dr. King had told her that, while Annie was a good wife from a financial viewpoint, he would like her improved in many ways. The letter from Miss Vandervoort had been discovered, and now Miss Garrett came forward with the indiscreet letter King had sent her. The day after the funeral, Clinton Lawson, Annie's brother, took the evidence to Simon Davidson, the county coroner. When it also emerged that Dr. King had purchased half an ounce of arsenic a few days before his wife fell ill, and later a quantity of morphine, the coroner did not hesitate: he ordered an inquest, empaneled a jury and had Annie's body exhumed. The body was placed on a door and carried to the schoolhouse, where, in the presence of the jury, a post-mortem was conducted by candlelight by Dr. Gross, Dr. P.R. Proctor and Dr. James Gilchrist.

Annie's body and organs were in healthy condition, except for the lungs, which presented a congested appearance, but not sufficient to cause death. The womb contained a healthy fetus three or four months old. The doctors were particularly interested in the stomach, which appeared congested and contained a dark fluid, and the bowels, which showed signs of inflammation. The stomach, obviously the key to the mystery, was removed and placed on an earthenware dish in the sight of the jury so that no one could tamper with it. When the inquest adjourned for the night, the coroner washed it, put it in a pickle jar, and took it with him to Brighton, where it was locked in a closet at Mr. DeLong's tavern, where the coroner stayed the night. "I kept the key in my pantaloons, which I did not take off that night as I sat up writing out papers relative to the inquest," Coroner Davidson would testify.

The next day, as the inquest resumed, the stomach took pride of place on the table in front of the coroner so that the doctors could better study it by daylight. Eventually, Davidson put it back in the jar, sealed it and dispatched it to Kingston, where a professor at Queen's University refused to examine it and sent it in turn to the University of Toronto. There, the much-traveled organ was finally examined by Henry Croft, a professor of chemistry. He found that it contained eleven grains of arsenic. Two grains can kill.

King might claim that the arsenic could have been added after death; to preclude such a defense, Croft immediately sent for the liver and kidneys. He found some arsenic in the liver, which, he said, could not have been added after death.

Meanwhile, King, returning from his rounds the day the inquest was called, got word of it and left home straightaway, saying he had to contact the authorities. At ten o'clock that night, John Vandervoort and his wife, Elizabeth, had already gone to bed when there was a banging on their door. A man they had never seen before, but who introduced himself as Dr. King, said he had an urgent message for their daughter. Melinda was called, and the two went into a room on their own.

An hour later, Vandervoort knocked on the door and asked, as any prudent father might, if the message was delivered yet. The answer was in the negative. Presently, the couple emerged. "My wife has unfortunately died," King explained. "They have got her body up and, in consequence of a likeness of your daughter being found in my pocket, a warrant has been issued for my apprehension, as well as your daughter's." They were accusing him of poisoning his wife, he said. It wasn't true, but he felt it would be wise if he took Melinda to her aunt's across the American border until things were straightened out.

Showing a surprising lack of discretion—and a vote of confidence in King's persuasive powers—the couple entrusted their daughter to this stranger they had just met, and saw the two ride off into the night.

Annie's brother, Clinton Lawson, was enraged at the news. He had himself sworn in as a deputy and, with a revolver and a warrant for King's arrest in his pocket, he too rode southward. Picking up the couple's trail, he crossed the St. Lawrence River and, at St. Vincent, on the American side, he learned of their location. Accompanied by a U.S. marshal, he approached an isolated farmhouse, telling the marshal to knock at the front door while he hung back. In a couple of minutes, Lawson saw King leap out of a back window and run toward the woods. Seeing his brother-in-law in pursuit, the doctor dashed into the barn. "We went in," Lawson would report, "and found him under the straw in a hogs' nest." Brandishing his gun, Lawson told him he would be shot if he ran. Lawson was asked at the trial if King came willingly. "No sir," he told the judge. And then he shook his head: "No, siree!"

King's flight to the U.S. had provided the prosecution with undeniable proof of *mens rea*, or guilty mind. But poisoning is notoriously hard to prove, and when, on April 4, 1859, large crowds converged on the town of Cobourg for King's trial, the presence of a dozen top-hatted and frock-coated pillars of the medical establishment, engaged to testify either for or against the accused, showed plainly that Dr. King would not go down without a fight. The medical faculty of Victoria University gave their students time off to attend the trial, believing, no doubt, that they'd learn more of a practical—and perhaps moral—nature in the courtroom than they would in the classroom.

King, according to a contemporary account, entered the courtroom "with a light, airy step, dressed in a gentlemanly manner in a suit of black broadcloth, with a gold chain across his vest." But most of the ladies who had arrived in their carriages to see the handsome young doctor had turned back at the sight of the crush.

Melinda Vandervoort was an early sensation in the witness box, claiming that it was Annie and not William who had asked for her likeness. "I never had any improper intercourse with Dr. King," she insisted. "I sent him [the] letter for amusement."

"Go down," said the prosecutor, Thomas Galt, severely. "I must read these letters, but not in your presence."

King made no good impression when he joined in the general laughter as the letters between himself and Miss Vandervoort were read.

With his first witness, the Honourable John Hillyard Cameron, KC, established the defense line. Professor Charles J. Hempel of the homeopathy college in Philadelphia, who had taught King, testified that in homeopathic medicine, "for the cure of disease we administer medicines which, if taken by a healthy person, would produce a like disease." For cholera morbus, for example, he would prescribe arsenic, which, if taken by a healthy person, would produce symptoms similar to the disease itself.

It was a defense more easily believed in the nineteenth century, when people commonly dosed themselves with small amounts of poison. For Asiatic cholera, Professor Hempel said, he had prescribed a fifth of a grain of arsenic, the dose to be repeated twelve to fifteen times in the course of twenty-four hours. "The patients have done well and recovered," he reported.

Annie's death, he suggested, was due either to nervous exhaustion or to the cumulative effects of arsenic. Prosecution witnesses had testified that arsenic is not a cumulative poison, but on that point, Hempel, who argued that it is, has been vindicated by modern knowledge.

A.H. Flanders, a Philadelphia professor of chemistry, testified that he would himself have prescribed arsenic for a pregnant patient experiencing pain and vomiting, and ascribed her death not to the poison but to her earlier fall from the buggy. He was hissed from the public galleries when he suggested that the arsenic found in Annie's stomach was introduced after death.

Dr. Thomas Nichol, a Canadian in practice for three years, offered himself as living proof of Hempel's and Flanders' theories. In 1855, he testified, he had given himself a third of a grain of arsenic three times a day for twenty-one days to gauge its effect. He had no symptoms until the eighth day, when he experienced fever, vomiting, thirst and violent purging. The symptoms persisted for three weeks after he stopped taking the arsenic. The rash young physician had also experimented with another poison, belladonna, and found that it produced paralysis in his legs. The bizarre testimony, supposedly, was intended to convince the jury of the medicinal benefits of arsenic. It was an ingenious defense, and apparently an effective one, because after an afternoon of deliberation, the jury was unable to agree—an unusual delay in that day and age. But, by ten the next morning, the foreman was able to announce a verdict: guilty with a recommendation for mercy. There can be no more socially dangerous crime than that of a doctor using his medical skills to commit murder. Seen in that light, the mercy recommendation was ludicrous; it can only have resulted from some sort of compromise in the jury room to arrive at a verdict.

The decision struck King like a thunderbolt. It was obvious that, in spite of everything, he had expected to go free, and he was struggling to control his emotions as he was led away. Two days later, brought back for sentencing, he looked "ashy pale" as Chief Justice Robert Easton Burns told him, "I cannot see that yours is a case in which such a recommendation [for mercy] is justifiable," before passing the death sentence.

The diary kept by an anonymous constable who guarded King during the two months while he awaited execution tells us that at first he would repeat over and over, "Oh, what an unfortunate man I have been! Is it possible I must be executed?" His death, he said, would finish his poor mother.

He was visited by a steady succession of ministers, with whom he prayed, and on May 20, the constable, who frequently joined in the prayers, could report, "Dr. happy now in the love of God." Dr. Norman Bethune, who had been a witness against him, now called on him regularly and laid down a program of exercises to keep his colleague fit.

Finally, sighing, "Oh, how I wish I had never married," King sat down to write his confession for publication in the newspapers. If his confession was intended as a warning to others, it must be counted a failure. It started well enough: "Having sinned against society as well as God, I feel it my duty to confess my guilt with deep humiliation and sincere repentance."

But humility quickly turned to callous self-justification. He had been cruelly disillusioned when he discovered after his marriage that Annie was not a virgin, he wrote. "The law may compel man and wife to life together, but I defy it to compel them to live together."

And then—and you can sense his spirits lifting—King turned to Melinda Vandervoort. "She was both lovely and loving. I looked upon her with all her personal charms and attracting graces and virtues, her attainments and literary acquirements, her mild and affectionate disposition...and it was as impossible for me not to love her as it would be to fly to the moon."

He still insisted that Annie's illness stemmed from her fall from the buggy and from her pregnancy, and solemnly denied giving her arsenic until she showed symptoms of cholera morbus.

"Here I may observe that the whole scientific world is deceived in reference to the cause of death...for I must assert that arsenic had nothing whatever to do in causing death." On her last evening, he wrote, Annie had asked him if he planned to marry Melinda.

"No," he replied.

"You are engaged to her," his wife insisted.

"You're crazy," he answered.

"Oh, that bitch! That bitch!" said Annie, finally revealing herself as properly resentful. And a few minutes later: "Oh Lord, take me out of this world. I don't want to live. Can't you give me something?"

"Now here was a temptation I could not resist," wrote King, expecting his readers to sympathize. For three weeks, he said, he had been thinking of ways to shorten her life, "yet I would never have killed her by violent means. But here was (something whispered to me) just what you want and you will not be guilty yourself. I said, 'Will you take anything yourself?' 'Oh yes,' she responded. 'The Devil said, try chloroform.'"

Just before daybreak, related King, as Annie's parents slept, he fetched a half-ounce vial containing about a drachm of chloroform, "which I gave her." In the morning, she was half-conscious as they got her out of bed and into a chair while the bed was made, but later she sank into a coma from which she did not recover.

King's "confession" was greeted with derision and anger. His talk of chloroform, in any case, does not have the ring of truth. Taken internally, it sears the throat and is difficult to swallow, and Douglas Lucas, director of the Centre of Forensic Sciences in Toronto, assured me that if it had been administered in the normal fashion, dripped onto gauze or cotton wool held over the mouth and nose, it is not likely Annie would have been semiconscious the following morning. And wouldn't her parents have smelled chloroform in the room? But the fact remained that, whether by arsenic or chloroform, Annie King was dead and her husband was responsible.

Snow coated the countryside as I walked up the hill outside the old Cobourg courthouse—now part of a senior citizens' home—where the scaffold was set up on June 9, 1859. Thousands had been trailing into town since the previous day, bringing picnics and making a holiday of it. Now, as King mounted the steps, they formed a sea of faces beneath him.

"It is very hard," began King, reading from a prepared text, "to be deprived of life in comparative youth."

"What about your wife?" shouted a voice.

As King urged them to take warning from his example, people began shouting to the hangman, "Get on with it!" The doctor brought his speech to an abrupt end, wiped his perspiring hands on his trousers and shouted, "I bid you farewell—a long farewell." He shook hands with his friends, kissed his brothers, then, after a mask was put over his head and his hands were tied behind his back, kneeled on the trapdoor for the rope to be placed around his neck.

A long sigh escaped the crowd at the thud of the rope. Suddenly, the bright summer day seemed not as festive after all, and people began drifting away without speaking.

And Melinda Vandervoort? She took up first with an American and then with a man in Montreal, finally returning to Brighton, where she lived under the scornful eyes of her neighbors. She reportedly died in a Toronto asylum in the late 1890s after taking to drink.

King—whose likeness can be seen in the carved face that crowns the front doorway of Victoria Hall, the Cobourg courthouse and municipal offices officially opened by Queen Victoria's eldest son the summer after King was hanged—was buried at his parents' farm in the hamlet of Codrington, north of Brighton.

It was there that I met Lloyd Ames, eighty-seven, who told me King was his mother's uncle. He was born in the King family home, and remembered Dr. King's gravestone well. He and his brother had stripped away the undergrowth long ago to note down the dates on the stone. But a few years ago, said Ames, his son, who had moved into the homestead, called him to say that while plowing up a field to put in strawberries, he had hit the gravestone, breaking it clean in half.

"Well," said Ames, "I went up there and I dug a hole somewhere else and I buried the pieces. I put 'em good and deep. Thing that happened so long ago, I reckon it's better let bygones be bygones."

Silk Pajamas for
the Chauffeur

The feeling was uncanny. Anna Landstein, who had lived in the Villa Madeira for thirty-five years, took me into the sitting room, and there was the armchair placed directly in front of the French windows in exactly the spot where Francis Rattenbury, one of Canada's best-known architects, was seated when he was bludgeoned with a mallet. In his later years, Rattenbury and his much younger wife, Alma, had traveled far from British Columbia, where he had achieved fame and fortune, to escape gossiping tongues. They ended up here, at Villa Madeira, a suburban house in Bournemouth, a genteel seaside resort on the south coast of England.

The house may be modest, but I have always thought the drama that played out here has the makings of grand opera: a tragic young woman, a young lover, an elderly, famous husband and a ghastly misunderstanding leading to a heartbreaking final scene. Verdi would have loved it.

Both Alma and Francis were larger than life, and that is what may have drawn them to each other. Rattenbury, who had been born in Yorkshire, was only newly arrived in British Columbia when he won a competition to design the gingerbread legislative buildings that still bring a touch of the fantastic to the waterfront in Victoria, the provincial capital.

Rattenbury, though, was a restless personality who could never stick to one thing for long, and when gold was discovered in the Klondike in northern Canada, he established a supply company, had steamers built and became a big name on the frontier. Marrying Eleanor Nunn in 1898, he took her, in typical Teddy Roosevelt Rough Rider style, over the rugged Whitehorse Pass, and they spent their honeymoon cruising Lake Bennett on one of his steamers.

Over the years, though, as Rattenbury tackled some of the choicest architectural assignments in the opening West—including Victoria's Empress Hotel, where English-style afternoon tea is still a tradition—his frantic bursts of energy alternated with curious bouts of lassitude. By 1922, when he was fifty-five, his marriage was at an end, and he was feeling like an old man.

At that appropriate moment, Alma Pakenham, slender, beautiful, vivacious, in her twenties and already married twice, came into his life, and Francis Rattenbury rediscovered his youth. Alma's origins were a mystery. Born in British Columbia in obscure circumstances to an English mother and, possibly, a German prospector father, she was described by one of her early teachers as "a brilliantly clever child." Musically gifted, at seventeen she appeared as a soloist with the Toronto Symphony Orchestra, playing both the piano and the violin in the same program.

In 1913, Alma married Caledon Dolling, a member of a prominent Ulster Catholic family, and when he joined up at the outbreak of the First World War, she followed him to England and secured herself a job at the War Office. Dolling was killed by a shell in 1916, and to bury her grief Alma signed up with the Scottish Women's Hospital, working as an orderly and stretcher-bearer, sometimes bringing in the wounded under fire. Twice wounded, she was the recipient of the Croix de Guerre.

When the guns finally fell silent, Alma, her sense of purpose gone, became one of those brittle, drifting flappers of the post-war years, briefly marrying Compton Pakenham, a former Coldstream Guards officer, with whom she had a son, Christopher, and then leaving her incorrigibly idle husband to return to her mother in British Columbia.

Meeting her for the first time, Rattenbury was enraptured. "Butterflies eat out of her hands," the architect wrote to his sister, and he later described her as looking like "a fragile Madonna." His first wife, though, would not budge from their grand house on Oak Bay in Victoria until he cut off the power, removed the furniture and finally made a cash settlement and agreed to build her another house. To Alma's intense displeasure, she had it built on a lot overlooking her old home.

But nothing could really spoil their early years of bliss. "Ratz," as Alma called her husband, built her a music room, and on December 27, 1928, a son, John, was born to them. The trouble was that starchy Victoria socialites, who had sided with Rattenbury's first wife in the bitter marital breakup, were not prepared to accept his new wife, even denying her membership in the Victoria Musical Society. Rattenbury quarreled with members of his profession, and in 1929, after he had lost a good part of his fortune in that disastrous year, the couple resolved to move to England and make a new start.

They settled in Bournemouth—as close to a carbon copy of Victoria as you could find—and moved into Villa Madeira, only a few minutes' walk from the seashore. The inside layout was as awkward as the outside was undistinguished, but it suited their purposes. On the ground floor, alongside the sitting room that opened through French doors into the garden, was a bedroom and bathroom, which Rattenbury, considerably slowed by age now, enamored of the bottle and no longer interested in sex, appropriated for himself, while Alma slept in an upstairs room she shared with the infant, John.

Soon, though, the unpredictable Ratz found new zest in promoting Alma's musical career. She had dabbled in song-writing in the past. Now he did everything in his power—contacting music publishers, making trips to London—to win acceptance for her songs. His efforts soon succeeded. Published under the name Lozanne, Alma's tunes, such "Dark-Haired Marie," sung by Peter Dawson, became hits. They met famous people such as Ambrose, the orchestra leader, and the tenor Richard Tauber, who visited the Villa Madeira.

And then Ratz, always fickle in his enthusiasms, lost interest in Alma's music and turned his attention to a local apartment development project. Increasingly deaf, his faculties sometimes impaired by alcohol, Rattenbury decided he no longer wanted to drive. In September 1934, George Percy Stoner, eighteen but claiming to be twenty-two, answered their advertisement in the local paper for a chauffeur-handyman. Stoner moved into the front upstairs bedroom, next to that of Irene Riggs, the maid-companion the Rattenburys had hired earlier. And the scene was set for tragedy.

F. Tennyson Jesse, one of Britain's preeminent writers on criminal matters, who attended the Rattenbury trial, wrote in the introduction to the official trial transcript, "Mrs. Rattenbury was a highly sexed woman and six years of being deprived of sexual satisfaction had combined with tuberculosis, from which she suffered, to bring her to the edge of nymphomania." Whether or not we accept Jesse's diagnosis, the fact was that Alma quickly became infatuated with Stoner and, while her husband slept in his bedroom downstairs, she brought the young chauffeur into the large main bedroom, being careful not to wake the sleeping child.

The following March, Alma made up a story about having to go to London for a minor operation in connection with her tuberculosis. Stoner accompanied her, and they stayed in adjoining rooms at the Royal Palace Hotel in Kensington. She took him on a shopping spree at Harrod's, buying him silk pajamas, a gray suit, and shoes and shirts. They lingered in town for three days, walking and attending theaters and cinemas, and returned to Bournemouth at around 10:30 P.M. on March 22. As he kissed her goodnight, Ratz, who had been drinking, asked her no questions.

Two days later, though, Rattenbury was feeling depressed. Not even a drive, with Stoner behind the wheel, to see a litter of puppies could cheer him up, and after tea he read aloud portions of a dreary novel in which the aging hero contemplates suicide. "You could admire a person doing away with himself because he was old and doddering," said Ratz as he closed the book.

Looking for a way to cheer him up, Alma phoned a business associate of Ratz's in nearby Bridport and arranged for them to visit the following day to discuss financial details concerning the apartment project in which the two men were involved. They would stay overnight at Bridport.

At 9:30 that evening, after a game of cards, she kissed her husband goodnight and left him sitting in the armchair in front of the French doors.

Forty-five minutes later, returning from her Sunday off, Irene Riggs let herself in through the front door. On the way to the kitchen to get herself something to eat, she heard heavy breathing. She knocked on the door of Rattenbury's bedroom, went in and found it empty. Then, oddly, she went up to bed without checking the sitting room. Heading for the bathroom a few minutes later, she saw Stoner leaning over the banisters at the top of the stairs. "Just checking to see if the lights are off," he said, before returning to his room. Alma, who had made Irene her confidante, joined her in her room a few moments later, and they chatted amiably about the plan to take Ratz to Bridport the following day.

Irene was still awake when, shortly afterwards, she heard a scream from downstairs. Running down, she found Alma in the sitting room with Rattenbury, who was slouched back in his chair, his eye blackened, his head a mass of blood. "Someone has hurt Ratz," Alma cried. "Telephone the doctor!" Her wartime training served her well. While Irene phoned, she ran to the bathroom, fetched a towel and wrapped it around her husband's head to staunch the bleeding. Then, as she tried to undress him, she sent Stoner to fetch the doctor.

At that point, Alma did something desperately foolish. She drank a stiff shot of whisky, threw up, then drank some more. By the time Dr. William O'Donnell arrived and ordered that Rattenbury be removed to a nursing home, where he could get proper treatment, Alma was tipsy. When Constable Arthur Bagwell arrived at 2:00 A.M. to investigate, she tried to dance with him and kiss him, and declared, "I know who did it. I did it! With a mallet!"

Returning to the house at 4:00 A.M., after doing what he could for Rattenbury, Dr. O'Donnell found police questioning the intoxicated Alma. Taking her by the arm, he marched her firmly upstairs to her room, gave her half a grain of morphine and saw that she went to bed. Two hours later, still incoherent, she was wakened on police orders and brought staggering downstairs. "Tell Stoner he must give me the mallet," she whispered to Irene as they took her away to the police station.

Yes, she told them at the station, she had hit her husband over the head with a mallet after he had dared her to kill him while they were playing cards. Challenged, she responded, "That's right, I did it deliberately, and I would do it again."

Her efforts to protect her lover were in vain. Rattenbury died three days later, and Stoner, along with Alma, was charged with murder. While in custody, he told a constable, "I watched through the French windows and saw her kiss him goodnight, then leave the room. I waited and crept in through the French window, which was unlocked." He added, "You know, there should be a doctor with her when they tell her I am arrested because she will go out of her mind."

He was not far wrong. Alma tortured herself with guilt. "The truth is," she told the prison governor, "it is my fault, absolutely."

When Frank Titterton, one of the singers whose recordings had brought Lozanne fame, visited her in Holloway Prison, he found her wan and worrying about her children, Christopher, who was now thirteen, and John, six. "Oh, I am so hungry for some music," she told him as he stood to go. He leaned forward and softly sang in her ear one of her best-known songs. She went into ecstasies, he wrote later.

In prison, she wrote a song for George Stoner that began, "By some mistake my spirit held you dear/ But now I wake in agony and fear." Her letters to her children had musical notes and little tunes at the end.

It was her closeness to her children, in fact, that finally brought her to see that nothing would be gained by persisting with the story that she had killed Ratz. In all likelihood, she could not save Stoner, and if she, too, was imprisoned or executed, her children would be motherless.

Some of the biggest rogues in British penal history—poisoners, child murderers and men who chopped up their wives into little bits—have stood in the dock of Number One Court at the Old Bailey. But it is probably fair to say that when Alma Rattenbury, still looking slim and younger than her reputed thirty-eight years, took her place in the dock beside the pale and surprisingly gentle-looking Stoner, she was among the most publicly reviled prisoners ever to stand on that spot. F. Tennyson Jesse wrote, "There was probably no one in England, and no one in court when the trial opened, save Mrs. Rattenbury, her solicitor and counsel, and Miss Riggs, who did not think Mrs. Rattenbury was guilty of the crime of murder." Attending the trial, Jesse was accompanied by the well-known actor Raymond Massey, who, long ago in Toronto, had attended kindergarten with Alma.

"In the box," wrote Jesse, "she was an excellent witness. Her voice was low and rich. She gave a great impression of truthfulness, and she was astonishingly well-controlled. Only a nervous tic in the side of her face, which jerked perpetually, betrayed the tension of her mind."

The evening her husband was attacked, she testified, Stoner had been angry about them going on the trip to Bridport the following day. He didn't like the prospect of Alma sharing a room with her husband. "He was very jealous of Mr. Rattenbury," she said in reply to a question. "Unnecessarily so."

Later, after her talk with Irene, Stoner joined her in her room. He seemed agitated and, when she asked the reason, "He told me that I was not going to Bridport the next day as he had hurt Ratz.

It did not penetrate my head what he did say to me at all until I heard Ratz groan, and then my brain became alive and I jumped out of bed." Stoner told her he had hit Rattenbury over the head with a mallet, which he had hidden in the garden.

The testimony that certainly did Alma the most harm concerned her making love with Stoner in the bedroom where John was sleeping. "Did you really choose the room where the child was asleep?" she was asked. She seemed surprised by the question. "Why not? The little boy was asleep. He was a sound sleeper... I did not consider that dreadful."

"You cannot have any feeling but disgust for her," Mr. Justice Christmas Humphreys told the jury. She was, he said, "a woman so lost to all decency, so entirely without any moral sense, that she would stop at nothing to gain her ends." We can almost imagine the wink as he told the members of the jury that they should not, of course, convict her simply because she was "an adulteress of the most unpleasant type." After going over the details of what he called the "orgy" in London, the judge left no doubt that he believed there had been a conspiracy to murder Rattenbury: "Do you believe that while they were in London the future was not discussed? Would not something have to be done with, or to, Mr. Rattenbury?"

As Jesse points out, the judge's prejudiced remarks were based on the odd assumption that Alma, a woman of the world with two children and married to an acquiescent and undemanding husband, would think of disposing of him so that she could marry the chauffeur, whom she now knew to be eighteen.

Turning to Stoner, Mr. Justice Humphreys cast further guilt on Alma by declaring, "Whatever your verdict may be in this case, his position is due to the domination of that woman over him."

By Friday, the last day of the five-day trial, Stoner, who had not given evidence, still sat apparently unmoved, his eyes down-cast. But Alma Rattenbury, observed Jesse, "looked twenty years older than she had on Monday. On the last day even her hands changed color, and were a livid, greenish white."

The jury returned their verdicts with merciful speed: Alma Victoria Rattenbury—not guilty; George Percy Stoner—guilty.

"Oh, no!" cried Alma, stepping forward as if there had been some mistake. Two wardresses grabbed her and helped her from the dock as the judge put on his black hat and prepared to sentence Stoner to death. Alma was free—but her freedom was of no use to her. She was booed by the crowd waiting outside the Old Bailey, but it hardly even registered. Stoner, the man she loved, would hang, and if she lived to be a hundred, she would still regard herself as responsible for his death, as well as that of her husband.

Four days after the trial ended, a farm worker, William Mitchell, saw a woman sitting on the bank of a river near Christchurch, just outside Bournemouth. She was writing when he first saw her, but when he looked in that direction again, she was walking toward the river. He thought she was going to pick flowers, but then he noticed a knife in her hand. At the water's edge, she crouched, then toppled in. Mitchell ran to the edge of the river and waded in, but she was already beyond his reach. "All this time, she was staring fixedly at me with a terrible look in her eyes," he would say. He threw her coat to her from the riverbank, yelling, "Catch hold of this." But as he did so, her head went back and blood oozed to the surface from a wound in her chest. "She turned her head and looked at me and uttered one long cry which sounded like, "O-o-h!"

In her suicide note, Alma had written, "Eight o'clock, and after so much walking I have got here. Oh, to see the swans and the spring flowers and to smell them... It was not intentional, my coming here. I tossed a coin, like Stoner always did, and it came down 'Christchurch.' It is beautiful here. What a lovely world, really...pray God nothing stops me tonight..." She had tried that morning to throw herself under a subway train at Oxford Circus, and later under a bus, but in both cases there had been too many people around. "It is beautiful here and I am alone," she concluded. "Thank God for peace at last. God bless my children and look after them."

George Stoner, in the event, was reprieved. He served seven years in prison and was then released to join the armed forces during the Second World War. He was at the Normandy landings.

When I visited Bournemouth in the late 1980s in the course of my research, I found that little had changed. George Stoner still lived in a pillared bungalow with his wife. In 1990, he had again come to public attention when, at the age of seventy-four, he admitted in magistrate's court to molesting a twelve-year-old boy in a public toilet. He was put on probation for two years.

It was growing dark as the keeper at the Bournemouth cemetery led me to the graves of Francis and Alma, and an evening breeze from the English Channel sighed in the pines overhead. But there was nothing to see. The graves are unmarked. Two lives that once sparkled and scintillated and engaged the interest of half the world are gone without a trace.

I made the ten-minute drive from the cemetery to Villa Madeira. Anna Landstein, who was eighty-three at the time, opened the door and invited me in. Little had changed. If Alma came laughing gaily through the French doors from the garden, the only thing she'd notice missing is the grand piano she brought with her from Victoria. When Mrs. Landstein and her husband came here from Austria and bought the house, they had no idea of its associations until an electrician, fixing the wiring, joked, "Do you want me to mop up the blood?" The murder never troubled Mrs. Landstein, whose husband had died several years earlier, until, following the airing of a television drama about the murder, someone threw a brick through the leaded front windows.

Bournemouth, though, like Victoria before it, does not seem to have taken to Alma. To those who knew her, she was a kind, affectionate and talented woman who was guilty, certainly, of bad judgment. But, as Mrs. Landstein wrote me in a subsequent letter, after thirty-five years in Bournemouth, they still say of her, "just as they say of poor Alma: 'She was a foreigner, you know.'"

Bloodstains on the Carpet

Policemen, for the sake of their own sanity, must sometimes develop a macabre sense of humor. Take, for example, the bathtub that serves as a drinking trough for horses at the stables of the mounted unit of the Lancashire Constabulary in Preston in the north of England. The tub was stained brown when I saw it, but the brass plaque above it shone brightly. It announced that this was the tub in which Dr. Buck Ruxton had, in September 1935, dismembered the bodies of his wife, Isabella, and the family maid, twenty-year-old Mary Rogerson.

Several of the cases in this book have featured white-collar professionals, doctors in particular, who have turned to murder. Generally, they are a tidy group. They don't like a mess, and their method of choice has generally been poison. But Ruxton, born in India to a French mother and Parsee father, applied a different area of his medical training to the business of murder: surgery. And that's what makes this a horror story, plain and simple.

You can still visit the scene of the crime: a handsome double-fronted Georgian house at 2 Dalton Square in the old city of Lancaster. No one has lived there since the events of 1935, and it now houses the town's planning department. It's easy to see how the central location, at the foot of a fine square dominated by Lancaster's Greek temple–style town hall, would appeal to the young Dr. Ruxton, arriving in town in 1930 to set up practice.

As the first person of color to occupy a prominent position in Lancaster, you might have expected he would encounter prejudice. But if the local establishment was cool toward the new doctor, the warm-hearted Lancashire folk took to him. He was soon known as the working people's doctor, and he had the largest practice in town. Even today, you'll find older people in Lancaster who say he was the finest doctor they ever had.

A good doctor Ruxton may have been; as a husband, he was a jealous tyrant.

Ruxton, who'd had his name changed by deed poll from Bakhtyar Hakim, had arrived in England from Bombay in 1925. He had medical degrees from London and Bombay, including a bachelor in surgery. It was while he was doing postgraduate work in Edinburgh that he was smitten by Isabella Kerr, a not very attractive Scottish woman with a long face and prominent teeth (of these, more later) who was managing a restaurant. Isabella, divorced from a Dutch sailor, was apparently in ignorance of the fact that Ruxton had a wife still in India when she married the handsome, emotional doctor. Before and while they lived in Lancaster, she bore him three children, Elizabeth, Diana and Billy. But Belle, as he called her, soon discovered that her husband was insatiably jealous, and she had only to talk to a man for him to fly into a rage and accuse her of having an affair.

Today, when we are more familiar with wife abuse, the pattern would quickly be recognized: Mrs. Ruxton twice sought protection at the police station just a few steps away across the square. "I would be justified in murdering her," Ruxton, who kept a revolver under his pillow, said on one of these occasions. A maid had seen him on the bed with his hands around his wife's throat; another had seen him attack her, crying, "You are a dirty prostitute." Her sister, Jeannie, said Isabella had tried to gas herself in 1931. He even told a police officer, "My wife has been unfaithful, and I will kill her if it continues."

In Lancashire, there are local writers prepared to say on the basis of their research that Mrs. Ruxton was flighty and gave Ruxton cause for anger. A play presented locally portrayed Ruxton as a victim of racial prejudice. To suggest that, in either case, this justified what followed shows cruel insensitivity.

In the final buildup to violence, Mrs. Ruxton, at the beginning of September 1935, traveled to Edinburgh with the family of Robert Edmonson, a young solicitor-in-training, and they stayed the night in a hotel. Ruxton was convinced she had slept with the young man, though Edmonson denied it in court.

On September 14, Belle, observing an annual rite, took the car and drove to the nearby resort of Blackpool, where she always met her sisters to view the famous illuminations. It was a jolly evening, with drinks, rides at the fair and laughter over memories of their growing up. But when Isabella left them, she was worried she would not reach home by 11:30, when she had told Ruxton to expect her.

What happened in the next six hours or so after Isabella Ruxton arrived home will never be known in detail. But a record of her husband's comings and goings the next morning, a Sunday, suggest strange happenings at 2 Dalton Square during the night.

At 6:30 A.M., Ruxton called on Agnes Oxley, who was supposed to clean house for him that day, and told her not to come, as his wife and the maid, Mary Rogerson, had gone on holiday to Edinburgh.

At 9:00 A.M., Winifred Roberts arrived with the Sunday news-papers and rang repeatedly; when Ruxton finally came to the door, he told her the Edinburgh story.

At 10:00 A.M., a woman delivering milk came to the door and noticed that the doctor's hand was bandaged. "I jammed it," he explained.

At 10:30 A.M., Ruxton went to a service station, bought four gallons of gasoline in cans, then bought a similar amount from another gas station.

At 11:00 A.M., Mrs. Isabella Whiteside arrived with her son, whom Ruxton was supposed to circumcise. He told her he must postpone the appointment because his wife was away in Scotland and, "There is just myself and the little maid, and we are busy taking up carpets."

All this while, of course, Ruxton had to deal with his children, the oldest age seven, as they woke up, demanding breakfast.

At 11:30 A.M., he arrived at the door of his friends Herbert Anderson, a dentist who lived six miles away in Morecambe, and his wife, to ask if they would look after the children for a while, as Belle had gone away on holiday. Mrs. Anderson asked about the bandaged hand, and Ruxton said he cut it opening a can of peaches.

At 4:00 P.M., whatever Ruxton had been doing in the house, he now felt it was safe to bring in an outsider. He called on Mary Hampshire, a patient who had not worked for him before, explained that his wife was in Blackpool and asked if she would help him clean up the house, as the decorators were coming the next morning. "Where is the maid?" she asked. On holiday, he replied.

What Mrs. Hampshire saw when she arrived at the house on Dalton Square would be of crucial interest in the trial. The carpets

in the hall and stairs were taken up, straw was littered everywhere, and the bathroom was filthy. The bathtub was stained a
brownish-yellow color. The doors to the bedrooms were locked,
but she noticed that, in the lounge, supper for two was laid out but
uneaten. In the small, paved yard, she noticed carpets, a shirt and
some surgical towels, all partly burned.

After she had swept out as best she could, her husband helped
her scrub the stairs. As they were leaving, Ruxton gave Mrs.
Hampshire some carpets and a suit. "You can have it cleaned," he
said of the suit. "I had it on this morning when I cut my finger
and it's badly stained." The next day, haggard and unshaven,
Ruxton asked Mrs. Hampshire if she would do some more cleaning. Picking up the suit he had given her, he offered to have it
cleaned. As he had been good enough to give it to her, she said,
the least she could do was have it cleaned herself. At that point,
Ruxton asked for a pair of scissors to cut out the maker's label.
When she went later to wash the carpet he had given her, the
water came away red.

Mrs. Hampshire was becoming suspicious. When she arrived
at his house that day, there was no cleaning to be done. "I sent for
you because you give me courage," the doctor said oddly. Where
was the mistress? This time, he said she was in London. "Doctor,
you are telling me lies," she said. "Yes, dear, I am," he replied
without hesitation. "I will tell you the truth. My wife has gone
away with another man and left me with the three children."

Ruxton told Mary Rogerson's parents an even odder story: did
they know Mary was pregnant? "Mrs. Ruxton has taken her away
to see if they can do anything about it." Mary's father said he
wanted her back regardless, and if Ruxton didn't bring her back,
he would go to the police. "Don't go to the police," he pleaded.
"I'll bring her back on Sunday."

The signs that something grisly had happened at 2 Dalton Square were, you would think, unmistakable. The neighbors saw Ruxton carrying parcels from the house and saw fires burning in the little yard at the back; the garbage men noticed that some of the carpets left out for them were bloodstained; and when Mrs. Oxley finally came to clean, she noticed a foul odor in the bedrooms, which were now unlocked. Why did no one call the police? Because a few bloodstains were not unusual for a doctor who performed minor surgery in his house. And who would suspect a popular and able doctor of being a murderer?

It was on September 29 that Susan Johnson, on vacation just over the Scottish border in Moffat, in Dumfriesshire, went on a walk she would never forget. Crossing a bridge over a ravine on the Edinburgh–Carlisle road, she paused to admire the scenery. In the valley below, she saw, to her horror, a package out of which protruded what seemed to be a human arm and hand. She hurried back to get her brother, who opened the parcel. It was, in fact, an arm, and inside were other remains wrapped in a torn piece of sheet. Police found another four bundles of assorted body parts, decomposing and infested with maggots, on the bank of the river, plus two heads wrapped in cotton wool, one of them tied up in a child's rompers.

Over the next few days, more than thirty parcels of remains were recovered from the ravine, some wrapped in copies of the *Sunday Graphic* and *Sunday News* dated September 15, 1935. A month later, a highway worker found a rain-sodden package beside the Glasgow–Carlisle road, five miles from Moffat. It contained a left foot. A week after that, another young woman out for a walk found a right forearm and hand wrapped in newspaper in roadside bracken half a mile from the ravine.

The dismemberment had been done by an expert; it was not clear at first, apart from the fact there were two heads, how many bodies there were. One of the heads was clearly that of a young woman; the other was thought to be a young man. Reconstruction and identification of the bodies would present one of the great forensic challenges of modern crime detection.

Just how tough a job it was becomes clear in a book published two years later, *Medico-Legal Aspects of the Ruxton Case*, written by John Glaister, a professor of forensic medicine at the University of Glasgow, and James Brash, a professor of anatomy at the University of Edinburgh, the two men who led the team of scientists involved. It is one of the grisliest and yet most fascinating books in the field.

The usual hack-and-slash murderer who dismembers the bodies of his victims uses a saw; for the expert, putting the parts back together is as simple as completing a child's jigsaw puzzle. In this case, though, the job had been done with a knife, with the bones being separated at the joints, and—to make matching almost impossible—skin and flesh had been removed, in many cases, from the bone. But the very skill with which the job had been done—the neat incisions, the knowledge of joint construction—revealed that the murderer had medical knowledge.

It is possible that no murderer has ever done a more thorough job of trying to prevent identification. Noses, ears and eyes had been removed, as well as the skin on the faces and scalps of the two heads, and some teeth had been extracted. One body was clearly female, but the torso of the other was missing, and the experts had to use bone measurements and skull characteristics to identify it as female.

In the end, though, the murderer had outsmarted himself. In removing certain features of the bodies, he had simply drawn attention to them. A bunion had been removed from one foot, for example, in exactly the place where Isabella Ruxton had a bunion. The tips of the toes of that body had been cut off, and Mrs. Ruxton had humped toes. The woman's distinctive large front teeth were missing. Skin and tissue had been removed from a hand belonging to the other body—in exactly the place where Mary Rogerson had a scar on her right thumb. Reassembled, the two bodies conformed in estimated age and height to the two missing women. Photographs of the two women matched when superimposed upon the skulls, while shoes belonging to the women fit casts made of the dismembered feet.

All the surgical skill in the world could not have made up for some slips made by the killer. A sharp-eyed policeman noticed that some of the pages of the *Sunday Graphic* in which body parts were wrapped were from a "slip edition" intended for delivery only in the Lancaster and Morecambe district. Both the child's romper and a blouse in which parts were wrapped were identified as coming from a parcel of clothing bought at a jumble sale and given to Mary Rogerson. Her stepmother even identified the patch she had put under the arm of the blouse. If there was even a shred of doubt, a comparison of fingerprints taken from Mary Rogerson's corpse with prints photographed over a period of eleven days in Mary's bedroom in the Ruxton house established identity once and for all.

In mid-October, even before identification of Mrs. Ruxton was definite, Lancaster Police Chief Henry Vann phoned Dr. Ruxton, told him they had some news of his wife and asked him to drop by. "I've just put the children to bed," said Ruxton. "No problem at all," said the chief. He dispatched a burly detective, who played babysitter while the interrogation of Dr. Buck Ruxton began. The doctor never returned to 2 Dalton Square. After two days of questioning, he was charged with the murder of Mary Rogerson.

On November 5, appearing on remand, Ruxton was charged further with the murder of his wife. It was as if something snapped. "It is impossible! It is a damned lie!" he shrieked. "It is damned rotten. My religion would not permit it." As he ranted on, the chairman of the magistrates called a five-minute recess.

Norman Birkett, the eminent lawyer who defended Ruxton at the Manchester spring assizes in 1936 (and who later sat in judgment at the Nuremberg trials), told an interviewer shortly before he died that the Lancaster doctor was one client in whose innocence he had difficulty believing. "Nobody could read, as I read, all the facts the prosecution was going to prove without feeling, well, this is a very difficult case," he said. "But it didn't make me any less eager to do everything that I could for Dr. Ruxton."

As no fewer than 115 witnesses, from garbage men to eminent pathologists, made their way to the witness box, Ruxton kept up a steady stream of notes and suggestions to Birkett, waving his hand to attract his lawyer's attention. When Mary Hampshire fainted in the witness box and had to be helped out for fresh air, Ruxton, the concerned physician, said, "She will be all right."

On the eighth day of the eleven-day trial, Birkett sent Ruxton a note, pointing out that it was hopeless to call medical evidence against the overwhelming case put forward by the prosecution. His wish would be to put Ruxton on the stand, he wrote, although Ruxton would, of course, then have to face the fire of cross-examination. "I entirely agree with you," wrote Ruxton in reply. "I wish to give evidence on my own behalf."

Ruxton, although he sometimes seemed on the verge of tears, was a surprisingly good witness. Asked about his stormy marriage, he said, "If I may put it in proper English, we could not live with each other and we could not live without each other." He rather spoiled the effect by adding a French proverb, "Who loves most chastises most."

To the charge that he had murdered Mary Rogerson, he flared, "It is absolute bunkum with a capital B, if I may say so." He was weeping as he added, "Why should I kill my poor Mary?" He still maintained that his wife had left him at about 9:00 A.M. that fatal Sunday, taking Mary with her. The copious bloodstains throughout the house and in the drains? From his cut hand, he explained. Or perhaps from a miscarriage his wife had suffered.

Ruxton was calm and collected as he shrugged off the questions of the prosecutor, J.C. Jackson. Was his wife unfaithful? "Yes," replied the prisoner. "It has been going on since 1932." But when cross-examination resumed the following morning, Ruxton went to pieces. Suddenly, he couldn't remember many of the facts. He stumbled, postured and wept. When Jackson confronted Ruxton with a cleaner who was prepared to say that the suit he had given Mrs. Hampshire had been cleaned and returned to him only shortly before the murder, Ruxton stammered, "My Belle does all the cleaning... I know nothing about it... I don't remember it."

As Jackson badgered him, Ruxton shouted hysterically, "Out of two hundred cases of confinement [births] in Lancaster, Dr. Ruxton has never written a death certificate."

"It would be better for you and everyone," the judge admonished him, "if you listened to the questions and tried to answer." At another point, Birkett had to tell his client to keep quiet and answer the questions calmly.

Jackson's final question left Ruxton floundering. "If that is the sheet from your wife's bed," Jackson said, pointing to the material that had been identified by an expert as coming from the Ruxton house, "can you explain how it got around the bodies at Moffat?"

"How could it be, sir?" said Ruxton helplessly.

Birkett made what he could of the few gaps in the Crown case. If murders had been committed at 2 Dalton Square, how was it that so many people had come and gone that Sunday morning and on subsequent days without suspecting it? And why, if Ruxton had transported those grisly parcels of flesh in his car or another car he'd rented around that time, had no traces of blood been found?

But Mr. Justice Singleton erased any doubts in the jury's minds by calling up the exhibits one by one—the bloodstained stair pads, the child's romper, the blouse. "Doesn't this establish the case for the prosecution as a case was rarely established before on circumstantial evidence?" he said. It was the work of an hour for the jury to find Buck Ruxton guilty.

"I want to thank everybody for the patience and fairness of my trial," said Ruxton, calm for once, before the judge sentenced him to death.

On the night of his execution, after his appeal failed, Ruxton wrote to Birkett, "Thanks awfully, old man, for all you have done." He left Birkett a set of silver fish knives and forks—perhaps not the most appropriate gift. Learned counsel gratefully declined the bequest.

The same night, Ruxton wrote to Vann, the police chief who had arrested him: "May I make a dying request? Oh please do be good to my children. You will not fail me, will you? Be a friend to them." He ended, "Dear Vann, I don't bear the slightest grudge against you. Shake hands. God bless you all."

On May 12, 1936, a gray, overcast day, large crowds gathered outside Strangeways Prison in Manchester, many of them demonstrating against the death penalty, as Dr. Buck Ruxton made his last exit.

The following Sunday, the sensational *News of the World* published a signed confession in Buck Ruxton's handwriting. It said, "I killed Mrs. Ruxton in a fit of temper because I thought she had been with a man. I was mad at the time. Mary Rogerson was present at the time. I had to kill her." The confession was dated October 14, 1935—the day after he was arrested. A reporter from the paper had seen Ruxton at his home shortly before the arrest. It was when he visited Ruxton in prison, supposedly, that the doctor had given him the confession in a sealed envelope, with instructions that it be opened only upon his death. If he was acquitted, it was to be returned to him.

If Ruxton had any hope at all of being found not guilty, he had taken an incredible risk. Why did he do so? The note certainly shows no sign of Ruxton's florid verbosity. But it was rumored that the newspaper had paid Ruxton £3,000 for the confession, a sum that would tidily take care of Birkett's bill for £2,000, while leaving any money realized from the estate for the upkeep of the children.

A fund was, in fact, set up for the children and, says Vann, "They all made good."

As for Ruxton, many have felt some sympathy for this emotional man who was governed by his passions. If Mary Rogerson had not witnessed the murder of Belle Ruxton, and the doctor had not disposed of the bodies in such a gruesome fashion, the case would have been no different from hundreds of crimes of passion committed every year, some argue.

I take a different view. A study of the plans of the house and its furnishings exhibited at the trial shows that Ruxton slept in the largest bedroom, while his wife was crammed into a smaller room with the three children, one of them having to sleep on a camp cot. This meant either that their marriage had, to all intents and purposes, ended and she no longer slept with him, or that Ruxton was used to keeping his wife in a state of subservience. His threats and earlier assaults against her would be grounds enough for prosecution today.

But it was the events of that September night that reveal Ruxton for the monster he was. The police believed that Mrs. Ruxton was strangled on the third-floor landing, outside her bedroom door. Mary Rogerson, opening the door of her room, would have been confronted by the sight of the doctor and his wife's body. If Ruxton had murdered in one blind moment of anger, wouldn't the natural thing be for him to feel remorse, to tell the maid to fetch the police? But Ruxton's first thought was to save his skin, and so he cold-bloodedly and viciously advanced on the cowering Mary Rogerson—his "little Mary"—hit her over the head with some object, fracturing her skull, and then, judging by the copious amounts of blood on the landing and down the stairs, slit her throat or stabbed her.

Again, there was a chance for remorse, a chance to give himself up. Instead, he carried the bodies downstairs to the bathroom located on a half-landing halfway up the main staircase and went about the ghastly business of draining the blood expertly from the bodies and reducing them to parcels of meat and bone, some of which, in the photographs produced in court, would not have looked out of place on a supermarket meat counter. Doctors at the trial estimated it took a minimum of five hours to dismember each corpse. The packages were then stored in the bedrooms, no doubt among the children's things, while Ruxton made his preparations for the drive to Scotland to dump most of the remains over the bridge.

Not the image of "the workingman's doctor," not the charming bedside manner still remembered in Lancaster, not even the picture of the loving father, thinking at the last of his children—none of this can erase those bloody images.

People who grew up in Britain in the 1930s remember that at school they would chant:

Bloodstains on the carpet, bloodstains on the knife,
Dr. Buck Ruxton has murdered his wife.

At the police stables, they told me that using the bathtub as a horse trough hadn't turned out to be such a good idea after all. Many of the horses refused to drink from it. I don't blame them.